TORNADO
F3
IN FOCUS

TORNADO F3

IN FOCUS

A NAVIGATOR'S EYE ON BRITAIN'S LAST INTERCEPTOR

DAVID GLEDHILL

FONTHILL

The views and opinions expressed in this book are those of the author and should not be taken to represent those of HMG, the MoD, the RAF or any Government agency.

Images in the book where attributed to UK MoD Crown Copyright are released for open publication under the terms of the Open Government Licence for public sector information.

Fonthill Media Limited
Fonthill Media LLC
www.fonthillmedia.com
office@fonthillmedia.com

First published in the United Kingdom and the United States of America 2015

British Library Cataloguing in Publication Data:
A catalogue record for this book is available from the British Library

Typeset in 10.5pt on 13pt Sabon
Printed and bound in England

Contents

The No. 65 (Reserve) Squadron weapons instructor Bob Burden in-cockpit.

Author's Note

I was closely involved in the story of the Tornado F3 from the moment I received my posting to join one of the first instructor's courses forming the new Operational Conversion Unit. During subsequent ground tours, I was responsible for modification programmes which took the aircraft from 'basket case' to a highly capable weapon system. Was it ever a fighter in the true sense? Probably not. Was it an effective interceptor, which is the role for which it was designed? Without a doubt.

Given my close involvement in modifications to the weapons and avionics and having managed elements of the operational test, I probably feel more responsibility for its progress than many of my peers.

Many talented individuals contributed to the turnaround in the aircraft's fortunes while many stood by and sniped. The staff in operational requirements worked relentlessly towards a better capability, often against the odds. Over the years I listened to much ill-informed debate; those who knew little, had never flown an air defence aircraft, or sought to pursue inter-service rivalries, often had the loudest voices. I hope that in recounting some of the politics and the reasons for some of the decisions, and by giving a reasoned assessment of how the aircraft matured, I may quieten some of the critics. They will never be silenced, but hopefully they will be better informed.

The topic of photographic quality was raised in reviews of my previous works. My photographs were never professionally staged. Some were even taken with a 'point and shoot' camera which just happened to be in my flying suit pocket at the time. In this age of digital photography we can afford to be more cavalier. I now snap away a series of shots and instantly review them. In those days, I used wet film so I had to be selective in the air. There would be a nervous wait for the negatives to see if any of the shots were memorable. It goes without saying that many of those that I include are well over twenty years old. If some are a little blurred or suffer from canopy reflections, I apologise. However, I feel that every photograph I have included, despite variable quality, in some way adds to the story. As always, I have avoided going into too much technical detail and I have tried to include anecdotes and stories which show key events in the F3 story from my own perspective.

I would like to thank a number of friends and colleagues: Steve Nicholl for penning the Foreword; Geoff Lee of Planefocus Ltd, a legend as an air-to-air photographer, for his permission to use his stunning images; Steve Smyth, Ian Black, Mark Wilson, Giz Taylor, Kelvin Harris, and Bob Burden for providing photographs to fill some gaps; BAE Systems and Selex ES for providing archive images; Neil Whitehead and Giz Taylor for providing insights into some operational aspects of the aircraft which were outside my areas of expertise; Rick Peacock-Edwards and Clive Duance for assisting with the draft; Chris Wilson of Jet Art Aviation for giving me access to ZE256 to capture the pictures for Chapter 2; and Simon Pulford for his work restoring ZD938 and the Tornado F3 simulator. Chris and Simon are typical of the enthusiasts who are dedicated to preserving our heritage for future generations.

As always, I lost good friends during my time on the aircraft. The F3 had an enviable safety record and there was little 'attrition' in the early years. In comparison with its predecessors, it was eight years into its operational service before the first F3 crashed, but inevitably crews perished, leaving gaps and memories on the squadrons. I would like to mention particular friends who will always be remembered: 'Jesse' Owens died when he was struck by the canopy in a high-speed ejection over the North Sea in 1995. Nige Morton and his pilot Ken Thompson who were killed when their F3 struck a hillside in Scotland in 2009. This was to be the final loss before the aircraft retired. Rob 'Banners' Bannister and Paul Brown; both friends who died of natural causes and were truly talented navigators and left us too soon. I would also like to mention Ian Weaver who suffered terrible injuries after he ejected from ZE862 in 1996. His courage and fortitude as he recovered from his injuries are an inspiration.

It would also be remiss of me not to make particular mention of my old friend Andy Lister-Tomlinson. 'L-T' was 'Mister Tornado' from the outset. His encyclopaedic knowledge was critical in shaping the development programme when others may have been less willing to accept the deficiencies he identified. His specialist expertise in weapons, the radar, and the data links, laid the foundations for the final version of the weapon system which eventually showed its true potential. When he finally pens his own account of the Tornado F3 story, it will lay more of the myths to rest.

The F3 was never truly loved but those who understood the eventual capability give it true respect. It gave twenty-five years of service to our country and, arguably, retired at the peak of its capability. The F3 is gone, but certainly not forgotten.

Foreword

Air Vice-Marshal Steven Nicholl, CB, CBE, AFC, BA, FRAeS.

In a number of ways this is an extraordinary book. It tells at least three separate stories of what David Gledhill himself describes as an unloved fighter, but one that, I could argue, was one of the most successful in history! I will try to justify that last statement in a moment.

The first story in this book is simply about what it is like to operate a complex fighter in the modern world. It describes the hard work behind what little glamour there is, but also the satisfaction and sometimes joy to be had in being part of an elite, working in an adrenaline-filled environment.

The second story is the equivalent story for a staff officer. And again it is a tale of hard work, little glamour, if any, and occasional satisfaction from providing the elite with whom you used to work with what they really need. David is extremely well placed to write both stories. One can only admire his memory, his vision, and his hard work in producing the stories.

The third story is, I believe, the most interesting and most important. It is the story of the constant battle between the users—in this case fighter aircrew—the politicians, and the Treasury. This is not a story of 'good guys' and 'bad guys'. It is so common for the military and aircrew in particular to view the Treasury as the 'bad guys' that I am tempted to say it is universal. But it is not universal; no one who has had a relative in need of expensive life-saving drugs can resent the Treasury trimming a percentage point off the defence budget to support health needs. And when one reads of teenagers killed in car accidents, one can almost support spending on speed cameras!

Nor are the aircrew always the good guys in this story. Of course they would love to fly the most capable aircraft, regardless of cost. But when cost constrained, they find it difficult sometimes to express precisely what they need, even without the vagaries of the intelligence 'threat'. Probably the biggest complaint about the Tornado (whether Ground-Attack and Air Defence variant) is that it lacks thrust, particularly when not using reheated power. However, that lack was driven by aircrew, in Operational Requirements, who set the combat allowance of fuel in the original specifications as 'two minutes at a maximum thrust' rather than, say, 'two minutes at 7 G'. The former drives designers to actively limit the maximum thrust. Had we chosen the latter formulation, we might have had an aircraft that could sustain combat G in unreheated power.

In this battle between users and the Treasury, it often falls to politicians to act as referees. And it is here that misunderstanding and miscommunication can create long-term problems. One area in which the British military can genuinely claim to be good guys lies in what the Army calls 'the moral component' of warfare. Even with limited equipment, a good team of highly motivated people can achieve wonders. You will read in this book many instances of that truism.

But the reverse is also true. Lack of appreciation, or simply perceived lack of appreciation, can de-motivate even the most capable team. When I finally joined the Tornado Force, as a fairly senior officer, they had not long returned from the First Gulf War. As you will read here, they had received none of the plaudits of their ground-attack peers and had slowly being relegated by their American counterparts to roles in the rear areas. Morale was low. On an exercise in Alaska in my first few months on the force, flying against US Air Force F-16s and F-15s, I quickly found the pervasive mind-set in the Tornado F3 Force lacked aggression and we were always on the defensive. We lost every engagement until I forced a situation in which an outstanding, aggressively-minded navigator, Ken Thomson, was given the lead. From losing 3–0 or 4–0 on every mission, we won 5–2! When, later, JTIDS (Joint Tactical Information Distribution System) gave a more general boost to morale as well as capability, very favourable kill rates against F-15s in exercises became a matter of routine.

Earlier I said that it could be argued that the Tornado F3 was one of our most successful fighters ever. What defines the world's best fighter? It is not the ability to put on the most impressive air display. Nor is it the ability to fly highest, fastest or, even, to turn tightest. While these elements are hugely relevant, the *national* objective must be an aircraft on which just enough is spent to achieve the defence objectives of the day. Remember that the Tornado F3 not only never lost a battle for real, but for a few years was a significant part of the front line in a war that was Cold but dangerous, and then played a role in the very different post-Cold War world of both peace keeping and peace enforcement.

For some twenty-five years, all this was achieved with expenditure that was never more than the bare minimum and often available long after the critical need had been identified. In fact, I could go further and say this bare minimum capability was achieved at no cost at all in the long run. The purchase of 165 Tornado F3s gave the UK and its defence industry the overall design lead in the Tornado. That and the resultant research work led to British-designed developments on Typhoon. In turn, that led to British industrial know-how that secured almost 20 per cent of the enormous Joint Strike Fighter joint programme with the United States. I suspect that the Treasury will take in more from the British work on the Joint Strike Fighter than it ever spent on the Tornado F3, which was critical to securing that work.

I cannot say that the Tornado F3 was my favourite aircraft, but I would rather have gone to war in it than any other I have flown regularly. I am proud to have been part of the Tornado F3 Force and I'm proud of the contribution it made to the front line in its day, which created conditions for an effective front line in the decades to come.

Dave Gledhill's book shows the hard work and occasional courage required of *both* front-line aircrew and staff officers. We can only hope for the same qualities in politicians directing the Treasury. I commend this book to those RAF personnel and anyone interested in aviation, defence, and procurement.

Tornado F2 ZD903 refuels from a VC10 tanker over the North Sea. (*Bob Burden*)

1

Developing the Tornado F3

Why does a country need a fighter? Although the UK has produced many capable fighting machines over the years including the Spitfire and, from a war-torn Europe, the Focke Wulf 190, it has also produced many dubious designs. The Tornado F2/F3 struggled to live up to its heritage. Regrettably, its tortured development is a study of errors despite the efforts of many dedicated individuals to rectify the deficiencies along the way.

The first task for an operational planner is to decide how to establish air superiority over the battlefield, or preferably, air supremacy. This means setting the conditions to prevent the opposing air force from operating in your airspace; to do this, capable air defence fighters are needed. Once control of the air is established, ground troops can operate unmolested without fear of air attack. The risks of failing to do this were evident during the Falklands campaign when Argentine Skyhawks, Daggers, and Mirages, although at the limit of their range, were able to attack ships in tactical areas with relative impunity. The commanders were simply unable to put sufficient fighters over the battlefield to maintain control. Losses were telling, despite the efforts of the Sea Harrier pilots. Destroying the attackers post-target was, at best, a draw, and the point was brought home on TV in the first media war. More recently, the trend of air superiority by default—in reality relying on the US—has made British military planners blasé about the risks of being unable to establish control of the air. Opponents have been either less well equipped with air defence forces or, like the Iraqis during both Gulf Wars and the Serbs during operations in the Balkans, less willing to employ them. Saddam flew his Air Force into the hands of his former Iranian enemies and during later operations even buried aircraft to avoid them falling into Coalition hands. He certainly failed to provide a credible air-to-air threat. More recent experiences during the enforcement of the Libyan 'No Fly Zone' using Typhoons may have quietened the detractors a little, but again, the Libyans put up little, if any, fighter resistance. Complacency among military planners is dangerous and air defence should always be the first priority.

The Tornado F2 was a classic example of specifying a product to fight the current war; at that time the Cold War. To show why, we must look at the way the UK's Ministry of Defence procures major equipment. A new operational requirements officer is asked to make a leap in thinking when he or she first sits down at a desk in the MoD. We were told: Don't set a requirement for the system which is needed now. Project ahead at least ten years and try to decide what will be needed for a future conflict. This immediately sets the first challenge as we have been unerringly poor at predicting where our military capability will next be needed. Who anticipated the Falklands conflict or the Balkans war? A requirement can only be set against an agreed threat scenario, so the first step is to decide how a new aircraft will be used and which threats it needs to counter. 'Stakeholders' analyse potential threat scenarios and agree a baseline. As the project develops, only the requirement which has been laid down is translated into the specification for the weapon system, even though scenarios change as the design matures. Once approved, to modify the baseline requirement invites resubmission and delay. Furthermore, to project ahead ten years, technology incorporated into the design must be 'on the shelf'. Any significant development will extend a project's life by years, and using radical new technology extends the project life beyond that timescale.

In the case of the Tornado F3, deployments to theatres such as Iraq could not justify a capability in the staff requirement, even though the aircraft was eventually used in precisely that way. The Cold War scenario over the North Sea drove the F2 design, yet hindsight shows that threats changed many times during that development period. With no automatic review, contractors reacted with glee when the requirement 'changed'. To the layman this may seem reasonable. How often has the media trumpeted details of a project over budget and unable to fulfil its intended role? Nimrod AEW1 and Nimrod MRA4 are prime examples of troubled projects that were cancelled at huge loss to the taxpayer as the aircraft failed to meet the specification. To the requirements officer, a ten-year lead time invites obsolescence unless safeguards are built in to adapt the design as it develops. To put the problem in context, would anyone expect a Formula 1 team to map out its plan for the coming ten seasons, to admit it did not intend to revise its car design to its competitors, and to publish its planned modification programme during pre-season testing? Of course not. To produce a world-beating design requires constant flexibility in all aspects of the procurement. For military programmes, scrutiny may compromise operational security, allowing opponents to match the new capability, and invite delays. Any suggestion that the programme is 'unwell' invites cancellation to meet relentless spending targets, and there is always a more deserving home for limited defence funds. For that reason, those responsible for projects soldier on, keeping deficiencies quiet, hoping for a turn in fortunes. Contractors are happy to acquiesce as change means work.

The Tornado Air Defence Variant, or ADV, was procured under these constraints, yet eventually it was developed into a very capable interceptor. Unfortunately, the final investment to turn it into a truly capable fighter was never made. Tornado

F2 followed on from some fine British fighters. The Hunter sits fondly in the memories of any fighter pilot who flew it. It was well matched to its peers, albeit relatively lightly armed with only guns and cannons. The Lightning was a superb airframe but woefully underdeveloped. Designed to launch from ground alert, it had only two air-to-air missiles with limited capability and was short of fuel on take off. How much more effective would an upgraded Lightning carrying four Sidewinder missiles have been? Radical ways to increase the fuel load such as conformal tanks were never followed through. Even so, its pilots loved it. The Phantom was a superb stop-gap purchase and was well armed with a good weapon load and carried a long-range pulse Doppler radar. Unfortunately, by the time it entered RAF service, its systems were already showing their age and were unreliable. It was not an agile fighter, it lacked the avionics to give the crew good situation awareness, and it required help from ground controllers to make it truly effective as an area fighter.

As the Tornado F2 Air Staff Requirement (ASR) 395 was being drafted, the British public had become aware of the deficiencies in the country's air defences. Newspaper articles in the mid-1970s warned that only seventy-seven frontline fighters were available to defend UK airspace—woefully inadequate against the might of the Soviet Union. The ASR asked for an interceptor to counter Soviet long-range bombers in an electronic war over the North Sea. There was no perceived need to counter escort fighters as designs such as the Su-27 Flanker were still grainy pictures in dimly lit vaults. The F2 had to be able to fly for a significant distance, set up a combat air patrol at 300 to 400 miles from base, and remain on task at medium level for a significant length of time, ready to intercept incoming bombers armed with long-range standoff weapons. Add to the mix political pressure to choose a European product and the choice started to narrow. To project combat power at a distance, small, highly efficient bypass fan engines would be needed. Fuel load would be critical. Cockpit automation was in its infancy and the workload was too high for a single pilot. Technology and computing power meant that two men were still needed to operate the equipment and to manage the tactical battle.

The airframe being developed to meet the NATO bomber requirement under the Multi Role Combat Aircraft programme became the prime candidate. To accommodate the medium-range air-to-air missiles, a 2-metre plug was installed aft of the rear cockpit of the Tornado GR1 design. Ironically, this proved to be a valuable addition to the airframe as the plug moved the rear cockpit forward, giving a much better view forward and down. The extra space was used to fit an additional fuel tank called the 'O' Tank, which increased the fuel load by 600 kg. The elongated fuselage proved much more aerodynamic and improved the handling, particularly in the transonic regime. Variable geometry wings conferred some advantages, particularly in the area of transonic and supersonic performance. The mantra trumpeted throughout the development was that the latest avionics would offset any airframe performance deficiencies and that the GEC Marconi Foxhunter radar was to be the key to that improvement. The true detection performance of Foxhunter was carefully protected for many years causing debate over its capability, but it was reported to be able to detect a bomber-sized target at 185 km and a fighter-sized target at 120 km. From personal experience, detections against an airliner flying at medium level over Europe were typically at 80 miles. This range was much reduced against a smaller fighter-sized target such as a Hawk fighter over the low flying areas in Wales, where ranges of about 30 to 40 miles were more likely. This was still a respectable performance when compared with the AN/AWG 12 in the Phantom, which in its day was a capable radar.

The perception that a close combat capability was irrelevant was based on the static positions of the players on the 'North Sea Chessboard' during the Cold War. From bases in Russia, the 1970s and 1980s era fighters could not threaten aircraft operating over the North Sea; the Mig-21 and Mig-23 series simply did not have the range. Even the later Mig-29 air superiority aircraft was a short-range point-defence fighter and would have operated within 100 miles of its base. Only the advent of the carrier-based Yak-38 Forger and the air-to-air refuelling capability of the Su-27 Flanker redefined the threat. By 1980, with Soviet Midas refuelling tankers able to push around North Cape, Tornado F3s operating on the outer combat air patrols might have faced a fighter threat for the first time. ASR 395 began to seem naïve, and as out-of-area operations such as Bosnia and Iraq became prevalent, the fighter threat underlined the myopic requirement.

The Tornado procurement was the first real example of full European cooperation in aircraft production, although there had been bilateral programmes before. Governments set up a coordinating agency known as the NATO Multi-Role Combat Aircraft Development and Production Management Agency, or NAMMA. This agency coordinated the nations' requirements and acted as the point of contact with industry. National representatives from the operational requirements branches and the procurement executives sat on committees which thrashed out a European Staff Requirement for Development document, or ESR(D). This was translated into specification documents and given to industry, which had formed a coordinating company known as Panavia to bring together the partner companies involved in the design and production. The original companies through mergers and acquisitions eventually became BAE Systems, EADS, and Alenia. A further company, known as Turbo Union, was set up by Rolls Royce and Fiat to coordinate engine design and production. Each nation was allocated a certain workshare on the project with lead nations taking responsibility for specific areas of the airframe.

The airframe weighed in at 31,970 lb (14,500 kg) empty, which increased to 47,500 lb (21,546 kg) at normal take-off weight, and 61,700 lb (27,986 kg) if fully loaded with missiles and external fuel tanks. The internal fuel capacity was 5,600 kg, but two 1,500-litre tanks could be carried on the inboard pylons or replaced by two 2,250-litre tanks to supplement the fuel load, increasing the load to 7,250 kg. For ferry fit, two 1,500-litre external tanks could be fitted to the forward under-fuselage stations, although carrying and firing missiles in that fit became problematic. The baseline capability was the Foxhunter radar, the

Skyflash Medium Range Air-to-Air Missile (MRAAM), the AIM-9L Sidewinder Short Range Air-to-Air Missile (SRAAM), and the integral Mauser 27-mm cannon. The semi-active missiles were carried on semi-conformal launchers under the centre fuselage with the infra-red guided weapons fitted to stub pylons mounted on each side of the inner movable pylon. Defensive aids to protect the aircraft in an electronic environment included the radar homing and warning receiver, or RHWR, which was eventually retrofitted to the GR1 bomber to replace the earlier and less effective radar warning equipment. In parallel, chaff and flare countermeasures were procured under a separate Air Staff Requirement. On a 'Stage 1 Plus' aircraft, a Phimat chaff dispenser was carried on a specially fitted outboard pylon and matched on the opposite side by a towed radar decoy pod (TRD), lovingly called the 'turd'. The Joint Tactical Information Distribution System (JTIDS) was included in the specification but would take some years to be deployed operationally, only entering service in 1995. Unit costs of the airframe are difficult to establish and vary depending on how the figures are calculated. Initial estimates suggested £21 million per aeroplane, but figures as high as £42 million seem unlikely.

The first flight of a Tornado F2, ZA254, was on 27 October 1979 at the British Aerospace factory at Warton, with three prototypes being allocated to the company. These were designated A01, A02, and A03—ZA254, ZA267, and ZA283 respectively—and first flew between August 1979 and November 1980. Of these, only A02 was a trainer variant. An additional aircraft, ZD899, AT001, went to the Aircraft and Armaments Experimental and Evaluation (A&AEE) Test Centre at RAF Boscombe Down to undertake the service clearance programme.

Using the batch production system, eighteen production models followed, of which eight were equipped as dual-control trainers and designated the Tornado F Mark 2. It was this standard which was first delivered to the RAF in March 1984, first at Warton, moving to RAF Coningsby to begin the first conversion courses on No. 229 Operational Conversion Unit in 1985. These airframes served for only eighteen months before the delivery of the next batch of aircraft which were upgraded to Tornado F Mark 3 standard. The first Tornado F3, ZE154, AT009 was delivered on 24 December 1985 and entered service early the following year. Plans were in place to return the Tornado F2s to RAF St Athan to be updated to F2A standard, which included refitting uprated Mk 103 engines to replace the original Mk 101s, upgrading the avionics to fit the dual inertial navigation suite, and adding extra stub pylons to carry four SRAAM (initially Sidewinder) missiles. The F2s were, ultimately, never modified due to lack of funding and a redefinition of the numbers of frontline aircraft required. Ironically, the F2s became donors to fix Tornado F3s that were damaged at the hands of a contractor during a maintenance programme and most never flew again. Formal entry to service was declared on 1 May 1985 as No. 29 (Fighter) Squadron was declared operational to NATO. In reality, No. 229 Operational Conversion Unit in its shadow No. 65 (Reserve) Squadron role had been declared to NATO some months earlier to meet commitments.

The prototype Tornado F2, ZA267. (*BAE Systems*)

An early production Tornado F3 on display at the Farnborough Airshow carrying the 2,250-litre fuel tanks and four Sidewinders.

The Tornado F3 was an improved version with significant changes in the cockpit, uprated Mk 103 Rolls Royce RB199 engines giving extra thrust in afterburner, and improved avionics. Mark 104 engines followed quickly, although they were downrated in service use to extend their life. The Mk 104 RB199s developed a very healthy 9656 lb of thrust in dry power and 16920 lb in afterburner from what was a very small and efficient engine. This disparity between relatively low dry power against a good performance in reheat shaped how the aircraft would be flown. The engine performance was a technical achievement, although lack of power was to blight the ultimate performance of the airframe. Plans to resolve this deficiency by fitting EJ200 engines developed for Typhoon never came to fruition. Of the 176 airframes that were built, 44 were fitted as dual-control trainers which were fully combat-capable. Despite major improvements under the combat sustainability programme in the 1990s, the aircraft was not re-designated as the Tornado F4. Perhaps the resistance from new F3 crews in making any links with its predecessor, the F4 Phantom, would explain this. More likely, politics would not allow the acknowledgement of a major upgrade.

The key to any fighter aircraft is its air-to-air weapons, and the original staff requirement envisaged a Tornado F2 with four Skyflash and two AIM-9L known in the software as MRAAM and SRAAM. A new version of Skyflash was developed, initially known as TEMP or the Tornado Enhancement Modification Programme standard. This version was further developed by Matra BAe Dynamics into the Super TEMP standard, which equipped most of the squadrons.

The Skyflash was a British-built derivative of the American Sparrow missile with a similar missile body but much improved capability. It entered service on the Phantom in the early 1980s, appearing in significant numbers in the mid-1980s. Housed in semi-conformal launchers under the fuselage of the Tornado F3, the new launchers were fitted with a complex hydraulic cradle which forced the missile out into the airflow even at high supersonic speeds or under negative 'G'. In order to mount four missiles, the launchers were staggered laterally, giving a slightly lopsided look when viewed from below. The Skyflash had a significantly longer range due to improved propulsion from the Aerojet Hoopoe motor, and further developments under the Super TEMP programme increased that range even further. Air-to-air missiles are not normally powered throughout their flight. The rocket motor fires once the missile separates from the host aircraft and accelerates it to supersonic speeds. For the Sparrow/Skyflash family, this was about Mach 2.8 above the launch speed. When the rocket motor burns out, hydraulic motors and batteries continue to power the electronics and the aerodynamic surfaces until it reaches its target. The initial acceleration is known as the 'boost phase' and the period afterwards, the 'coast phase'. If designers can increase the available fuel, it is possible to maintain the cruising speed of the missile for longer. This is called the 'sustain' phase. For the TEMP standard, the concept was 'boost-coast'. Once the larger Hoopoe motor with a longer burn time was fitted, the Super TEMP became a 'boost-sustain-coast' missile achieving a longer range. It was fitted with a Marconi-designed monopulse seeker head which performed well against electronic jamming—the environment in which the F3 would have to fight. Skyflash was easily identifiable by the black strip antennas down the centre body of the missile for a new fuse designed by Thorn EMI, again a huge improvement over its predecessors. Despite all these improvements, Skyflash still had a fundamental weakness. As a semi-active missile, the radar had to be locked to the target for the duration of the missile's flight. Even though the Foxhunter radar used track-while-scan to track multiple targets, when it was locked-on, those targets were memorised. Once back in wide scan it took some time before the tracks were updated and a further lock could be successfully achieved. Predicted impact points were quite close to the Tornado F3 so it was difficult if not impossible to break lock at impact and reacquire a further target for engagement before the minimum range of the Skyflash. This meant only one head-on shot was possible. Additionally, such attacks were tactically questionable. If the missile failed or opponents were engaged, the Tornado crew would be forced into close combat against potentially more agile opponents.

Crews were already familiar with the AIM-9L which had been in service for some years. Using infra-red guidance it tracked hot metal such as the jet pipes or even the leading edges of the wings, which were warmed due to surface friction. In flight, coolant from bottles in each missile launcher lowered the temperature of the seeker heads, making them more sensitive. There was sufficient coolant for a typical sortie but it had to be managed for longer QRA missions. Two AIM-9Ls were fitted on the inboard side of the pylons on the F2, but with the introduction of the F3, two further stubs were fitted outboard, increasing the SRAAM load to four. The Sidewinders, like the Skyflash, were controlled by the missile monitoring system (MMS) in each cockpit and could be jettisoned in emergency by either crew member. As the weapon was introduced into service on the F2, little work was needed to validate its basic performance. Some early firings by BAE Systems had proved the release, separation, and jettison functions. Development of weapon system functions such as head-up displays and tactical displays had been achieved using acquisition heads. These were dummy missiles which contained only the tracking elements of the missile, but without power supplies, autopilot, warhead, or motor. The development firings proved the interfaces and functionality of the new MMS, that the displays in the cockpit were correct and that the firing sequence was controlled correctly by the weapon system.

The gun was a Mauser 27-mm cannon and was the same weapon fitted to the Tornado GR1/4. In order to accommodate an integral air-to-air refuelling probe on the left side, only one gun was fitted on the right-hand side under the cockpit. The gun was internally mounted and accessed through external panels. The ammunition was held in a tank inboard of the gun and spent cases were caught in another tank alongside as the gun fired. The Mauser is a single-barrel revolver type weapon carrying 27-mm rounds which, for the air-to-air role, were armour piercing. For training, non-explosive ball ammunition was used. Most of the 2.3-metre barrel was hidden from view, and only a short section protruded into the airflow with its prominent blast deflector. The 180 rounds could be fired at either 1,000 rounds per minute or 1,700 rounds per minute, leaving the barrel at just over 1,000 metres per second. With its lower rate of fire, the gun had a stuttering sound when fired, unlike the 'whizz' of the SUU-23 gunpod on the Phantom. Being internally mounted, there was a satisfying smell of cordite in the cockpit after firing.

The weapons were upgraded later in the F3s service life. The Advanced Short Range Air-to-air Missile (ASRAAM) was fitted in June 2002, followed closely by the AIM-120B Advanced Medium Range Air-to-air Missile (AMRAAM) in June 2004 and, finally, the AIM-120-C5 in September of the same year. The first level of AMRAAM integration was the Capability Sustainment Programme (CSP) in 1999–2002, but it took some time to convince a sceptical Air Plans that adding AMRAAM without the mid-course guidance was too little, too late, and would invite continuing obsolescence despite significant cost. The final upgrade under the AMRAAM Optimisation Programme followed adding the data link providing mid-course guidance between 2003 and 2004. Ironically, it was delay in the Typhoon programme which ensured that the work was essential to retain credibility and capability.

The Tornado F3 was to replace the Lightning and the Phantom in RAF service but, as always, plans matured during its service life. The aging Lightning was already difficult to support by the time the F3 entered service. The Phantom was

A Skyflash is fired from a Tornado F2. (*Geoff Lee*)

A Sidewinder is fired from a Tornado F3. (*Geoff Lee*)

The Mauser 27-mm cannon.

scheduled to run on for some years but was retired early in 1992 to give a 'Cold War windfall' to the air planners. Retiring a fleet of aircraft offered huge savings to the defence vote and was seen as a way to stretch limited defence funds. Sadly, the windfall was not used to equip the F3 better to meet the revised post-Cold War threat, and savings were diverted elsewhere.

Despite early promise, the Tornado F3 failed to secure many export customers. The only overseas order was for twenty-four to Saudi Arabia under the Al Yamama contract. A number of nations assessed the F3, but even our staunch ally Oman cancelled an order before delivery. Compared to competing designs, the F3 was expensive to buy and operate, and suffered from its reputation. A further twenty-four airframes were leased to Italy in 1993 to act as a stop gap, pending the introduction of the Typhoon. Italy already operated the Tornado GR1 and it was a relatively easy step to introduce the F3. The airframes were returned to the UK for disposal in 2004.

There was much debate about whether the aircraft retired early, but its eventual retirement date was quite close to the one planned as the Typhoon's introduction to service was progressively delayed. A planning date of 2010 was brought forward to 2009, but eventually slipped back to 2011 to dovetail with the Typhoon build up. On retirement in 2011, the final standard of the Tornado F3 was a very capable weapon system, but despite this, it could never shake off its much maligned reputation.

2

Operating the Tornado F3

The Tornado F2 delivered to the RAF in 1985 was a radically different aircraft to the one that retired in 2011. Many felt the F2 was the wrong aircraft to meet our needs. The majority of aircrew probably favoured the F-14 Tomcat. After all, the UK had often been described as a large aircraft carrier and the Tomcat, with its long-range AN/AWG 9 radar and AIM-54 Phoenix, Sparrow, and Sidewinder missiles, had excellent combat persistence and a respectable turning performance. The F-15 was a strong contender but experience in the early 1980s was that the F-15A, which the UK would likely have ordered, was still immature for single-seat operations, particularly at very low levels, although ex-single pilots might disagree. Hindsight proved that the F-15C became a superb fighter in all respects, but not without significant development. The F-15E was little more than a concept at that time but would have been ideal. UK pilots were also invited to fly the F-18 which was also Sparrow armed, but it was felt to be short on fuel for the longer range missions. An F-16 with a stern hemisphere capability didn't meet the specification and, despite its agile performance, would have been a backward step. Whatever the options and whatever the opinions, there seemed little likelihood that the procurement decision would change. The F2 was delivered to the RAF and the myths and legends began.

For me, the introduction to service of the Tornado F2 coincided with a series of visits to the British Aerospace factory at Warton in Lancashire. I had already received a posting to the new aircraft as an instructor, and at the time we had been evaluating the BAE Systems Air Combat Simulator being developed at the factory. Being on site, a visit to the Tornado F2 production line was a must. Despite the misgivings, it was hard to disguise the eager anticipation of inspecting and critiquing the new fighter type, which was to be our mount for the foreseeable future for better or worse. If nothing else, the cockpits were new and shiny!

The production line was an unusual affair. The major sections were manufactured by companies from the partner nations in Italy, Germany, and the UK, and the sub-sections were brought together for final assembly at Warton, where the individual elements were mated. The forward and rear sections were the responsibility of

BAE Systems, the centre section DASA of Germany, and the wings Alenia of Italy. The sections were fed in at the beginning of the production line and slowly came together during progress down the track. Each Tornado was designated with a company production number that identified the variant. As an example, AS054 was a single-stick ADV whereas AT080 was a twin-stick ADV; A for air defence variant or ADV, S or T for the variant, and the number being the position on the production line. The components wore the pale yellow undercoat for most of this time until assembled, when the complete airframe moved to the paint shop to receive the UK air defence grey livery.

Aircrew reactions to the new aircraft were mixed and depended largely on background. Most pilots who made the transition had flown either the Lightning or the Phantom in RAF service, with most having either Hunter or Hawk experience during their weapons training. Each of those types was considerably different to the Tornado in both design and role. Rick Peacock-Edwards, an experienced Lightning and Phantom pilot and the first Tornado F3 squadron commander, gave his assessment of the F3 from a pilot's perspective shortly after its introduction to service.

> The aircraft is a delight to fly. The cockpit working environment is pleasant and has more space than its predecessors. The first thing that strikes you is the quietness; it is quiet enough to have a coherent conversation between front and back seaters without use of the intercom. The controls are extremely well harmonised and the aircraft feel is approximately 30% lighter than the GR1. The result is an aircraft with light controls which feels every bit the fighter it is. Handling is effectively carefree and control inputs are protected from exceeding limits by a spin prevention and incidence limiting system. This is a most effective system in which pilots have great faith. Those who have seen the F3 perform will have been left in no doubt that it is an aircraft with an excellent turning capability. With the use of reheat, it climbs to height as impressively as the Lightning. It has a good supersonic performance and is quite the nicest supersonic handling aircraft that I have flown. The low level performance is outstanding; acceleration from 250 knots to over 600 knots takes approximately 25 seconds. At sea level it can go supersonic without the use of reheat and the low level turning performance is particularly impressive. It can loop at 250 knots and, thanks to the thrust reverser system it is capable of stopping in under 2,000 feet on landing.

Praise indeed. Most the navigators at the early stage of the programme were ex-Phantom, although there was still a smattering of experience of other types. A select few had been lucky enough to fly state-of-the-art fighters on exchange duties in the USA and Europe and were, perhaps, the harshest critics. Unlike the Typhoon where the cockpit design was directed by the Cockpit Working Party, an aircrew-led body subordinate to the NATO Eurofighter Management Agency (NEFMA), there seemed to have been little liaison with frontline aircrew and the designers of the Tornado cockpit. Destined only for RAF service, decisions that normally required international consensus were delegated to the UK for the fighter variant. Regrettably, many aspects were a direct inheritance from the Tornado GR1, even though they might not be optimised for a fighter. This led to frustration at first, but as deficiencies were uncovered, change would prove inevitable and lead to a more effective design. The frustrations were not one sided, however, and in a discussion with a design engineer he explained that if he asked the opinion of ten different aircrew on a given topic he would receive ten different views. Perhaps this explained the reason for frontline aircrew being excluded from the procurement process.

Criticism from those who had flown the F-15 or F-16 bordered on dismissive and reflected disappointment at a lost opportunity. There were to be no reclined ejection seats or side-mounted control columns in the RAF; tradition seemed to be the watch word. That said, for the first time in an RAF fighter aircraft, the pilot would rely on the head-up display, or HUD, as the primary flight instrument, although it was difficult to visualise its role with the Tornado sitting dormant on the factory floor.

My personal view is that the F3 was a step forward but not the major leap which had been made with the latest generation US fighters which I had flown as a NATO Tactical Evaluator. On first impressions, the Tornado F2 was a delight to fly. The cockpit was well ventilated and the air conditioning worked, unlike the Phantom, giving a much more comfortable working environment. The ejection seats were more comfortable than earlier seats and could be raised high in the cockpit, giving a better all-round view. In the back, the fuselage extension meant that the navigator could see forward and downwards to well aft of the wing line. The single-piece canopy was clear of intrusive ironwork to interrupt the view from the rear cockpit in air combat. This meant it was much easier to keep track of the 'bogey' when engaged. Unlike the Phantom, the canopy was too large to guarantee that it would separate in the event of an ejection, so a miniature detonating cord broke the plexiglass cover into two large sections. The wavy line ran along the centreline of the canopy and is seen in many airborne pictures. The canopy was opened and closed using a selector on the left wall of the cockpit, but as it moved, both crew lowered their visors in case it should detonate accidentally. A loud horn accompanied the action and the sound became a feature of the Tornado flightline as it blared out across the airfield. The canopy rails were much lower than earlier aircraft and were less intrusive, but a 'bubble' canopy such as that fitted to the F-15 Eagle was not part of the final design. Aircrew flying equipment was redesigned to improve its survivability. There were the traditional G suit and leg restraints, but the lifejacket sprouted sleeves. Onto these were fixed arm restraints on the upper arm. Cords ran down behind the lifejacket stoll and tucked away between the legs. On ejection, both arm and leg restraints drew tight, pulling the limbs into the seat and preventing flailing in the airflow, reducing the risk of injury during a high-speed ejection. Quite soon after the aircraft entered service, the Mark 4 flying helmet was introduced which was a much lighter design and far more comfortable to wear. To add a final touch of luxury, a voice-activated microphone meant the intercom was quiet when dormant. Each of these small factors improved life in the cockpit.

The front cockpit was a very traditional layout dominated by the floor mounted, centrally positioned control column and the head-up display, or HUD. Despite a prominent electronic head-down digital display (EHDD), it was still principally an analogue cockpit with lots of 'hard' switches. For once, however, the word 'auto' featured prominently on many of them. BAE Systems were trying to persuade the aircrew that the computer really did know best and that it could be relied upon to make many of the routine selections and to control systems safely in the event of failures.

In the Tornado F2, the main computer that ran the electronics was a paltry 32 kb, updated to 64 kb shortly after introduction to service, and it was some years before it reached the heady capacity of 128 kb. The single colour (green) displays were driven by basic wave form generators, and hard keys at the edge of the displays allowed the selection of sub routines through menus on screen.

The role of the centrally positioned EHDD was limited. A single rotary control allowed the pilot to select the rear cockpit display of his choice and a further range scale selector allowed him to zoom in on an area of interest. Options quickly disappeared in an early software change, leaving the pilot with the choice of one of the two displays which the navigator had selected in the rear cockpit. The plan display gave a tactical overview, although the F3 lacked the moving digital map of the Tornado bomber. Most pilots preferred this to give 'situation awareness', but whether this or the radar display was of greater interest depended on the stage of the intercept.

The Tornado F3 front cockpit.

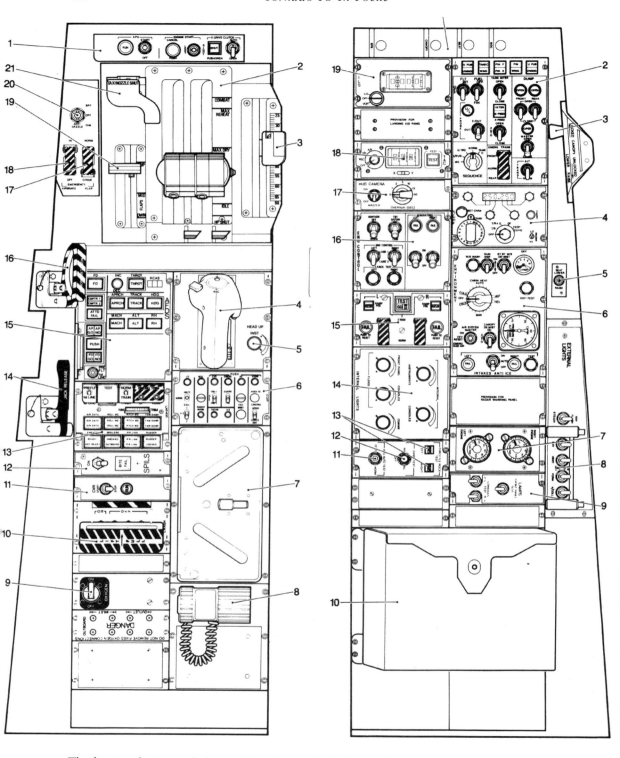

The front cockpit console layout. (Decodes are in the Appendix). (*UK MoD Crown Copyright,* *1985*)

The HUD became the focus of activity in the front cockpit. The Lead Computing Optical Sighting System in the Phantom was a rudimentary affair and really only provided sighting symbology for gun aiming. The HUD in the Tornado F2/F3 was a quantum improvement and was the first example of a comprehensive integrated weapons display in a British fighter. The Lightning had been innovative in some of the weapons displays and controls, but the Tornado was a major step forward and a generation ahead of the Phantom. Controlled by an electronics unit in the main avionics bay, the HUD consisted of a pilots display unit which was centre-mounted at eye level. Symbology projected onto a combining glass in the windscreen was easily visible, albeit with a narrow field of view compared to later fighters such as Typhoon. To aid debriefing, a small periscope on the side of the unit allowed the display to be recorded by a HUD camera to the onboard video recording system. A pilot's control panel selected the modes and, most importantly, de-cluttered the display. As the primary reference for instrument flying, in the rare event that HUD integrity was in doubt, the display would 'occult' (flash) and pilots were warned to cross check with the head-down instruments. In a concession to the 'Navigator's Union', the HUD display was routed to a TV tab in the rear cockpit and gave the navigator a forward view past the front ejection seat for the first time, albeit in glorious monochromatic green.

The HUD was a complex instrument with a number of modes. It provided dynamic flight parameters at all times such as heading, height, and speed in digital format and an energy management display allowed the pilot to adjust the flight profile using the 'SEP' bars (specific excess power). In other words, the pilot could see visually from the HUD when he had spare performance in hand. For navigation, steering bars in the HUD gave cues to fly a track towards a nominated waypoint (a line on the ground between two navigation points) set by the navigator. Flying a groundspeed would guarantee meeting a time on target, although it was rare for air defence crews to need pinpoint timing accuracy, unlike during ground attack operations when it was essential.

Significant was the provision of comprehensive weapons displays. In missile mode, the symbology, which hitherto had been displayed on a radar display buried in the cockpit, was now visible 'heads up', allowing the pilot to concentrate on the tactical situation outside the cockpit. Launch success zones for the missiles were prominently displayed; the allowable steering error, vital to launch a successful radar missile shot, was displayed along with a relative speed scale showing combined closing velocity with the target. A target designator box aided visual acquisition by showing where the radar target should appear in the HUD field of view. An additional lock symbol appeared when the radar was locked-up, allowing a radar-guided missile to be fired. The SRAAM diamond symbol changed depending on missile acquisition status. As the Sidewinder acquired its target, an open diamond showed where the seeker head was pointing and 'closed' once it acquired. The acquisition tone known as the Sidewinder 'chirp' was heard in the headphones at the same time.

In gun mode, a radical new concept called continuously computed impact line, or CCIL, was implemented. In this mode, a sixteen-dot line starting from a fixed gun cross showed the predicted impact points of sixteen shells fired at 0.1 second intervals. By using a ranging wheel, the pilot could programme the estimated wingspan of the target and match the actual range in the HUD. When locked, a range circle wound down giving precise radar range to the target. This gave a huge improvement in accuracy, coupled with an internal mounting which allowed better harmonisation; using accurate radar and computing, the gun scores were excellent from the outset. Not surprisingly, it would have been impossible to introduce such a radical new feature without ironic comment from the pilot community. During the earliest armament practice camps, CCIL was described as trying to 'thread wet spaghetti up a wildcat's ass'. Even so, it worked and it worked well.

In combat, further short-range radar lock modes allowed the pilot to override the navigator's controls to allow the radar to be locked visually in highly dynamic close combat situations. Shot opportunities could be fleeting and it was difficult to predict these in the rear seat, while from the pilot's vantage point they were much clearer. The pilot used the castellated selector on the stick top to enter the preferred mode. A call of 'my radar' would transfer control allowing the combat modes to be employed. There were four main air-to-air override modes:

- Pitch plane scan, or PPS, in which the radar entered a two plane scan in an area from -10 degrees to +50 degrees. The radar would automatically lock to any target inside 5 miles.
- Radar acquisition zone, or RAZ, was steerable and searched out to 5 miles and would automatically lock to the first target detected. RAZ was known colloquially as 'the sausage' due to the symbol which was displayed in the HUD.
- Boresight acquisition mode, or BAM, centred on the weapons. Boresight would also lock to any target detected inside 5 miles. In this mode the pilot pointed the aircraft at an opponent in order to aid radar acquisition.
- HUD acquisition mode, or HAQ, was a more complex mode using the pulse Doppler mode and scanned rapidly from +8 degrees to -6 degrees in a narrow azimuth band around the nose. A box symbol showed the search area.

HOTAS or 'hands-on-throttle-and-stick' had been present in simple forms on earlier fighters but in the Tornado F3 the level of sophistication increased. To make full use of the HUD, routine switch changes could be made without taking the hands from the throttles and the control column. Initially, the moding was 'clunky' and there had been insufficient interaction with front-line crews. Much work was done by the Operational Evaluation Unit to optimise the modes and give pilots the most ergonomic solution. The stick top was redesigned and fitted with an enlarged head similar to that found on the F-18. This introduced a 'hard selector' to the left of the pilot's thumb allowing MRAAM to be selected by pushing forward, the gun to be selected by pulling backwards, and SRAAM to be selected by pressing down, giving missile selection on a single button. The trimmer was retained on the stick top but a castellated selector for the air-to-air radar modes appeared opposite the target acquisition enable button for the SRAAM. The trigger remained on the rear of the stick top in the natural position for the trigger finger. Although a 'slaved' mode allowed the Sidewinder heads to be designated by the radar, a sequencer which allowed the pilot to page through each SRAAM sat on the rear of the left throttle and worked in conjunction with the target acquisition enable button on the stick top. The combination of automatic and manual modes gave the pilot a great degree of control over the missiles before launch, which was particularly useful if an opponent used infra-red decoys. In keeping with the philosophy of giving tactical displays prominence, the radar warning display was given a position high on the right of the front panel in the pilots scan, opposite the missile monitoring system.

'Data overload' was to become a well-known phenomenon in the cockpit, as a vast amount of highly accurate information was suddenly available to the crew both in the HUD and on the TV displays. Although highly accurate, data had to be read, analysed, and assimilated, leading to potential saturation. Analogue gauges give an instant impression of a value, whereas numbers have to be read on a digital display. It was of little use if an over-worked pilot flew the aircraft into the ground while digesting complex data from the flight systems telling him he was about to do so.

Moving around the cockpit from left to right, the least important instrumentation and controls were relegated to the rear of the consoles. It was a known phenomenon that leaning down to select systems immediately after take off, particularly in a turn, would induce disorientation known as 'the leans', and aircraft had been lost after pilots became confused. Any switch which may be needed during these critical phases of flight was moved to a more prominent position and, for the first time, a number of traditionally front seat functions were moved into the back cockpit where the workload was lower just after take off. This included the Identification Friend or Foe (IFF) control box and duplicate radio controls. Other items such as the fly-by-wire control panel which was not used in flight were located to the rear left.

The throttles and wing sweep lever fell naturally to hand as the aircraft was designed to be operated right handed. Like earlier fighters, once through the idle stop, the engines could be exercised in the military power range through to maximum military power. There the similarities ended. Unlike the Phantom where the throttles were rocked outboard to select reheat, doing so in an F3 selected the thrust reversers and lift dump devices. This was a key difference which ex-Phantom pilots were quick to appreciate during conversion, although there were a few embarrassments along the way.

The 'swing wings' were a novelty for new crews. Having seen the wings being installed at the factory I knew they were a true feat of engineering. The wing pivot was milled from a block of titanium and freeze treated before being inserted.

Once in place it was a major task to remove them. The wings rotated around this pivot and a complex series of linkages ensured that the pylons which carried the missiles, fuel tanks, and defensive aids pods, rotated in harmony and stayed aligned with the airflow. A complex gearing mechanism ensured the wings moved in unison—asymmetric wing sweep was a phenomenon that no one wished to flight test. Although an automatic wing sweep and manoeuvre devices mode was built in (AWSMD), it was never cleared for use in the RAF so the wings were selected manually using the lever in the cockpit and the speed limits monitored by the crew. With the wings fully forward in 25 wing, the turning performance was at its best but the speed limit was lower. The wings were brought back to the cruise detente, first to 33 wing which was also never officially cleared for the F3 and then to the midpoint of 45 wing. For high speed flight, 58 wing was virtually fully swept. A stop at 63 wing allowed large tanks to be fitted without striking the tail, and the final position of 67 wing, which was fully swept, gave the maximum speed capability. Although interim positions could be selected, they were not officially cleared for flight. One of the more interesting emergencies which had to be practiced was a wing sweep failure. This gave a stringent crosswind limit of 10 knots. If the wings failed in one of the swept positions the approach speed could be as high as 217 knots, some 65 knots faster than a normal approach. The angle of attack on approach was much higher than normal so the approach angle seemed abnormal with the cockpit sitting high, restricting the normal view of the runway. In the event of a wing sweep failure, the thrust reverse and lift dumps could be pre-armed but they could not be used until the speed dropped below 200 knots, nor could the brakes be used at such high speeds. This left an uncomfortable intervening period until the speed dropped off and the end of the runway came ever closer. An alternative might have been to use the approach end cable, but the speed limit was 165 knots making the option hard to use. Invariably the aircraft would pass over the cable too fast. Happily, I cannot recall such a failure ever occurring as the wing sweep mechanism was extremely reliable.

At the rear of the left console was the crash bar which was only used in the event of a crash so did not need a prime location. Immediately forward were the switches for the voice recorder and the Spin Prevention and Incidence Limiting System, or SPILS. This system gave 'carefree handling' by limiting the effect of demanded control inputs to those which could be delivered by the airframe. The computer analysed the pilot's demanded control movement and fed the 'request' to the fly-by-wire computers. If approved, the electronic 'brain' would give the pilot the demanded manoeuvre. After a little initial scepticism, most pilots began to respect the system and realised that under all but extreme conditions it would keep them out of trouble. One of the first OCU instructors became totally convinced of its value after nearly departing the aircraft from controlled flight during a break into the circuit. Having turned the system off, he increased the 'G' during the break manoeuvre and the aircraft reacted violently. For a few moments the crew thought it was out of control, but the aircraft settled back into normal flight downwind. The instructor suddenly became keen to use SPILS throughout the flight envelope from then on.

Immediately forward of the SPILS was the control panel for the control and stability augmentation system (CSAS) or fly-by-wire system. CSAS was another new phenomenon for the Tornado. The control surfaces were not connected directly to the control column so when the pilot demanded an input, like SPILS, a series of electronic commands passed from the stick via electronic lines to the 'black boxes' of the quadruplex fly-by-wire system. After a series of checks and balances, the computer decided what control input would maintain stability and controlled flight, and whether it would give the pilot his demanded control input. For the first time, an aircraft could not be flown efficiently without the help of the computer. At least the Tornado F3 was a relatively stable design, unlike the F-16 which was designed to be unstable and could not fly without computer assistance. A secondary control system called 'Mech Mode' was the back-up and proved just how badly a Tornado F3 handled in its reversionary flight mode. The aircraft was sluggish and could really only be recovered to base; it was impossible to fight in this mode. The CSAS had to be checked regularly pre-flight using an onboard built-in-test system. Once initiated, a series of dramatic and violent control inputs were fed in as the flight controls rattled away, checking out the operation of the system. For the first year a CSAS BITE (built-in-test) was run on every sortie, but it was a spine jarring event and must have been nearly as detrimental to the fatigue life as an air combat sortie. Very quickly, aircrew pleaded with the engineers to reduce the frequency of the check, ostensibly to save stress on the airframe. In reality, it was to ensure that the frequency of dental work among Tornado aircrew did not begin to creep up. The autopilot control panel sat outboard of the intercom box and the pilot's hand controller finished off the left console.

The centre panel was a departure from the traditional fighter cockpit layout. With the HUD available, the flight instruments were relegated to the lower left-hand side and the normal centre position was dominated by the EHDD. Engine instruments were grouped on the right-hand side. Above and to the left was the missile monitoring system with the radar homing and warning receiver display above and to the right. Some key flight system functions were grouped on a centre pedestal, along with the trim gauges, and controlled by a gang bar. Tactical displays had replaced basic flight instruments.

To the front of the right-hand console sat the telelight panel which gave indications of a malfunction of aircraft systems. The crew were warned of a problem by a flashing red caution light which illuminated in both cockpits. Emergencies were broken down into red light and amber light problems depending on severity. Major failures such as a gearbox failure or hydraulic failure brought up a red caption. Additional combinations of amber captions would confirm which system had failed. Lesser emergencies that would have an effect on the mission but, *in extremis*, might be safely managed without returning to base, brought up single amber warnings. Although the F3 was a simpler aeroplane to operate than its predecessors, its flight reference card drills still ran to eighty-three pages, and crews were evaluated in the mission simulator every month to ensure that the correct way to handle each drill was understood. Unlike its predecessors, there were fewer emergencies which were likely to result in the loss of the aircraft if properly managed. There was, however, one strange anomaly concerning the battery. In the event of a double generator failure—rare, admittedly—a veritable Christmas tree of warning captions would illuminate. A red 'AC' and 'DC' caption was seriously bad news, particularly if operating well out into the North Sea at night. If attempts to reset the generators were unsuccessful, systems which provided an electrical drain were slowly shed. Many of the systems which required high power usage were the avionics controlled by the navigator in the back cockpit. The warnings in the cards were particularly dire:

> Battery endurance approx 20 mins; thereafter, engine shutdown is impossible and uncontrolled engine runaway occurs.
> If both IN [inertial navigation units] not switched off, battery life reduced to approximately 7 minutes.

In a bizarre piece of design logic, if the engines lost electrical power they spooled up to greater than 100 per cent until self-destruct! Suffice to say that a double generator failure resulted in some snappy work in both cockpits and an immediate recovery to the nearest airfield before the F3 committed suicide.

The right console held the main systems and lighting controls. A fuel control panel, engine control panel, cabin conditioning and fuel temperature gauges were placed towards the front. Additional avionics, including the instrument landing system, the HUD camera control, and a duplicate radio and RHWR control panel, took the remaining space. Bizarrely, the TACAN (radio navigation) control box was in the front cockpit and no one could see an obvious reason for why it was not in the back cockpit. Perhaps the logic was that it could provide an emergency 'get you home' facility if the navigator withdrew his labour! In defence of the designers, cockpit layout was always a thorny issue and it was impossible to please all of the people all of the time. There was never 100 per cent agreement, even among the experts on the OEU, and debates continued long into the evening in the bar.

For the navigators, the rear cockpit was a radical change with the focus of activity around the two electronic TV tabular displays, or TV tabs. This was the first shift towards a modern digital cockpit. Gone was the archaic radar display of the Phantom, wedged into the gap under the instrument panels. It had been replaced by TV screens at eye level. Rather than poring over a small screen which had seemed to be an afterthought, navigators now sat upright with tactical information in clear view. It was a huge improvement not to be bent double when pulling 'G' in air combat manoeuvring.

The centre panel flight instrument cluster had attitude, heading, height, and speed information displayed on analogue instruments below the TV tabs. Largely superfluous, the information was replicated on the TV displays where it could

The electronic head-down display (EHDD).

The pilot's view through the head-up display (HUD). (*UK MoD Crown Copyright, 1991*)

The front cockpit telelight panel. (*UK MoD Crown Copyright, 1991*)

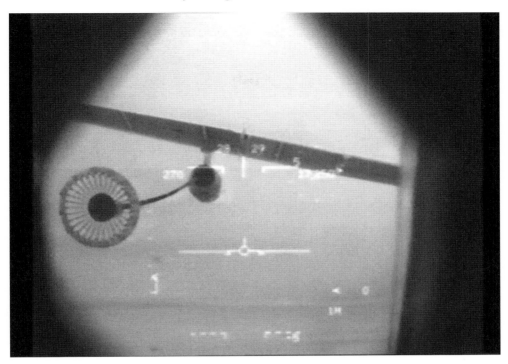

The refuelling basket from the pilot's perspective through the head-up display.

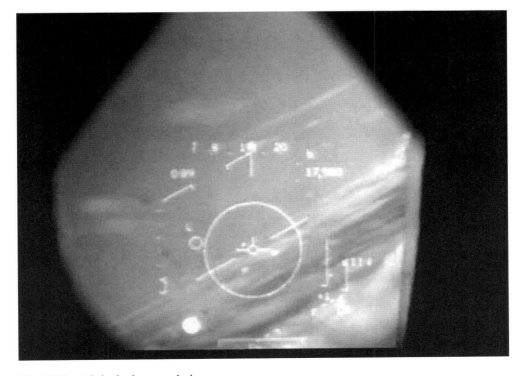

The HUD with locked-up symbology.

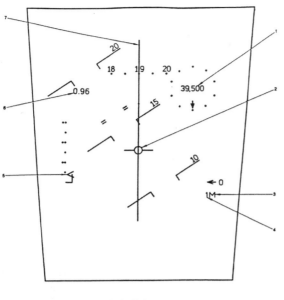

1 AIRCRAFT HEIGHT
2 AIRCRAFT SYMBOL(VV)
3 WEAPON TYPE (M=MRAAM)
4 NUMBER OF WEAPONS REMAINING
5 ANGLE OF ATTACK SCALE
6 AIRCRAFT SPEED (MACH NO.)
7 RADAR CENTERLINE

Pitch Plane Scan

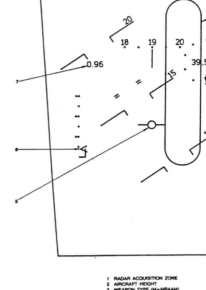

1 RADAR ACQUISITION ZONE
2 AIRCRAFT HEIGHT
3 WEAPON TYPE (M=MRAAM)
4 NUMBER OF WEAPONS REMAINING
5 AIRCRAFT SYMBOL(VV)
6 ANGLE OF ATTACK SCALE
7 AIRCRAFT SPEED (MACH NO.)

Radar Acquisition Zone

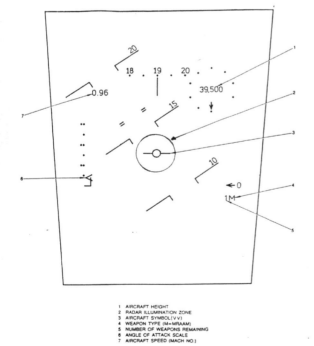

1 AIRCRAFT HEIGHT
2 RADAR ILLUMINATION ZONE
3 AIRCRAFT SYMBOL(VV)
4 WEAPON TYPE (M=MRAAM)
5 NUMBER OF WEAPONS REMAINING
6 ANGLE OF ATTACK SCALE
7 AIRCRAFT SPEED (MACH NO.)

Boresight Acquisition

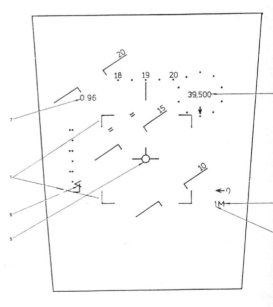

1 ACQUISITION ZONE
2 AIRCRAFT HEIGHT
3 WEAPON TYPE (M=MRAAM)
4 NUMBER OF WEAPONS REMAINING
5 AIRCRAFT SYMBOL (LOCKED)
6 ANGLE OF ATTACK SCALE
7 AIRCRAFT SPEED (MACH NO.)

HUD Acquisition

The HUD air combat modes. (*UK MoD Crown Copyright, 1986*)

The throttle box and wing sweep lever.

The pilot's modified stick top.

The pilot's radar, homing, and warning display. The engine instruments are below.

The pilot's missile monitoring system panel.

The wing glove box with the wings swept.

be better assimilated. For the first time the navigator had a fuel gauge which was absolutely essential in air combat given the rates at which fuel was used in full afterburner. The analogue gauge sat in easy view immediately in front of the navigator's eyes on a small panel above the TVs. In later software iterations, vital fuel figures also appeared as a prompt on the tactical display. 'Bingo' fuel could be programmed into the main computer, and as the fuel dropped below a pre-determined level, an additional flashing prompt appeared in the centre of the display. This was impossible to miss and gave the crew a final warning of when to disengage and return to base. An angle of attack gauge, which was useful in air combat, completed this cluster. To the left of the main panel by the navigator's left knee was the radar data control panel which operated the routine radar functions. In the centre was the data link control panel for the Joint Tactical Information and Distribution System, although this did not appear until the mid-1990s. A blank panel was a feature of the early F2s and F3s, although it was used to house defensive aids control panels fitted during the Stage 1 Plus programme. Once installed, the JTIDS panel dominated the cockpit, giving not just datalink information but secure communications via a keyboard and screen.

Other control boxes and panels were arranged on the side consoles in traditional style. Basic mission data was pre-planned on the ground and loaded during start up and the tactical data could then be modified in the cockpit using the hard key sets below the TV tab screens. As each menu was called up, tags appeared on the screen directly above the nine unmarked white keys with a different function for each sub-menu. Further rows of 'hard' keys below selected a main function on that particular TV tab, taking the navigator back to a top level menu. The main functions were 'PLN', 'NAV', 'VAS', and 'RDR' for plan, navigation, visual acquisition system, and radar. Other hard keys allowed the navigator to select secondary functions, and test and sub menus. Once airborne, new data or amendments could be inserted into the computer using a freehand typing mode.

For crew cooperation purposes, the radar display was normally called up on the left-hand TV tab with the 'God's Eye' tactical plan display on the right. This meant that the pilot could easily select the display of interest. As in previous fighters, the radar scanner in the nose of the aircraft was operated using the navigator's hand controller from the back seat. In the single sticker, this controller sat on a centre pedestal at waist height. It was used in conjunction with the radar display control panel, or RDCP, on the left-hand side of the front bulkhead above the left knee, and the main radar control panel, or RCP. This panel housed the on/off switch and frequency selectors for the main radar channel and the continuous-wave (CW) radar channel. Twenty-four channels could be selected manually with a further eighteen channels for the CW radar, which guided the MRAAMs. In addition, a random channel selector mode could be programmed into the main computer, giving an element of frequency agility which was extremely useful in the electronic battle. By using the hand controller, the navigator set routine functions such as scan widths, elevation patterns, and lock modes on either display. On the Tornado F2, the hand controller was a simple affair lifted straight from the Tornado GR1 bomber, offering only a few simple switches. As the 'Stage 1' radar design was finalised, a new hand controller was produced providing the ability to select thirteen key radar functions using switches on the controller. The main controls to operate the radar scanner were along the top of the hand controller. A toggle switch allowed the navigator to cycle between tracks in the read out line, which showed track data on the TV tab. Alongside, a vertical toggle switch moved the scanner up and down in elevation, and to the right, a further selector put the radar into highlight mode and could command it to lock automatically. Next to the thumb on the left-hand side was an insert switch which, when pushed forward, entered tracks into 'track-while-scan' once designated on the TV tab. By pulling the same switch backwards, a display of target height appeared next to the tracks on the radar display. By interrogating the track electronically using the IFF system, a friendly track would turn into a number rather than a letter on both radar and plan displays. Interlocks could then be set which prevented the crew from firing a missile at a friendly track. The lock trigger which set the radar into single target track remained on the rear side of the controller. Once selected, the radar locked its beam onto the target and a MRAAM could be launched once inside parameters. The final button was to the lower left and was originally intended as a chaff/flare release button. It was superseded by the controls on the grab handles but was used for other functions at various times. The age of the computer game had arrived in the back cockpit.

At the forward end of the left console, tucked away in the corner, was the display and control unit for the radar homing and warning receiver, or RHWR. This position low in the cockpit was a throwback to the Phantom cockpit where the RWR occupied the same ill-considered position—to repeat the mistake in a newly designed cockpit was careless and unnecessary.

On the right console were the main avionics. A telelight panel replicated the systems warnings but the rear cockpit panel was optimised for functions more relevant to the back seater. The key red light warnings were still displayed, as were amber warnings for the main systems, but items such as amber warnings for avionics functions were unique to the rear panel. Below this was the IFF interrogator—it was the first time that this equipment had been installed in a British fighter. All aircraft carried a Mode 1 and a Mode 3 IFF transponder. Military aircraft were also equipped with a special code known as Mode 2, which transmitted a reprogrammable code unique to the specific aircraft. The interrogator could be programmed with codes of the day for exercise or operations. By pressing a switch on the hand controller, the navigator could interrogate a potential threat aircraft electronically in Modes 1 and 3. A Mode 4 facility, which was even more secure, was added later. Until the advent of more advanced interrogation systems, the lack of a response did not allow the Tornado crew to declare a contact hostile. It was merely an indicator and there were much more complex procedures to do so. Moving back along the panel down the inboard side were the controls for the onboard recording system and mission data entry facility, the flight director, the twin inertial navigation controller, and the controls for the computer and graphics. Outboard was the IFF control box, the communications panel, the VHF/UHF radio, and the HF radio box.

On the left console, in addition to the radar control panel, or RCP, and a little used compass control panel, sat the major new innovation for a back seater. The missile monitoring system, or MMS, was a duplicate of the pilot's MMS in the front cockpit and allowed missiles to be selected, tuned, and jettisoned. This was the first time such functions had migrated from the front cockpit and allowed the workload to be shared. An electronic display showed which missiles were fitted and on which station, their status, and which one was nominated for firing. In addition, if there were any failures of the weapons or their pylons, the display would highlight the problem. The emergency radio was also located in the back, but in the early days it was a relatively simple device which operated on a single frequency.

Such was the increase in space that a small receptacle was provided in the console to house flight documents such as the *en route* supplements—essential material for a navigator, even in the digital age. Later in the aircraft's life, another JTIDS data panel joined these units. Outboard on the console were the brightly coloured handles which allowed the navigator to jettison the canopy either explosively, or to unlock the canopy manually. These were in addition to the normal canopy selector.

Bracketing the TV tab displays on either side were the grab handles designed and fitted during Operation 'Granby'. These allowed the navigator to pull around in the seat to 'Check 6' in air combat. Fitted diagonally at the side of the TV tabs, they were equipped with chaff and flare release buttons at the top and bottom of each bar. The navigator could dispense self-defence countermeasures from the rear cockpit while still holding a bogey in visual sight when looking over his shoulder during an air combat engagement. The timing of when countermeasures were 'popped' was critical as they had to bloom in the case of chaff and ignite in the case of a flare at the appropriate moment if they were to be effective in decoying an incoming missile. For the pilot, the dispense button was on the throttle, so always within easy reach. Had the original back-seat hand controller been used, it would have been unreachable in combat. By putting a dispense switch on the grab bar, it was always to hand. Simple ergonomics, but slow in coming.

One of the big improvements for the Tornado F2 was to have been the inclusion of a visual acquisition system, or VAS. RAF fighter crews had long coveted the TV Sensor Unit, or TVSU, which was fitted to the F-14 Tomcat, a system similar to the USAF F4E TISEO. This gave US crews the ability to track a target passively. After locking the electronic/visual sensor to the radar, once acquired, an image of the target aircraft could be seen at ranges significantly beyond visual range, at which time the radar could be switched to standby. This also allowed visual identification in sufficient time to engage with a longer range missile before being pulled into a combat engagement. A similar capability was envisaged for the F3 which would have allowed a passive approach behind a target. TVSU was hugely expensive and relied on an optical sensor mounted under the nose and was also something of a 'dragmaster', incurring an aerodynamic penalty. For the RAF Phantom, a low-technology optical sight known as the telescope sighting system, or TESS, had been fitted, but the F3 was earmarked for a more technological solution. Once cued by the track-while-scan, which was less likely to trigger an enemy radar warning receiver, the visual sensor would be locked on and a profile could be flown as if the radar had been providing full tracking data. Under these circumstances, the radar would only be needed to support a MRAAM firing so could remain in standby or search mode for much longer. It would also have aided Quick Reaction Alert operations as the crew could close into an offset identification position, preset by the navigator on the Visident Offset Control Panel (VOCP). By selecting an azimuth angle and elevation angle, the steering commands would position the aircraft at that point in space 200 yards from the target. The glossy brochure seemed impressive, but after a series of initial discussions in which a technician offered some blurry computer images of projected VAS capability, the function quietly disappeared from future plans, never to reappear. As with many projects, it was not clear at the front line why it was dropped. The plans were never resurrected during my time as the fleet manager for the F3 avionics. The F3 retired from service without a VAS capability and the VOCP was used purely with the radar.

The vast majority of the 165 Tornado 'Air Defence Variants' that were originally ordered were single-stick aircraft, and on the squadrons, only one trainer variant was normally held on strength. For the Operational Conversion Unit, however, where many more sorties required a flying instructor to sit in the rear seat during pilot conversion sorties and check rides, a much higher proportion of twin-stick aircraft were needed. For the OCU, the ratio was about 1:1 of each type. The rear cockpit of the twin-stick aircraft was radically different and required major changes to the cockpit layout. The design was carefully developed and gave the flying instructor in the rear seat the ability to carry out virtually every function needed to fly the aircraft. Very few systems were available exclusively in the front cockpit of a trainer variant with most duplicated in the back. Flying instructors, known as QFIs, became confident in their ability to fly the jet, even if the front seater became incapacitated—this led to an interesting opportunity for some fortunate navigators which I will describe later. The TV tabs were shifted to the right-hand side of the bulkhead to allow the placing of ancillary flight instruments to the left. These included a more comprehensive set of flight instruments, landing gear indicators, a 'G' meter, and a series of controls down the left glare panel. Most important was the provision of a hook selector and low pressure fuel cocks to allow the engines to be shut down from the back. Engine instruments were replicated on the lower main bulkhead to the right of the back-seater's knee. To make room for the control column, which was mounted in the centre of the floor, the navigator's hand controller was shifted across to the right-hand console and the adjustable footrests on the floor were replaced by rudder pedals. On the left console, navigation and radar functions were relegated to the rear of the console, making them harder to reach when conducting intercept missions. This

The rear cockpit of a single-stick (strike) version.

The TV tabular displays.

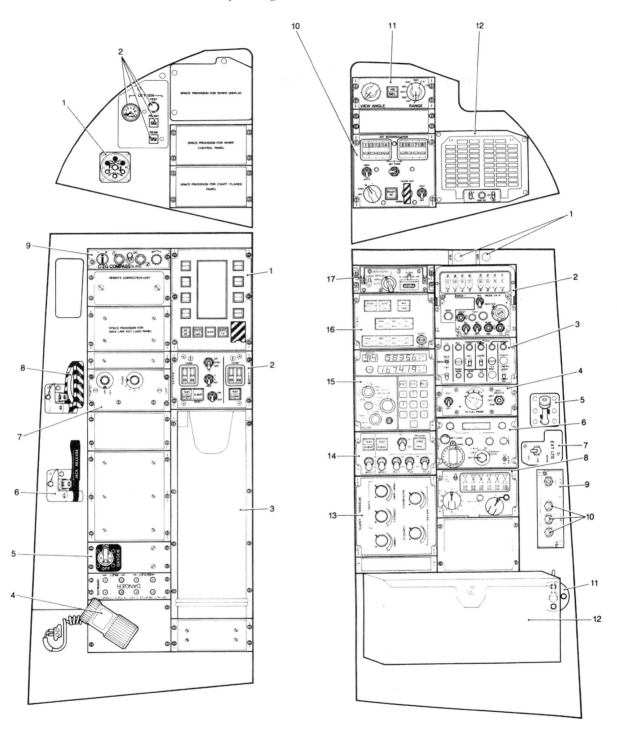

The rear cockpit console layout. (Decodes are in the Appendix). (*UK MoD Crown Copyright, 1985*)

The rear cockpit analogue instruments in the single-stick 'strike' version.

The radar data control panel.

The radar control panel.

Hard keys on the TV tabs allowed the navigator to select functions and input data.

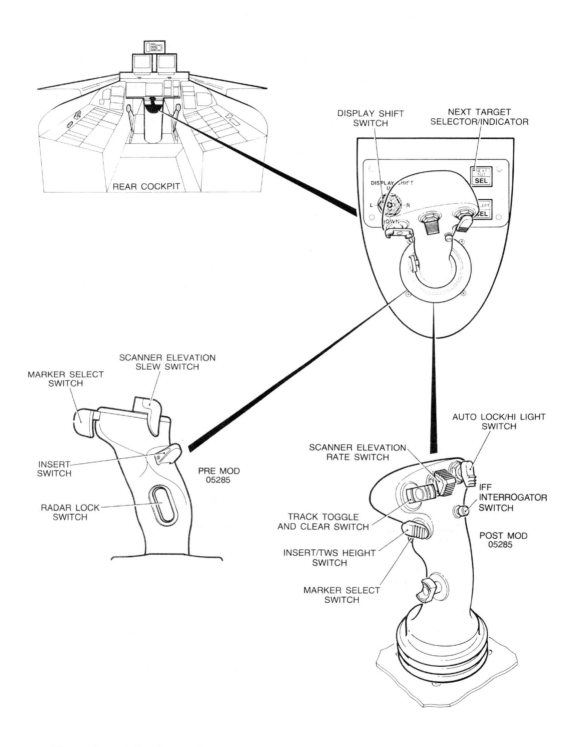

REAR COCKPIT

DISPLAY SHIFT
SWITCH

NEXT TARGET
SELECTOR/INDICATOR

DISPLAY SHIFT

SEL

SEL

MARKER SELECT
SWITCH

SCANNER ELEVATION
SLEW SWITCH

INSERT
SWITCH

RADAR LOCK
SWITCH

PRE MOD
05285

AUTO LOCK/HI LIGHT
SWITCH

SCANNER ELEVATION
RATE SWITCH

IFF
INTERROGATOR
SWITCH

TRACK TOGGLE
AND CLEAR SWITCH

POST MOD
05285

INSERT/TWS HEIGHT
SWITCH

MARKER SELECT
SWITCH

The navigator's hand controller functions. (*UK MoD Crown Copyright, 1987*)

The original navigator's hand controller.

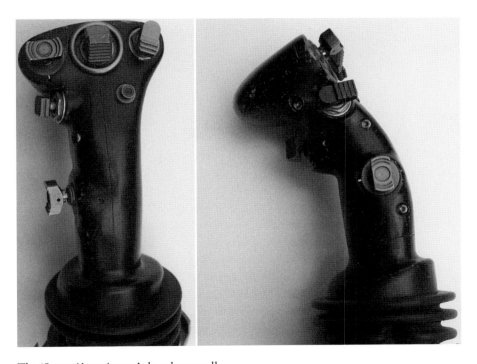

The 'Stage 1' navigator's hand controller.

Left: The dual inertial navigation system control panel.

Opposite above: The IFF interrogator and the IFF control panel.

Opposite below: The rear cockpit missile monitoring system control panel. (*UK MoD Crown Copyright, 1986*)

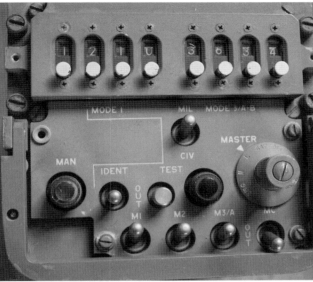

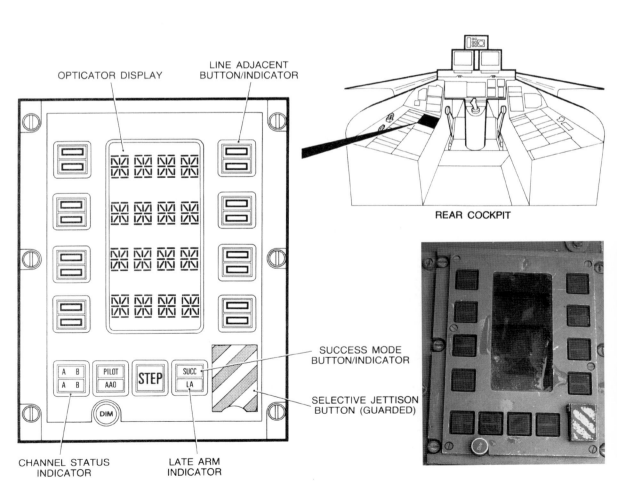

OPTICATOR DISPLAY

LINE ADJACENT
BUTTON/INDICATOR

SUCCESS MODE
BUTTON/INDICATOR

SELECTIVE JETTISON
BUTTON (GUARDED)

CHANNEL STATUS
INDICATOR

LATE ARM
INDICATOR

REAR COCKPIT

The grab bars which also mounted dispense buttons for the chaff and flare system.

was to make way for the throttle quadrant and wing sweep lever, which had to take the natural position to fall to hand for the instructor pilot. These changes affected OCU navigator instructors most as they would have to adapt regularly to two radically different cockpit layouts with switches and displays in completely different positions.

The most significant change in cockpit design was the fact that for the first time everything was software controlled. I could fire up the Phantom simulator today and, despite the fact that I had not flown the aircraft for thirty years, most of the functions would be familiar and the knobs and gauges would work as I remember them on my final sortie. The same could not be said for the Tornado F3. Firing up the main computer after only three years away, I was faced with brand new displays with soft keys operating functions which were suddenly unfamiliar.

Like the Phantom, the main radar display was known as a B Scope. The baseline (at 0 miles range) was expanded to cover 60 degrees either side of the nose. This allowed targets at close range to be interpreted. In conventional sector scan radars, those targets would otherwise have been closely packed in the base of the 'cheese wedge', and it would have been impossible to manoeuvre the aircraft precisely at close range to achieve an interception. By opening out the baseline, the position of targets close to the aircraft's nose were more easily interpreted and a controlled final turn could be flown. Much more tactical information appeared on the new radar display. Unlike the Phantom, as soon as a target was entered into track-while-scan, it 'associated' and showed as a tadpole with a vector. A lettered block was tagged with a short proboscis which showed a rough heading for the designated track. The full flight parameters of the track were then repeated in the 'read out line' at the base of the display. As more tracks were added, becoming B then C and so on, the navigator could 'toggle' between them to see precise flight parameters for each track down to quite accurate levels of detail. A small elevation display to the right of the radar showed a rough disposition in height, centred on the F3's flight level. Individual tracks were shown at a range and azimuth offset from the Tornado's extended centreline, giving a graphic depiction of the target's position in space. This allowed the crew to set up a tactical intercept into weapons release parameters. As the navigator hit the IFF interrogator switch on the hand controller, a friendly IFF response would change the track designation. Later, as the Joint Tactical Information Distribution System was fitted, the system was refined. Tracks annotated L, M, and so on originated from a JTIDS 'cross tell'. This meant that an E3 Sentry mounting an airborne early warning barrier could send information about tracks outside the Tornado's radar coverage direct to the crew's tactical display.

The quantum leap forward was the provision of the 'God's Eye' tactical view called the Plan display. For the first time, the individual tracks were transferred from the radar and displayed on a north-orientated tactical grid, providing a clear picture of the battlefield. Using a cassette tape, the navigator loaded this tactical information into the main computer after pre-programming missile engagement zones, tanker towlines, navigation routes, combat air patrols, air force bases,

The rear cockpit of a twin-stick 'trainer' variant.

The rear-seat control column stick top, similar to the original front-seat control column.

The repositioned navigator's hand controller in the trainer variant.

and TACAN beacons on the ground station. For the first time, the crew had excellent situation awareness of any tactical information which may affect an intercept. Instead of blundering inadvertently into a live missile engagement zone, the boundaries were clearly shown on the displays. Crucially, a 'Bullseye' could be shown, which when used with a cursor, gave a range and bearing from the reference point and allowed the crew to report and identify potential hostile contacts accurately to their ground controller.

The final display which was rarely used was the navigation format. A fixed circle showed the aircraft's position in relation to a planned track. While it was excellent for bomber crews, it was rare for a fighter crew on UK air defence tasks to have to approach CAP, or any other navigation reference on a precise heading. Ironically, it would have been extremely useful for low-level operations in RAF Germany during the Cold War. For air defence operations, the plan display was much more flexible for area navigation, although the lack of a moving map which the Tornado GR1 crews enjoyed was a limitation. Over the sea this was not a problem, but in the overland role it became a severe limitation. Even for air defence, relating targets to ground features was important and the 'electric string', as the navigation lines were known, were just short of the mark. Although navigation lines could be used to replicate land features, the small onboard computer had inadequate power to run a full moving map or even a basic landmass simulation. For that reason, the display had to be interpreted to give precise navigation accuracy. It was only the advent of JTIDS, which required more accurate navigation data for target correlation, that led to the provision of ring laser giro inertial systems and GPS navigation. Along with that came a landmass simulation. The last Tornado F3 crews were much better served in this area.

The following pictures taken from early open source training material show the three types of displays.

The displays, when run in the benign environment on a test bench in the factory, were impressive. However, the reality was that operating the early Foxhunter radar was much more of a handful for the first navigators. In the first screenshot, a four-ship formation is flying ahead of the fighter at 25-miles and 53-miles range respectively. The lead pair is hostile and showing letter designations. The trail pair is flying wider but closer to the fighter. This display would suggest two enemy aircraft being followed by a pair of friendly fighters. All four tracks are in full track and being updated by the Foxhunter radar. The navigator has designated track B as the target of interest, and 'B' is shown in the read out line. The elevation scan on the right shows a tight grouping in height, although it is impossible to read each track's height accurately from this display. To do so, the navigator would toggle through the tracks in the read out line.

Once new aircrew had familiarised themselves with the cockpit, it was time to fly. The pre-flight start sequence was similar to that of other two-seat aircraft types. The crew walked to the aircraft together and while the pilot completed the external walk around, the navigator completed a few checks in the back cockpit before climbing into the front cockpit to apply external power. Back in the rear cockpit, he or she brought up the main computer and the wave form generators before beginning the alignment sequence for the dual inertial navigation platforms. As the inertial system aligned, mission data prepared on the cassette preparation ground system was loaded into the main computer via a data loading device on the right-hand console. For the modern generation the system would seem archaic as it used a cassette tape as the storage medium. For the 1980s this was cutting edge technology, not least because, in playback mode, it allowed crews to listen to music on a long and otherwise boring transit sortie. I was eternally grateful for the function on my ten-hour transit to Oman. With both crew strapped in and the ejection seats armed, the pilot started the small auxiliary power unit or APU, which was then used to power up the first engine. The complexity of the start sequence was readily apparent in the fact that the drills to complete the process

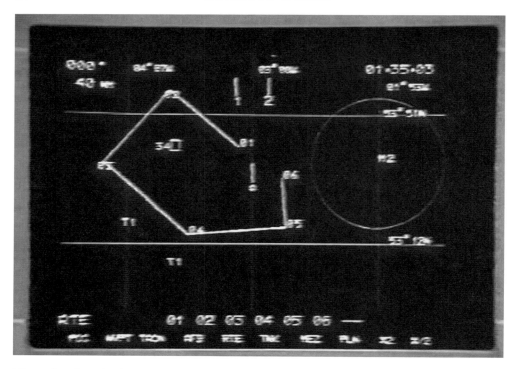

The early 'Plan' display. (*UK MoD Crown Copyright, 1985*)

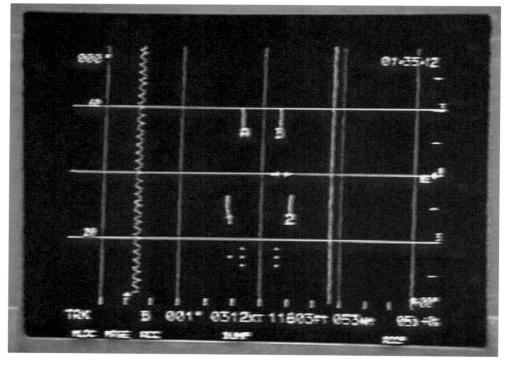

The early radar display. (*UK MoD Crown Copyright, 1985*)

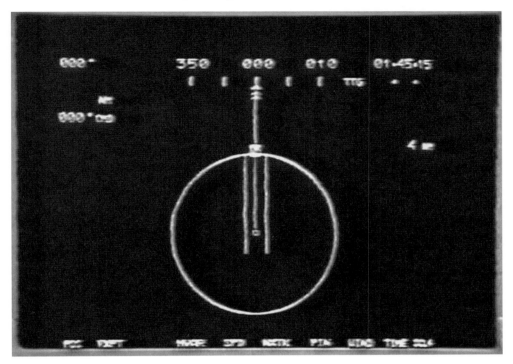

The early navigation display. (*UK MoD Crown Copyright, 1985*)

extended to fifty-five pages in the flight reference cards. In contrast, the actual start sequence was simple. After selecting the start button for the first engine— the right was always started first— the throttle was advanced through the idle stop. Monitoring the oil pressure, the RPM rose to about 65 per cent before stabilising. At this stage, the fuel flow, which was also used to cool systems, was redirected. It was important to confirm that the recirculation change over valve, or RCOV, had operated correctly. If not, pressurised fuel could be flowing through the incorrect pipes causing damage to the engines. After starting both engines, the pilot checked the various airframe functions such as the wing sweep, the flaps, the manoeuvre devices, and the airbrakes. At this stage the CSAS built-in-test was run if required. In the back, once the inertial navigators had aligned, they were placed into the navigate position, the navigation computer was engaged, and built-in-tests were completed on the radar, RHWR, IFF systems, and defensive aids.

Once all the formation had checked in serviceable, the formation leader called for taxi clearance from Air Traffic Control before taxiing to the in use runway. The engines were quite powerful and a facility known as taxi nozzle reduced the effective thrust, allowing the pilot to hold a slower taxi speed. As the formation moved along the taxiway, the pre-flight checks were conducted on a 'challenge and response' basis with the navigator calling out the checks from the flight reference cards and the pilot making the final switch selections to prepare the aircraft. For take off, afterburner was always used with mid flap, and once safely airborne, the undercarriage was retracted before reaching 250 knots and the flaps were retracted. The afterburner was cancelled normally at about 300 to 350 knots, and the formation climbed out to the normal operating altitude. In the air, given that the aircraft could be configured with a wing sweep as far forward as 25 degrees and as far back as 67 degrees, the Tornado F3 handled like two different aircraft. It took only seven seconds to move the wings from fully forward to fully back. Fully forward, 25 wing gave the best performance for take off, normal climb, range flying, loiter, low-speed flying, range descents, approach, and landing. Although not officially cleared for use in the F3, some pilots felt 33 wing gave better performance for range flying. Between 450 and 550 knots, 45 wing was the optimum setting and was used for higher speed cruise. The compromise here was that at the more swept wing positions, turn performance suffered. As the wings moved aft, despite manoeuvre slat being available, turn performance fell off, and even more so with increased altitude. Beyond these wing positions the aircraft was configured for high-speed flight. High subsonic speeds above Mach 0.9 required 58 wing, but the optimum speed range was quite small, ranging from M0.88 to M0.95. A 63 wing detent allowed the large external fuel tanks to be carried at high speed without risk of contact with the 'taileron'. If fully swept, the rear of the tanks fouled the leading edge so a mechanical interlock prevented this. The final position, fully swept at 67 degrees, was for sustained supersonic flight. Surprisingly, the aircraft was still manoeuvrable in this condition although turns were much wider, even at high 'G'. Even at these speeds, the cockpit was quiet and the aircraft felt responsive and seemed to be in its element. Decelerating, pilots had to be aware of a tendency for a marked increase in roll rate, which could occur as the spoilers deployed between the 58 and 45 wing settings. There were also some limits on when the airbrakes could be used as they were quite large and could have a significant effect on the handling characteristics and trim. Much effort had been put in to give the aircraft 'carefree handling'. The Spin Prevention and Limiting System, or SPILS, worked with the fly-by-wire computer to limit the demands placed by the pilot to prevent the aircraft overstressing or entering an unsafe area of the flight envelope. It was turned on before flight and remained selected throughout. It was only turned off during the downwind checks prior to landing. With SPILS on, the pilot could be confident that he would achieve the maximum performance that the airframe was able to deliver at any given time.

The carefree concept extended to the engines, and the improved reliability of the RB199 ensured that the engines could be operated at any power setting throughout the flight envelope. This also included the ability to slam the throttles open or closed. A slam from idle to maximum dry took about four seconds. In the opposite sense, a slam closed may have resulted in a period of 'sub idle'. If the pilot then tried to push the throttles forward at that moment, it was possible to surge the engine. This risk was most evident in air combat manoeuvring, but despite the warnings, surges were quite rare, albeit extremely dramatic, and the RB199 was extremely well behaved. A final engine position was known as 'Combat'. This maximum reheat selection allowed a higher turbine blade temperature, giving extra combat thrust at higher levels just when you needed that extra help, but at the cost of reduced engine life.

For best turn, the wings were selected fully forward and the leading edge slats and manoeuvre flaps were extended. At low level, this gave the Tornado F3 a respectable 19 degrees per second turn rate, although this fell somewhat short of the 26 degrees per second for an F-16. To sweep the wings, the flaps had to be retracted before the wings would travel, although the leading edge slats were still available at greater wing sweeps up to 45 degrees. For that reason, fighting the F3 became a compromise between speed and turn performance. One thing was sure, it was quite difficult to take a visual missile shot against a Tornado F3 coming through the fight at a high Mach number with the wings fully back.

Initial impressions as pilots transitioned to the F3 were often positive and it was some time later when frustrations crept in. Development of the fly-by-wire scheduling meant that the responses to stick demands were uniform and consistent throughout the flight envelope at all wing sweeps and all stores configurations. With SPILS engaged, pitch and roll authority reduced with increasing angle of attack (AOA). Stick forces were deliberately increased above 12.6 units AOA; with rapid stick movement, this gave the pilot feedback in the more challenging areas of the envelope. AOA limits were determined by the limit of stick movement or by CSAS limiters. At this stage, the CSAS computer simply prevented the pilot from demanding additional performance. The RAF, in its wisdom, decided not to use the automatic wing sweep and manoeuvre devices (AWSMDS) and many felt that this was an unnecessary limitation which more comprehensive testing could have avoided. There was nothing wrong with the system and it was often used on delivery flights when crews worked to the manufacturer's flight rules. In a bizarre decision early in the service life, it was decided to inhibit the system and remove certain elements. For Saudi operation the system was cleared for flight, and many pilots who returned from duties in the Kingdom expressed amazement at the RAF impasse. During my own time in MoD, my pilot colleague attempted to reinstate the AWSMDS but was thwarted by the high cost of the retrofit and the intimidating flight clearance proposals. The impasse was bizarre given that the manufacturer had already approved it for flight through its own rigorous flight safety regime. With the lack of funding, a perfectly capable system was not cleared for RAF use. For that reason, RAF pilots operated the wings in manual mode, checking speeds carefully as they approached the limits and manually sweeping the wings to the appropriate settings. Although this required constant attention, mistakes were relatively rare. Navigators monitored the wing position from the back seat as it was particularly obvious when pilots forgot to sweep the wings. At 450 knots a call of 'Wings' would often go from back to front even though the pilots were attuned to the need. The aircraft would often send its own reminders as 'wing buzz' was obvious at higher speeds if a pilot neglected the wing sweep lever. It was much later when we learned that the implications of failing to sweep the wings in a timely fashion could be catastrophic.

Back in the circuit the aircraft was docile. There were two main landing techniques. The pilot flared the aircraft onto the runway giving a gentle arrival unlike the 'controlled crash' in a Phantom. The normal landing used thrust reverse, which was selected by rocking the throttles outboard. The left throttle pre-armed the lift dump system while the right throttle pre-armed the thrust reverse. By preparing these selections before touchdown, once the weight was on the wheels they would immediately slow the aircraft. Lift dump popped the spoilers out into the airflow, killing the lift on the wings. To engage the thrust reverse, the throttles were advanced as if increasing power, but the thrust was diverted forward acting as a brake. The stopping performance was a vast improvement over previous types which relied on brake parachutes, and the F3 could come to a halt in a staggeringly short distance. Landing on the 'numbers' on the easterly runway at RAF Coningsby and using full reverse thrust, it was just possible to stop before reaching the lazy runway—mere hundreds of feet. During this time, the noise in the cockpit was at its highest since the thrust reverse was extremely loud. As the thrust reverse bit, the aircraft would oscillate quite markedly about the lateral axis, giving rise to the term 'riding the white rhino'. A normal thrust reverse landing was much more gentlemanly. Once below 90 knots there was a risk of ingesting debris into the intakes due to the airflow flowing forward from the 'buckets', so the thrust reverse had to be cancelled when the warning horn sounded. This led to an immediate lull in the noise and a return to sanity. The downside of thrust reversers was that they were incredibly heavy and the weight penalty impacted adversely on normal airframe performance. The most obvious penalty was that F3s were always dirty, a function of the oily exhaust gases passing forward over the base of the light coloured fin.

A much more serene arrival was to use aerodynamic braking. After a normal approach at a high angle of attack, the aircraft was settled onto the runway on its mainwheels and the throttles reduced to idle. The pilot had the option to use lift dump, but in either event, the taxi nozzle was opened, killing the thrust from the engines, and the nose was raised by easing back on the control column to 18 units angle of attack. This nose-high attitude, which gave the aircraft a surprisingly elegant profile, was maintained as the speed fell off, and at about 100 knots, the nose was allowed to drop gently onto the runway before braking to taxi speed. Although it required a longer roll than full thrust reverse landing, it was much more stylish, and the fact it was even possible in an F3 surprised a few F-15 pilots.

An ergonomic anomaly emerged quite early in the F3s life. As fighter crews, we wanted to sit as high in the cockpit as possible and by raising the seat to the upper limits of its travel, the navigator was now sitting quite high above the cockpit canopy rails. With the slight bulge in the canopy (note slight), the view into the 6 o'clock was vastly improved, and with the slimmer wings, the view behind and below was also better. As with most improvements it was not without compromise. It was discovered that by raising the seat so high, the upper straps adopted an unnatural angle that forced the navigator's shoulders down, causing possible back problems if forced to eject. The design position had been for the seat to sit much lower in the cockpit. For air defenders, the new gains were not given up easily and the edict that navigators should adopt the lower sitting position was received badly. Most who were enjoying the better view into the 6 o'clock preferred to take the risk although would have preferred some time to motor the seat lower in the event of a pre-meditated ejection. In the front cockpit, similar wobbles ensued as the doctors suddenly decided that pilots over 6 feet tall could not safely operate in the ejection seat. This was ironic given that early efforts had been made to accommodate short pilots. Such chicanery caused massive frustration among crews, particularly given the vast size of the cockpits.

The grey paint scheme on the consoles was a little easier on the eye compared to the black colour scheme in earlier fighters. Ergonomics was important and with the displays at eye level, for the first time the navigator could sit back in the seat in relative comfort rather than huddle forward over a tiny radar screen. The positioning of the navigator's hand controller on a centre pedestal in the single-stick aircraft made for a natural working position. Until the arrival of the modified hand controller which allowed many of the radar functions to be selected on the controller, the navigator still had to lean forward to reach the radar control panel. Although it was within easy reach on the right console, once aligned, there was little in-flight management of the inertial navigation system. The inertial platforms were allowed to drift, and rather than update the actual platform positions, the present position of the F3 was updated in the main computer which was used to drive the tactical displays.

The radar homing and warning receiver, or RHWR, which warned the F3 crew if they were being illuminated by a threat radar, was not available in time to fit the Tornado F2, but began to appear quite early in the F3's service. By the late 1980s, most aircraft were fitted. Different radar systems operate in different areas of the electro-magnetic spectrum. The large ground-based early warning radars operate at the lower frequencies, airborne intercept radars and ground mapping radars are usually found in the area known as 'I' Band, and surface-to-air missiles in the 'I', 'J', and 'K' bands. Warning receivers have to detect the signals from the surveillance and tracking radars and give the crew a warning on a cockpit display to allow them to activate jamming systems, employ countermeasures, or to employ tactics to defeat a potential threat. Radar warners are also useful to identify friendly radar systems. RHWR was a major step forward over the old 'crystal video' receiver fitted in the Phantom which offered a wide open 'ear' on the electronic environment. The new warning receiver used a newer technology called a 'scanning superheterodyne' receiver to search the electronic spectrum. Controlled by a software program written by the manufacturer and extremely clever programmers at the Air Warfare Centre, the receiver scanned through the bandwidth according to a pre-determined strategy. If it found something of interest, it dwelt on that signal and analysed it in more depth, producing detailed parametric information. The signal was then displayed on an electronic screen with a vector and a tag which identified the threat type. Two types of display could be selected. One which displayed the threats along a baseline from 60 degrees left to 60 degrees right of the nose, looking very similar to the radar display making it easier to match a threat to a track displayed on the TV tab. The more common display was a 360-degree circle around the aircraft with potential threats being displayed as vectors around the host Tornado. By strobing the threat with a toggle switch on the control panel, either the pilot or the navigator could bring up the precise parametric details of each threat including an identification of the type. The least welcome tag was a small question mark, classified as an unknown, which meant the analysis had been inconclusive and the identification would be left to the crew.

Buried on the lower left hand side of the rear cockpit the threat warning display was difficult to read, although the pilot was better served as it sat high on the main control panel on the right. For the navigator, a stand-alone display was redundant and it would have been preferable to integrate the warning information provided by the RHWR into the tactical displays. With more consideration at the design stage, threat-warning data could have been provided on the radar screen to identify a radar track, but the warning system was designed and produced by GEC Marconi rather than by the aircraft manufacturer, BAE Systems, and weapon system integration was in its infancy. The display unit was eventually moved during the Operation 'Granby' modification programme to a position adjacent to the TV tabs, and fitted with a glare shield bringing the display into the navigator's scan. The ultimate integration was never funded despite efforts during my time as the avionics sponsor in the MoD's Air Defence Department. While the information provided by RHWR could have been integrated into the tactical displays, at the post-design stage the work was costly. As always, the modification was technically feasible and the company would have been happy to do the work but it was classified as an enhancement by the planners and, frustratingly, could not be funded under post-design contracts. It had to enter the fray with all the other annual proposals for improvements and failed to attract funding. Crews, therefore, continued to the end with stand-alone displays, which added to the cockpit workload. Sometimes, having reprogrammable software did not mean that it would be reprogrammed.

The Joint Tactical Information Distribution System, or JTIDS, arrived later and provided data on any track which was introduced into the recognised air picture by any platform operating on the Link 16 network. This included E3 airborne early warning aircraft, ground radars and ships as well as other fighters. This data was then displayed on the tactical screens in the F3. The original requirement was to fit a capable 'Class Two' terminal to each operational Tornado F3. During one spending round in the MoD, planning staffs were looking for 'offsets' to fund the AH64 Apache helicopter and it was decided to reduce the buy of JTIDS terminals in order to divert funding to the helicopter project. The decision was taken to equip just the two squadrons at RAF Coningsby and to operate the remainder of the fleet as non-JTIDS platforms. The naivety of this decision was graphically demonstrated when the innovative nature of the new data link became evident

The re-positioned RHWR display above the TV tabs

The RHWR control panel.

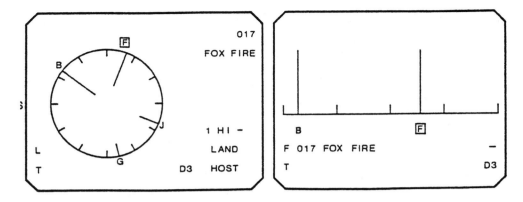

The RHWR displays. (*UK MoD Crown Copyright, 1986*)

after it was introduced. It revolutionised F3 operations and it was immediately evident that the effectiveness of the F3 force would be adversely affected unless it was embodied fleet wide. There would be a mini fleet of F3 crews with superb situation awareness and the rest who were effectively blind and unidentified. In a bizarre example of MoD politics I then spent two years justifying full fleet embodiment for a requirement which had been endorsed many years earlier and was already a huge success in service use.

On the ground, the operational ground support equipment was another step forward and made mission preparation much more efficient. A Cassette Preparation Ground Station or CPGS was provided to prepare mission data before flight. The mission computer could display a number of pre-programmed tactical data points. A number between 1 and 30 designated a navpoint (NAVPT). NAVPT 30 was eventually programmed as the bullseye which was the main reference and reporting point for a Fighter Area of Responsibility. It had a special symbol on the display looking like a target symbol. Navpoints could be connected by programming a route and would be shown as a line on the plan display. Numbers from 31 to 51 were designated as 'Air Force Bases' (AFB), although a civilian airfield could be programmed and each base was identified by a three-letter designator. Numbers from 52 to 64 were allocated to TACAN radio navigation beacons and could be cross-referred to the AFBs. The beacon identification and its channel number were also annotated. Five tactical air-to-air refuelling brackets could be set up and were designated T1 to T5. A datum position, orientation, and height, amplified the information. Finally a Missile Engagement Zone or MEZ could be displayed as a circle on the plan display. In addition to providing tactical information, a navigation function allowed a deployment route to be planned using forecast wind velocity. This could all be printed out and carried on a kneeboard in cockpit. Old habits die hard and at that stage, some of us still needed the comfort of hard copy despite the advent of the digital age. Once stored onto a cassette tape it was taken to the aircraft for loading into the main computer.

It was important to record the displays for subsequent analysis at the sortie

The Joint Tactical Information Distribution System (JTIDS) control panel. (*Ian Black*)

debrief. In the Tornado F2, an interim recording system, which the navigator carried out to the aircraft, recorded a single display onto a VHS video tape. This was only ever a temporary stop gap as, like many other new features, the entry to service of the final fit was delayed for a year. Even so, in another bizarre procurement decision, the recording medium was the 'Phillips 2000' protocol, which seemed to have been adopted as widely as Betamax! This meant that all the replay equipment had to be procured specifically and was almost exclusive to the Tornado F3. Those responsible joked that it was to improve operational security. In practice, it meant that it was almost impossible to find a replay suite away from base that could allow the crews to debrief mission tapes. For a detachment, the replay suite had to be transported to the deployment base at some cost and quite often the less capable VHS interim suite was used in preference to the final system as VHS replay systems were more common. Compatibility aside, the Direct Data Video Recorder or DDVR was an excellent debriefing aid. The onboard recording system captured the output from the EHDD, TV Tab 1, TV Tab 2, the HUD, and the RHWR. Each could be individually displayed at full size or on a composite screen showing all five displays simultaneously. The cockpit voice track was captured and could be backed up by the cockpit voice recorder cassette. When coupled with system time it was possible to reconstruct engagements in precise detail and missile and gun shots could be assessed accurately.

Despite the technological advances, it is an understatement to say that the standard of cockpit ergonomics delivered to RAF Coningsby on 5 November 1984 was a disappointment to the aircrew. The crews on the Operational Conversion Unit, who at that time were the ones with most exposure and experience with the aircraft, began to catalogue the problems. As the Operational Evaluation Unit formed, this team took up the challenge to become the corporate conscience. Careers were made and ended as the truth behind the problems became public. It was to take nearly five years before the basic fixes could be designed and implemented, and only the onset of the First Gulf War provided the impetus for swift action which was long overdue. The final standard would take many more years to bring to fruition.

3

The Arrival of the Tornado F2 on No. 229 Operational Conversion Unit

For some years, a small Course Design Team had been attached to No. 228 Operational Conversion Unit, the Phantom OCU. They were a cadre of new instructors destined to fly the Tornado F2 who had maintained flying currency on the Phantom by undertaking instructor duties while waiting for the new aircraft. When not flying they were designing the basics of the syllabus which would be used to train new crews. The official reformation of No. 229 Operational Conversion Unit, the selected number plate for the new unit, was on 1 November 1984, but the Course Design Team had started work back in 1981. At the start of the manufacturer's course at the British Aerospace factory at Warton, they were subsumed into the newly formed No. 229 OCU, joining the new commanding officer and his first instructors.

Training for the Tornado F2 and subsequently the F3 was to be radically different to the training for the ground-attack Tornado. As the RAF was the only customer for the Air Defence Variant, a completely independent training regime was set up at RAF Coningsby. The crews who would fly the bomber trained initially at the Tri-National Tornado Training Establishment, or TTTE, at RAF Cottesmore before continuing to national training units for weapons training. TTTE only flew the Tornado GR1, and the conversion-to-type lasted many months, even without weapons training. It was decided not to add F2s to the TTTE fleet, but to complete both the conversion and the applied phases at RAF Coningsby. The advantage was that ground school and conversion training, which took months at Cottesmore, would be completed in just six weeks at Coningsby, and would be specific to the new variant. In fact the whole air defence course, including the radar and air combat phases, would last just four months, at which stage the bomber crews would just be starting weapons training at the Tornado Weapons Conversion Unit.

In the months before the first deliveries, a core of those first instructors was taught the rudiments of operating the Tornado F2. Although not a full syllabus, the first manufacturer-delivered training covered the essential elements to allow follow-on training to begin back at Coningsby. No. 1 Tornado Service Instructor Aircrew Training (SIAT) Course began on 4 February 1985 and ran until 29 March 1985, with No. 2 SIAT Course following a month behind. Each course had two pilots and two navigators, and the newly qualified crews took the opportunity to validate some of the new training profiles that would be used on the OCU course. Aircraft availability was limited so the flying rates were not impressive, but it allowed the select few to get a head start on their future colleagues before training began in earnest at RAF Coningsby. In parallel, selected unit groundcrew were being trained in servicing procedures at Warton—an equally challenging task.

The first airframes, ZD901 and ZD903, were delivered on 5 November 1984 and arrived at RAF Coningsby in close formation to much fanfare. ZD901 (AA) was flown by the BAE Systems test pilot Jerry Lee with Air Vice Marshal Ken Hayr in the rear cockpit, who at that time was the Air Officer Commanding No. 11 Group. The other Tornado F2, ZD903 (AB), was flown by David Eagles with the new No. 229 Operational Conversion Unit Commander, Wing Commander Rick Peacock-Edwards, in the rear cockpit. Quite appropriately, the formation was escorted into RAF Coningsby by Phantoms from No. 29 (Fighter) Squadron heralding the new era. As with all subsequent deliveries from the factory, as soon as the media cameras stopped clicking, the aircraft were taken to the OCU hangar and stripped down to their constituent parts to be accepted by the RAF engineers. This process was always a mystery to aircrew as the aircraft had literally just been built, although it provided essential training for the maintenance personnel in a number of critical engineering procedures. Another less obvious but equally essential task was to decide how to park the rapidly growing fleet of Tornados in the hangar. At one stage as many as fifty F2 and F3 airframes had arrived at Coningsby, waiting for squadrons to form, and space became tight. Once reassembled, the new airframes were passed on to the squadron aircrew for acceptance flights. Neither of the first aircraft was fitted with radar on delivery but both were twin-stick aircraft and were used to begin basic pilot conversion exercises pending arrival of the much-heralded Foxhunter radars. The third Tornado F2, ZD902, 'AC', was delivered in short order by the first RAF crew on 29 March 1985. The duty fell to the Boss, Wing Commander Rick Peacock-Edwards, and the senior navigator from the Course Design Team at the conclusion of the manufacturer's course. Over the following month, the test pilots from Boscombe Down took the opportunity to fly the RAF's own airframes and build their experience to allow them to initiate the in-service testing schedule which was planned.

After the initial work-up sorties, the BAE Systems-trained instructors ran the first Staff Conversion Course, after which the combined strength of brand new instructors ran the second Staff Conversion Course, who in turn ran the third Staff Conversion Course. This group of instructors from the first three courses formed the inaugural OCU staff and then enjoyed a period of consolidation before the first true Squadron Conversion Course began in 1986. In a very short time, the new instructors who had been declared 'cleared to instruct', readied for the arrival of the crews who would populate the newly reformed No. 29 (Fighter) Squadron, which was destined to become the first operational squadron. For course graduates, qualification on the RAF's newest fighter was marked with the presentation of a certificate for passing the milestone. No qualification would be complete without an obligatory badge for the flying suit. Given the delta shape of the Tornado F2 and F3, the badge showed a Tornado with its wings swept set in a huge red triangle worn on the left arm to compliment the squadron operational crest on the right arm.

The OCU was structured in a similar way to its Phantom predecessor. On arrival, students were taken under the wing of the Ground School Flight, which operated the synthetic training aids and, eventually, the simulators. A four-week phase dissected the aircraft systems in great depth and introduced the students to the aircraft using part task trainers and mission simulators. As had been the custom for many years, once schooled in emergencies, the students moved over to the flightline for the flying phase.

The conversion phase began with a demonstration of the handling characteristics in all regimes of flight. The pilot instructor flying in the rear cockpit took the new pilot through turns at all speeds, aerobatic manoeuvres, and on into transonic and supersonic handling. Much to the consternation of the 'Navigator's Union', some flying instructors (QFIs) were 'allowed' to operate the radar, providing an early look at steering and weapons information. If the truth be known, some became quite adept, but this could never be admitted in public. After a 'first

The Tornado F3 badge presented to new crews on graduation from the OCU course.

solo' with a staff navigator, a number of sorties of formation flying and low-level navigation exercises followed before completing 'convex', with night flying and an instrument rating test. This awarded pilots with a 'white' rating which allowed them to fly in a cloudbase as low as 400 feet and in marginal visibility. Some of the more experienced pilots went straight for a 'green' rating which allowed them to operate down to 200 feet and in even more marginal visibility. The test for a 'green' rating was more stringent and was a challenge on a new aircraft type. For the navigators, the conversion phase was quite short and the spare time waiting for their pilot crew member to complete the planned sorties was taken up with training sessions in the Tornado Air Intercept Trainer, or TAIT. After two familiarisation sorties flown predominantly at low level in the low flying areas, plus two close formation sorties, the phase culminated in a night navigation exercise, flown as a student crew, operating the navigation equipment.

Next came the basic radar phase which taught the fundamentals of intercepting a single target using a single fighter, and included the profiles to visually identify an airborne target, known as a 'visident'. These profiles were flown at medium level and then at low level. Much earlier than in the Phantom syllabus, pairs targets were introduced so that the new F3 crew began to use the enhanced radar capability as it was intended to be used, namely against multiple targets often provided by Canberras of No. 100 Squadron. Again, these profiles were flown at medium level before being repeated at low level.

A short air combat phase followed in which the rudiments of 'similar' combat were explored or, in other words, air combat against another Tornado. Crews transitioning from the Phantom or the Lightning were already experienced in air combat skills so would find this phase less of a challenge than *ab-initio* crews. For that reason it was some time before *ab-initio* crews were allocated slots on the conversion course.

The advanced radar phase, which completed the course, included low-level day tactics and intercepts against a supersonic target but progressed quickly to two Tornado F3s versus four Jaguars in the low flying areas, culminating in a two versus two dissimilar air combat sortie against the Lightnings from Binbrook. Using a variety of external targets was a feature of the early flying, but in order to maintain a tighter control of standardisation, this feature was soon replaced with Canberra and Hawk targets or flown against another Tornado F2/F3 so that opponents could replicate the syllabus threats. Hawks would fly in from the tactical weapons units and briefings could be held face-to-face with the opposing Hawk pilots, allowing greater control of how the sortie was run. Appropriate training points could be drawn out more easily debriefing together rather than relying on a sketchy telephone debrief.

A routine training sortie consisted of a comprehensive briefing during which the staff pilot briefed the student crews on the sortie domestics and how to get to and from the play area, followed by the staff navigator briefing the crews on the parameters and techniques of the intercept profiles. Once complete, the crews would don their flying clothing and walk to the jets. After a thirty-minute start up routine, the mission would be flown, sometimes over the sea under the control of an intercept controller, but often in the low flying areas in Wales, operating autonomously at low level. Later, as it entered service, the control might be provided by the E3D Sentry operating from RAF Waddington. The sorties followed a carefully scripted profile drawn from a syllabus guide, designed to reinforce each element of the training. Once back on the ground, and after signing in the aircraft and debriefing any faults with the engineers, a comprehensive debriefing picked out the relevant learning points. After a short summary of the 'domestics' from the pilot, the staff navigator would dissect each intercept and evaluate the student's performance with input from the staff pilot where appropriate. Each run was analysed using the digital data video recording suite (DDVR) and the techniques were assessed during a debrief lasting typically thirty minutes. For an air combat sortie debrief, the pilot would have a much greater influence, concentrating on handling as well as weapon system aspects. Once success against the objectives had been analysed, the final decision on whether the student crew had achieved a 'DCO', or duty carried out, was made before the sortie was written up for the record. On completion of the syllabus, new crews were awarded the coveted certificate, qualifying them to fly the RAF's latest combat aircraft.

There would be many diversions during the early days of No. 229 OCU, not least of which was the task to provide nine aircraft for Her Majesty's Birthday Flypast, and further aircraft for sales tours of the Middle East. The European consortium was keen to secure export sales and visits to Bahrain, Qatar, The United Arab Emirates, Jordan, and Oman were all on the schedule. In between trips, the instructors studied hard to understand the new aircraft and its systems,

OCU crews brief for a training sortie. (*UK MoD Crown Copyright, 1985*)

The 'out-brief'. (*UK MoD Crown Copyright, 1985*)

Tornado F2s of No. 229 OCU prepare for a sortie.

OCU crews debrief after a training sortie. (*UK MoD Crown Copyright, 1985*)

This is to Certify that

Flt Lt D Gledhill

has successfully completed

No. 2 Squadron Conversion Course for

TORNADO F2

Date JUN 86

Wg Cdr
OC 229 OCU

And after the pain—the qualification.

and worked on the ground training aids to become adept at delivering the new syllabus. The new equipment made the analogue systems that had been used to train Phantom crews seem extremely dated. A computer-based training system that described each of the aircraft systems in outstanding detail using modern computer graphics was introduced to support the ground school phase. This was a first for the RAF and was extremely well designed and equally well received. Part task trainers introduced the crews to the new avionics using keyboard display trainers that replicated the functions of the TV tab displays. Although similar to the actual equipment, the processors in the KDTs were designed in the computer dark ages and exhibited the speed of a dormant sloth. Even so, it allowed navigators to get to grips with the complexities of the computer menus and sub routines of the new displays and controls in the quiet of a classroom environment. Once mastered, it would be easy to put the routines into practice in the air—or not! One of the biggest steps forward was the provision of the Tornado F3 Air Intercept Trainer, or TAIT, which was produced by the defence contractor EASAMS and installed in 1985. Two basic cockpits provided all the essential switches and displays to allow crews to complete intercept profiles in a classroom setting. The shirt-sleeve environment meant that profiles could be run repeatedly to give quick and effective tuition in the techniques which the crews would use in the air. The computer-controlled mini simulator was way ahead of its Phantom equivalent, which most crews were familiar with, and the training environment allowed rapid progress to be made. A staff navigator instructor from the flying staff sat at a central control console with the student pilot in the front cockpit to the right and the navigator in the back cockpit to the left. Intercept profiles could be set up replicating the sortie that the students would next fly in the air. This meant that every flying event was rehearsed before the wheels ever left the ground. The instructor could critique the methodology, but more importantly, because he was sitting immediately next to the student, he could see how the student was operating the weapon system and correct mistakes at an early stage. This close scrutiny was impossible within the confines of a fast jet cockpit and ensured that bad habits were caught and corrected early. The TAIT provided a unique training facility.

In contrast, the Tornado F3 simulator, which was an essential part of training on an operational aircraft, was a huge disappointment. The simulator was well behind the aircraft in its introduction to service and was not installed at RAF Coningsby until 1986 and even then went through a long acceptance process. One RAF pilot, a member of the simulator staff, worked hard with the company to replicate the actual handling characteristics of the F3, which were far from realistic at first. Through long hours of debriefing passing on his experience of the real aircraft, the simulator designers were able to get the 'box' to handle in a vaguely realistic way. In the interim, a simple cockpit emergencies and procedures trainer was rushed into service to give a stop-gap capability. The cockpit emergencies procedures trainer, or CEPT, lacked the full mission avionics of the simulator, although the basic aircraft systems were replicated. It was vital that new crews were drilled in how to react to systems failures; the lack of a simulator in which to practice could have been a serious flight safety risk at such a formative period in the aircraft's introduction to service. Although the gauges, functions, and warning lights worked in the CEPT, the lack of mission avionics meant it was impossible to practice the air defence role, so it was only used to practice simple emergency procedures. When it was finally commissioned, the major deficiency in the new mission simulator was that, despite the advent of excellent computer graphics to give an immersive experience, in an example of unfathomable procurement myopia, the simulator was specified without a visual system. Due to the fact that the Phantom simulator had operated for years without visuals, and despite the fact that it was the accepted norm for other fast jet types, it was decided that air defenders did not need a visual system. This was despite the fact that the air defence force had operated principally at low level since the late 1970s. Although the improved avionics simulation allowed intercepts to be flown, the absence of a world outside the cockpit made it unrealistic and of limited value as a training vehicle. Effectively, every training intercept in the simulator was flown at night or in cloud. Crews were in danger of training in a false environment and the risk of 'simulatoritis' was real. There were many attempts to retrofit visuals but it was very late in the aircraft's life before a system was finally fitted, albeit only to the simulator at RAF Leuchars. The Coningsby and Leeming simulators retired without enjoying the capability. At Leuchars, a large curved screen gave 120-degree coverage around the cockpit up to 60 degrees in elevation. The computer graphics eventually offered a good representation of the local area which finally allowed Tornado F3 crews to train in daylight; ironically, just about the time the main effort on operations was at night.

Sometime after the start of the OCU courses an additional training aid was funded. A system known as 'Joust' was developed by the Defence Evaluation and Research Agency, originally as an aid to scientific analysis. It provided computer consoles which could be programmed to replicate virtual Tornado cockpits. These could be pitted against other consoles that replicated Soviet fighters and bombers, which were considered to be the prevalent threat. 'Joust' allowed crews to develop and practice tactics and procedures against these potential threats in a controlled, albeit slightly artificial, virtual environment. Various tactics could be flown and kill successes validated before the weapons instructors took those profiles into the air for a reality check. Many of the new operational techniques were rehearsed and developed on 'Joust' before being fielded.

As experience built, the new Tornado aircrew took the opportunity to explore the full performance envelope of the jet. In order to maximise the performance, OCU training missions were flown without external fuel tanks. This still gave a respectable one hour forty-five minutes on a typical low-level intercept sortie—more than enough to achieve the aim. This was one area where the F3 more than met its specification. It had excellent persistence at low level and was frugal with its fuel and could complete the same number of intercepts in a clean configuration as a Phantom carrying two external fuel tanks. Predictably, profiles that required

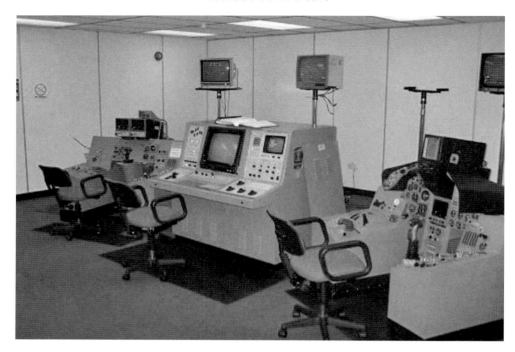

The Tornado Air Intercept Trainer. (*UK MoD Crown Copyright, 1985*)

The 'Joust' control room. (*UK MoD Crown Copyright, 1995*)

The Tornado F3 Mission Simulator.

reheat such as high flyers, supersonics, or air combat, were much shorter in duration as the fuel flow increased markedly when operating in reheat.

Inevitably, putting the new airframe through its paces led to dire warnings from No. 11 Group Headquarters air staff during the first year. Aircrew who had been constrained by fatigue-invoked limitations on the Phantom and Lightning were overjoyed to be flying a new airframe. After a few months of spirited 'stunting and bunting', during which many opponents wished to test the turning capability of the new airframe, the squadron statisticians began to spot an ominous trend. The anticipated life of an airframe was dictated by the fatigue index (FI) usage. Typically, the Tornado F2/F3 was expected to use 100 FI over its service life and would be upgraded every 25 FI by returning to RAF St Athan for structural modifications which would extend the airframe life. Not surprisingly, the first airframes to be delivered did not have fatigue meters as the production of this device was also delayed. Most assumed that fatigue would not be a problem for some time, and the Tornado GR1 force had operated for some years without an issue, although their profiles were less demanding fatigue wise. When fatigue meters were installed some months later, a different picture emerged. Initially, there was a collective intake of breath as figures were calculated, but there was to be some good news. While the fatigue use was high, an error in the fatigue formula meant that what was looking like a disaster was tempered by the recalculation due to an excessive safety factor. Even so, one Tornado F2 had accumulated almost 10 FI in less than one year's flying. This was somewhat short of the line needed to meet a target of 100 FI over the planned twenty-five-year life. The 25 FI programme had yet to be finalised, let alone implemented, yet this airframe was in danger of being grounded to bring it back in line with its intended use. The rate of consumption of airframe life began to be carefully monitored and controlled. The horns were reined in and a more sustainable flying regime was implemented.

The arrival of No. 4 Squadron Conversion Course brought reality back to the temporarily relaxed environment of the OCU. The air of a squadron began to fade, the rate of continuation flying slowed, and the rigidity of the conversion syllabus re-imposed a strict discipline to the daily flying programme. The 'sausage machine' which had been a feature of life on the Phantom OCU reasserted itself, and graphs appeared on the wall of the Flight Commander's office showing course targets against squadron declaration dates. Rigid flying rates were implemented to meet the tasking. Despite the renewed sense of efficiency, there was one 'elephant in the room', namely the Foxhunter radar, which was about to provide the greatest challenge to the new fighter force's capability, and a headache to fleet planners.

An integral part of the introduction to service was the validation of the weapons performance; in the absence of the Operational Evaluation Unit which had yet to form, the early work fell to the OCU. The Skyflash missile had undergone development testing during a company-led programme. The first unguided firings were from a US F-4J Phantom at the Pacific Missile Test Centre at Point Mugu in California in 1976, leading to full envelope validation over the following two years. The unguided firings were followed in 1979 by further separation testing from an F-16 fighter, again in America. On this occasion, the missile was launched at Mach 1.6 at 28,000 feet to validate supersonic separation, albeit under more benign conditions from an F-16 rail launcher than the semi-conformal housings of the F3. The first guided firings from a Tornado came some years later, after the first F2s had been delivered to RAF Coningsby. The manufacturer conducted a series of development firings from a prototype on the weapons range at Aberporth in Cardigan Bay in Wales. The target was a Jindivik remotely piloted vehicle flying from the research facility at Llanbedr. The profile was a beyond-visual-range head-on firing against the subsonic target and resulted in a 'dead hit'. Shortly afterwards the Qualified Weapons Instructors on No. 229 OCU were tasked to run the first missile practice camp (MPC). Before the firings the Foxhunter radars were carefully prepared and their individual performances analysed by the specialists. As the airframes deployed to RAF Valley, rigorous testing ensued, leaving nothing to chance. Rick Peacock-Edwards remembered the first firings well, particularly as he pulled the trigger for the first in-service Skyflash shot. He recalled the preparations vividly:

> We had to complete the MPC and missile firings (both Sidewinder and Skyflash) in order to be declared operational to SACEUR on 31 Dec 86. A lot of hard work went into the preparations for the MPC both in the air and on the ground, in particular on the QWI and engineering sides associated with getting all the relevant profiles and clearances sorted. The Senior Engineering Officer was working 24 hours per day. On 13 October 1986, I carried out the first RAF Skyflash firing from a Tornado F2, ZD 936, with a weapons instructor in the back seat. The profile was a head on shot with the fighter at 3,000 ft and the target at 800 ft. I remember the day as being scattered cloud and I do not recall seeing the target as we were fairly intermittent IMC [Instrument Meteorological Conditions]. The missile firing was a complete success.

This was the first time a Skyflash missile had been fired using Foxhunter in its primary Frequency Modulated Interrupted Continuous Wave (FMICW) pulse Doppler mode to support a beyond-visual-range shot. It was a landmark event and a huge relief that it had been a success. Immediately, the weapons specialists began sifting through the enormous amounts of data which had been collected by the range instrumentation to begin building a picture of the weapons capability of the aircraft in its air defence role.

Firings by the first operational squadron followed in November 1987. RAF Coningsby was in the midst of a tactical evaluation exercise, known as TACEVAL, during which the newest F3 squadron, No. 29 (F) Squadron, was being evaluated for the first time flying its latest mount. An aircraft had been loaded with a full warload of four Skyflash, four AIM-9L Sidewinders, and the Mauser cannon, ostensibly as a weapons loading demonstration. As was the norm, once the weapons were loaded the crew checked in on the Wing Operations frequency, as yet unaware that they had been selected by the evaluation team to fire a missile. Instead of downloading the weapons, the crew were scrambled on a westerly

A Tornado F3 in formation with a Jindivik remotely piloted vehicle prior to a missile firing. (*Geoff Lee*)

vector. For anyone who had sat on Quick Reaction Alert this could mean only one thing: a no notice missile firing at the Strike Command Air-to-Air Missile Establishment (STCAAME) at RAF Valley. The Operational Conversion Unit was also involved in the exercise in the guise of No. 65 (Reserve) Squadron, the shadow numberplate for the OCU. As the squadron held a NATO commitment to generate aircraft for exercises, it could just as easily have been an instructor crew nominated for the firing.

There was a buzz of anticipation as results began to filter back. The firing had gone well but the initial debrief came later in the bar as we celebrated 'endex'. The crew were keen to recount their story. The navigator was an experienced Phantom back-seater, but must have felt more than a moment of apprehension with limited F3 experience. The profile was a typical QRA firing in which the launch aircraft approached the Jindivik from behind. What caused some alarm was that a stern shot would rely on the pulse radar mode which, at that time, was notoriously unreliable. The reassuring fact was that the firing point was only about a mile behind the target so detection was not an issue as the short pulse mode was able to find the target out to 5 miles. The problem was that lock tenacity of the F3 pulse radar was abysmal at that time, yet the Skyflash would rely on the radar to track the target and provide guidance. It was a relief to hear that it had hung on to the target throughout the missile time of flight.

Had there had been any major differences over previous types? The bar chat was incisive: 'What did it sound like' and 'Did it go bang?' Evaluation of how the 'wiggly amps' had performed would be left to the weapons instructors and would be debriefed later. The navigator explained that the biggest difference was due to the new Fraser Nash launcher. The eject rams had been considerably beefed up for the Tornado and were 'agricultural' pieces of equipment. The rams had to be able to force the Skyflash away from the underside of a Tornado F3 which might be travelling at supersonic speeds or pushing negative 'G'. Under such conditions it took an enormous effort to force the missile away from the fuselage into clear air and to ensure a clean separation. The crew described the noisy clunk as the rams and the scissor shackle extended. Unlike the Phantom, however, there was a further massive clunk as the rams were retracted into the housing. Apparently this feature, which no one had anticipated, led the crew to believe that a second missile had left the aircraft! The crew were extremely conscious of the problem of being too hasty. There was a long delay—up to four seconds—between trigger press and the missile being ejected into the airflow. In the heat of a missile shot, this was a lifetime, and it was so easy to think the missile had misfired and pull the trigger again. This had been proven by a No. 29 Squadron Phantom crew some years before who had launched two Sparrows in error during a QRA firing. It was a mistake all air defence crews were keen to avoid. The most satisfying debrief point was that there was absolutely no difference in the terrific noise as the Skyflash motor fired up. The missile still sounded just like an express train as it was boosted up to its supersonic cruise velocity in a cloud of exhaust smoke. The sight of the 'smoking telegraph pole' streaking away from the jet is a sight that no pilot or navigator who has fired a missile will ever forget. I know I won't.

This was another defining moment. The first operational squadron had fired a live Skyflash from a fully armed Tornado F3 for the first time. Not only that, but the crew had used a radar mode in which, up to that point, we had little confidence. As the missile was a warshot round there would be little telemetry, and it emerged later that there was no film of the firing due to a problem in the chase aircraft. The analysis of how Foxhunter had performed would come after careful assessment of the radar data from the range, but in the weapons arena, the F3 was proving to be a success. We received the results some months later and our weapons instructors prepared detailed briefings of the firing. All had gone well and weapons performance seemed to be a positive aspect in a sea of radar gloom.

The first in-service AIM-9L firings had also occurred during the No. 229 OCU missile practice camp. These firings were much less problematic given that Sidewinder was a less complex missile and was less affected by the troubled Foxhunter. Even so, the software controlled Sidewinder acquisition modes had to be validated, as did the operation of the missile management system. If I recall correctly, the first firing was in 'slaved mode', which was the normal operating mode. As Foxhunter swept the sky, the seeker heads could be primed to follow. Once locked, the Sidewinder heads pointed directly at the target of interest. If the pilot then selected 'SRAAM', the missiles would already be pointed and primed and would immediately acquire the target, meaning an instant launch was possible. The crews would be confident that the missile had acquired the target because of the Sidewinder tone in the headphones. This aural tone, fed to the crew, would only sound if the missile could see its heat source. Unlike the 'growl' of the earlier AIM-9G, the AIM-9L generated a much lighter 'chirping' noise. An academic firing profile was much more controlled than an air combat firing, and the shot was set up carefully by the range controllers and the firing crew. For a Sidewinder shot, in the absence of an acquisition tone, the firing would be aborted. With a tone detected, the missile success was down to the normal probability of kill, as it did not rely on the radar. AIM-9Ls were fired against another Jindivik drone that towed a huge infra-red decoy flare which would attract the AIM-9L seeker head. The missile tracked towards the flare rather than the drone, thereby saving a huge bill for a destroyed target. The more astute will notice that the AIM-9L could, therefore, be decoyed easily by a flare; this was a huge problem operationally, although the Jindivik flare was enormous and persistent, and unlikely to be fitted to an operational aircraft. If a target launched infra-red countermeasures, known as flares, against the attacking Tornado F3, the missile could be defeated. It was some years later before infra-red counter-countermeasures were incorporated into the AIM-9L in the form of the SWIFT and the AIM-9Li modifications.

The AIM-9L firings demonstrated a new phenomenon which was a feature of the Tornado design. On the Phantom the Sidewinders were carried on launcher rails on pylons that were fitted below the wings. On the Tornado F3 the pylons sat beneath its high-mounted wings, virtually at eye level to the crew. Behind the line of sight when carried on the rails, the missile, once launched, passed the cockpit just as the rocket motor boosted to cruise velocity, streaming a huge smoke trail and disappearing into the distance at Mach 3. By day this was a dramatic sight, but crews tasked with night firings were emphatic—it was truly spectacular, or words to that effect.

Despite the successes, the growing army of detractors were slow to publicise the promising weapons capability which was so essential for a fighter. The bad news about Foxhunter performance was by then dominating the headlines.

As the Tornado work-up programme gained momentum, there was another significant milestone as the Phantom era came to an end at RAF Coningsby. With an increasing flying rate and demands on airspace becoming unmanageable, the decision had been taken to move the Phantom OCU to RAF Leuchars in Scotland where more training airspace was available. Headed by the squadron commanders, the aircrew and groundcrew from each unit were pictured in front of their respective aircraft to record the event. In a powerful example of how the air defence strength of the UK had been increased, ten Phantoms and ten Tornado

Commemorating the service of Nos 64 (Reserve) and 65 (Reserve) Squadrons. The photograph was taken at RAF Coningsby just before the Phantom OCU moved north to RAF Leuchars. (*UK MoD Crown Copyright, 1986*)

F3s were pictured on the main dispersal at RAF Coningsby, representing just half the strength of their respective units. There was a greater significance to the photograph. Some years earlier, when both Nos 64 and 65 Squadrons had been flying Javelins, a similar picture had been taken, and it was a unique opportunity to recapture a historic event. In April 1986 the Phantoms headed north, leaving the two hardened dispersals at RAF Coningsby to numbers No. 29 (Fighter) Squadron and No. 5 (Army Cooperation) Squadron with their new Tornado F3s. The re-equipment programme at RAF Coningsby was completed when No. 5 Squadron was declared operational in February 1988.

4

The Foxhunter Radar Saga

There was much speculation, bordering on derision, at the state of the GEC Marconi Foxhunter radar which was fitted to the Tornado F2 when it first arrived at RAF Coningsby. As with most stories, there is some truth and some fiction.

British radar companies had been sidelined in the radar design business for some years before Foxhunter arrived. Ferranti designed the Air Intercept Mark 23 radar which was fitted to the Lightning. Innovative for its time, the AI23 was a monopulse radar but lacked the pulse Doppler mode which allowed targets flying at low level to be detected against background clutter. With the selection of the Phantom in the 1960s to take over as the UK's main air defence fighter, British radar companies were relegated to a support rather than design role. The Phantom arrived equipped with the American Westinghouse-designed AN/AWG 11/12 radar, licence built by Ferranti, but were only contracted for maintenance and post-design upgrade work. Foxhunter offered a potential leap in capability over the AN/AWG 11/12, and had it worked as envisaged from the outset, it would have been a major advance in capability.

Foxhunter started life as a research project at a government agency, The Royal Signals Research Establishment at Malvern. Full development began in 1976 and a contract to design the new radar was awarded to GEC Marconi who had, up to that time, never produced an air intercept radar and certainly nothing as complex as Foxhunter. The radar was undoubtedly conceived in the sterile environment of a laboratory, and on the test bench the performance seemed impressive. Even though the Tornado airframe left prospective crews rather underwhelmed when compared to American fighters, the potential of the new weapon system offered hope. It was sold as the justification for selecting the Tornado F2 over its US peers.

To understand the problems of Foxhunter, some simple radar theory is needed. The most effective means to detect an airborne target would be to use a continuous wave of radar energy which when reflected from the target would give the strongest return. In order to process the transmitted information which

Foxhunter radar displayed at Newark Air Museum.

is reflected from the target, a radar set uses a receiver to listen to the response. A radar set cannot transmit and receive at the same time, so it chops the signal into pulses and the receiver listens for the response during the period between the pulses. In human terms, if we talk loudly so that a distant colleague can hear us, unless we stop talking we probably won't hear the reply. For pulse radar, the spatial coordinates of the returned signal are measured to give range and bearing. In a pulse Doppler radar, the velocity of the target, or range rate, is calculated by measuring the Doppler shift. However, in search mode it does not measure range, and without range, it is hard for an operator to set up an intercept. Additional information is needed if a pulse Doppler return is to be of use.

Foxhunter is known as a 'high PRF' radar. The pulse repetition frequency (PRF) is the number of pulses transmitted per second and determines how effectively a radar detects a target. In Foxhunter's case the rate of transmission of pulses—the repetition—is high. Once responses are received they are processed by clever electronics and the range is calculated by working out how long it has taken the pulse to travel to and from the target. At this point, scientists begin scribbling unintelligible mathematic formulae on the 'chalkboard' to explain why. Powerful high PRF radars are excellent for long-range detection but can be susceptible to electronic noise known as sidelobe clutter. High PRF radars, therefore, work well against the type of relatively high-speed bomber target that might approach a fighter from head on, which was the type of target envisaged for the F3 and is why this design was chosen for Foxhunter. They are less capable in the short-range air combat environment because a highly manoeuvrable target generates reduced Doppler shift as it passes through the beam in an evasion turn. Foxhunter struggled with this type of agile target, which was typically the type against which operational crews trained.

In squadron use, an operational crew was more likely to be meeting a formation of Jaguar bombers at low level than a Vulcan bomber flying in a straight line towards them. Even when a Vulcan acted as a target, the crews demonstrated amazing agility at heights above 50,000 feet, giving Foxhunter an equally hard time. Whether the crew of a Bear or Badger bomber would have done the same is moot. However, and crucially, in a tailchase situation where the Doppler shift is small, the Foxhunter had difficulty processing the signals accurately, meaning detection behind a target in the pulse Doppler mode was poor. Most air-to-air radars fitted to American fighters used a medium PRF (MPRF) mode. This gives much-improved resolution and tracking at shorter ranges and when a target evades. The downside to this mode was that there were ambiguities in the responses from the target which had to be resolved by clever electronic processing. A MPRF dual mode modification was later developed by GEC Marconi but was not adopted by the RAF. I will explore some of the reasons later.

The antenna which was selected was of the 'twisted cassegrain' type. This is a parabolic antenna in which the feed is mounted behind the concave main parabolic reflector dish and is aimed at a smaller convex secondary reflector in front of the primary reflector. It gives the Foxhunter its unusual dustbin-shaped scanner dish. The design works extremely well in an electronic jamming environment demanded by the specification as it has low 'sidelobes'. When a radar set transmits, it produces a powerful main beam but also a number of associated beams called 'sidelobes' which radiate either side of the main beam. When a countermeasures scientist tries to produce signals to jam air intercept radars, he can rarely produce enough power to jam the main beam so he tries to attack the processor by jamming through the sidelobes. The Foxhunter designers thought that by using this technology they could make the radar less vulnerable to electronic jamming. A twisted cassegrain antenna is problematic in that it has a narrower beamwidth and, therefore, a higher gain or power than a normal front-fed antenna. Given the specification and to achieve long-range detection, the design engineers produced the high PRF radar to improve the resistance against electronic countermeasures. It seemed a logical choice but neglected to address how the radar would be used in service. As we were to find out so quickly, this configuration struggled against large formations which evaded in order to avoid detection and engagement. It also struggled in the highly dynamic environment of air-to-air combat.

The truly innovative feature of Foxhunter was the adoption of a new technology to provide the look-down capability in pulse Doppler mode. The Radar and Signals Research Establishment at Malvern had been investigating a new technique known as Frequency Modulated Interrupted Continuous Wave, or FMICW, which showed promise for use in airborne interception radars. The frequency of a continuous wave signal was varied over time and the frequency of the returns from the target compared with the emitted pulse. By combining the signals, responses known as 'triplets' were produced which gave both range and velocity of the target. This was a huge leap over the Phantom pulse Doppler mode which had to be locked on to a target before it could give range information. For the first time, the radar would show target range in pulse Doppler search mode without the need to lock on. This allowed for the adoption of track-while-scan to track multiple targets in search. After lengthy descriptions of this technique, squadron aircrew adopted the term '[Expletive] Magic', or FM for short! FMICW was pulse Doppler on steroids.

It is now history but, despite the promises, the equipment delivered to the front line proved to be under-developed and inadequately tested in the air. The early standard of the radar earned the nickname 'Blue Circle' but the real reason is often lost. It was not a reflection of the actual performance of Foxhunter once it was fitted, although that accolade may have also been deserved at first. 'Blue Circle' was a well-known concrete manufacturer of the day and the first 'Foxhunters' were, literally, lumps of concrete ballast fitted *in lieu* of the radar to maintain the centre of gravity in the absence of a radar pack. Despite the delays in radar deliveries, the decision was taken not to delay deliveries of the aircraft from the factory at Warton to the front line. This was a sound call because with all new combat aircraft there are engineering programmes to complete and engineering training to be undertaken so the arrival of the jets allowed the Air Force introduction to service programme to begin. For the first few months, none of the shiny Tornado F2s had radars. By the time I arrived on No. 229 OCU to attend the second in-house instructor course, or No. 2 Staff (Squadron) Conversion Course (SCC), the 'Y List' radars had begun to roll off the production lines at the GEC Marconi factory in Milton Keynes. With company guidance and assistance, the RAF engineers fitted the radar packs into the nominated aircraft and it was with some trepidation that we fired up the transmitters for the first time. At first glance, all seemed well. The horror stories had yet to develop. The radar worked and plots appeared on the brand new TV tab displays. Unlike the Phantom, radar faults were less prevalent and, certainly, catastrophic transmitter failures were rare. Sadly, this early optimism was to be short lived. Contrary to legend, by the time the first true course began training, almost 70 per cent of the aircraft were radar equipped. There were nearly enough sets to have fitted all the aircraft but the early radar packs had to be returned to the GEC Marconi factory for upgrading to the latest hardware standard, called, paradoxically, 'W List'. By feeding the radar production line it left gaps at the front line, and it was only towards the end of 1986 when enough surplus sets were produced to fulfil the commitments. Even then there was much competition between the OCU and the first squadron to lay claim to the limited supply, particularly of upgraded radars. OC 229 OCU wanted the best radars to train the new crews. OC 29 (F) Squadron wanted the best radars to declare his new squadron operational. The company wanted to catch up with the production and modification schedule. There were other strains because, despite promises from the No. 11 Group Headquarters staff to allocate Hawk trainers to act as airborne targets, initially, few were forthcoming. The conversion course needed targets to train against so, reverting to tradition, Tornado F2s were co-opted to fly as targets for training sorties, and these sorties were allocated to the 'Blue Circle' aircraft. On a positive note, this meant more hours for new crews, but for navigators it was unproductive flying without a radar. Twin-stick trainers were selected to be non-radar jets as they spent much of the early months with a pilot in the back cockpit teaching handling skills as new pilots converted onto type. For instructor navigators it meant plenty of 'stick' time once in the operating area. The intercept profiles could be achieved successfully without radar so the impact on the course progress was minimised by managing the fleet and allocating appropriate aircraft to the task.

In the meantime, weapons instructors were grappling with the Foxhunter radar performance, and as the 'Y List' radars were fitted to the F2s, the system was evaluated informally. The navigator operated the radar differently to earlier types. In the Phantom, a single-scan pattern was centred at the anticipated height of the target. Once the target was detected, it was relatively easy to track by careful manipulation of the scanner using an 'artistic feel'. It was unusual or careless to lose contact with the target as the display was analogue and instant. With the Tornado, a much wider scan pattern was employed and the display was processed. This turned 'set handling' or manipulation of the radar controls from an art into a science. When using the full 120-degree azimuth scan, the coverage in height was expanded by employing a multi-bar raster scan. By employing multiple elevation passes, a larger volume could be searched more methodically. Unfortunately, this meant that the target may only be detected on one of every four sweeps as the radar nodded up and down automatically as it scanned. Once a target was detected, a processed target return, or 'plot', was displayed and entered into the track-while-scan system manually. The target would turn from a small block into a fully established track with a vector and a track allocation letter. The track information giving target flight parameters would appear in the 'read out line' at the base of the TV tab display. Once the radar had generated the track it would associate with each subsequent 'hit' on the track and update the information. If the association was subsequently lost or the parameters changed enough to make it seem like another target, the track block would 'contrast invert', showing that the computer was unsure and was predicting where the track should be. This memory tracking became infamous and was the root of many issues.

For the first months the displayed information was accepted on trust. If a plot was entered into track-while-scan and it associated and the information seemed accurate, crews were happy. At long range, the short periods of memorised information were acceptable as the additional data from track-while-scan made the task seem easier. At face value, situation awareness had improved markedly. The addition of the airborne IFF interrogator provided instant position on a friendly

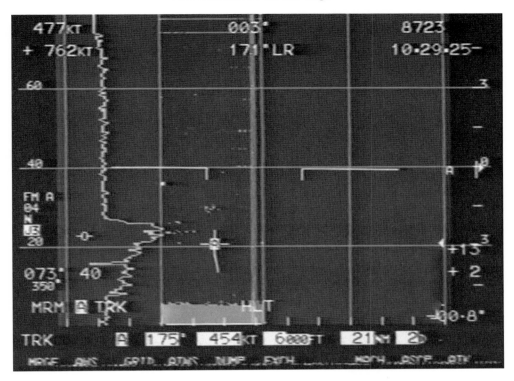

The radar attempting to lock to a target. The information is contrast inverted, meaning it has not yet gone into full track. (*UK MoD Crown Copyright, 1985*)

track, further boosting confidence, albeit artificially. The 'read out line' on the TV display, which is where target information was displayed, became compulsive viewing, giving precise indications of the target flight parameters and offering more information than most navigators had expected in their wildest dreams. Although, it was easy to be seduced by the track-while-scan, the complex displays, and the massive increase in target data which the radar provided, the problems with the early radar standard became increasingly obvious. With a processed display, rather than seeing a solid 'blip'—a target in air defence speak—the return was displayed as a small, synthetic rectangular block. Unfortunately, Foxhunter not only produced the target plot, it produced many more returns which were totally unrelated to anything in the real world and were a figment of its radar data processor's imagination. This 'internal noise', which it generated as it struggled to analyse potential targets, was erroneously displayed as false targets on the TV display. Instead of the one target which you knew you were intercepting, a whole gaggle of phantom 'wingmen' appeared around the real target appearing as a formation. In a training environment only a single target was present, but in a real combat situation you could not know. This led to the need to sample individual, often false tracks, to determine validity. The real target would eventually form a track whereas the false targets would enter memory mode and had to be cleared

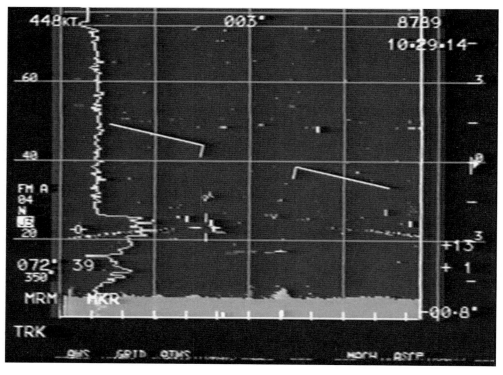

Raw plots seen in FMICW search mode but some are 'false plots'. Only one target is present. (*UK MoD Crown Copyright, 1985*)

from the system, adding to the navigator's workload. Only when the actual target was designated could the intercept proceed.

With a track established the display was impressive. A proboscis or vector on the track box showed the rough heading. A small proboscis meant a slow target and a long one meant a fast target, giving instant tactical awareness. The information about the target was in the 'read out line' at the base of the radar display, giving the target's heading, height, speed, range, track displacement, and 'G'. For someone used to the limited information from the Phantom radar, this was truly magic as most of those parameters had traditionally been calculated using mental arithmetic combined with a touch of 'that looks about right'.

Once into an engagement, opponents would rarely make life easy and allow an intercept to proceed benignly. In the test environment, engineers used simple scenarios but with real targets approaching at combined closing velocities of 1,000 mph, events were more pressing. Poorly designed software meant that navigators could not type fast enough to keep up with the changes and became overloaded. It was a most unsatisfactory situation which was exacerbated by a further deficiency. As Foxhunter reacquired its target, the track block would jump to its new position and reassociate. At first, this constant jumping around was confusing as it led to periods of nervous anticipation as the navigator waited for better quality information to plan the intercept. Jumps in azimuth of up to ten degrees were not uncommon and would negate the mental calculations of displacement, height, and speed, which were still critical to determining the intercept geometry. Often it would be back to square one and a frustrated navigator would have to re-plan the intercept. Of course the reason for the period of memory tracking might be because the target had turned rather than poor processing, but Foxhunter was expert at keeping those clues to itself.

At longer ranges, the automatic functions coped, but unfortunately, as the range closed inside 20 miles, just as the navigator was setting up the front sector Skyflash shot, the low data rate caused increasingly lengthy periods in memory, even when the scanner was precisely positioned. Less than perfect scanner handling by the navigator invariably meant a lost contact on the target. With the Phantom radar, this would have been recoverable. With a raw display, moving the scanner to the correct position would have re-established contact, allowing the navigator to lock on to the target and fire a missile. With the processed displays of the Tornado F2, it was a lottery. Sometimes it would reassociate and sometimes it stubbornly refused. All should have been recoverable had the lock function been more robust. Once a lock was demanded using the navigator's hand controller, the radar would attempt to point to the last known position of the memorised track, but unfortunately, the moding was poorly conceived. On the earliest standard of Foxhunter, the radar would point only to that position in space, but by then the target might be elsewhere. After some ponderous electronic thought and with no target to lock on to, Foxhunter reverted to search mode. This left the crew inside the point at which a safe tactical disengagement could be flown. The crew had no option but to continue to a visual merge with little idea of the target's position, leading to a poor entry with no situational awareness.

Eventually, this problem was resolved by redefining the lock rules and allowing the radar to search around the last known memorised position until it found the target, when it would then lock. Simple and effective, it was some years before this modification could be implemented into the software, leaving crews embarrassed and frustrated in the meantime. Had a quick fix been possible, much of the early frustration might have been alleviated. Entering a fight behind a Skyflash missile was a good way to begin a combat engagement. Entering a fight without visual contact was a recipe for disaster.

If intercepting a single target with a 'Y List' radar was a challenge, once multi-target intercepts were introduced, the flaws in the design and the questionable implementation of the software modes became even more evident. At some stage in the design process, either the operational requirements staff or the design engineers had decided that an 'attack store' would be a tactical revolution. The concept was sound in a laboratory where targets always behaved and tactics were simple. Unfortunately, the concept was not tested in the heat of air combat before it was delivered. The idea was that once the navigator had entered the tracks into the TWS and had identified the formation type, he or she would formulate an attack plan. A typical formation was known as 'card' formation where a pair of tactical aircraft would fly in 'battle' formation, line abreast between one and two miles apart, followed by another pair a few miles behind, hence the term 'card'. A standard attack against such a formation would be to approach on one side of the formation and attack the leading target with a front sector Skyflash before relocking to the trailing target on the same side. Once each of those missiles had destroyed its target, a stern conversion could be conducted onto the trailing target on the far side of the formation if the tactical situation allowed.

The first pair would be designated 'A' and 'B' and the trailing pair 'C' and 'D', so the attack plan that was entered into the a store was A:C:D. Once the first missile had destroyed its target, a simple button press would select the next one, bringing up its data into the read out line, followed by the third. Simple! All would have been well, but no one briefed the target pilots that they had to remain on the same heading and allow themselves to be engaged without reacting. After the simplest of navigation turns, the attack plan became history as the formation now presented a different aspect to the fighter. The carefully crafted plan was thrown out of the window; the data was manually deleted from the computer and the whole process was begun again. The software routine was fundamentally flawed

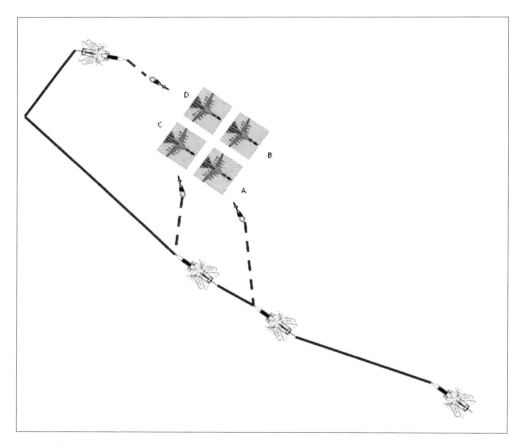

A typical 'sort' plan against a card formation.

as tactics had to be responsive to the tactical air picture. The 'A Store' was quietly dropped from subsequent software loads and a more user-friendly solution was implemented.

As the raft of deficiencies in the design were catalogued, alarm bells began to sound. Many of the basic capabilities of the AN/AWG 11/12 in the Phantom, which crews had become used to, had been lost in translation. The assumption that track-while-scan would offer a good stern hemisphere capability allowing crews to remain in that mode throughout an intercept proved wrong, although it would have been a significant step forward. The reality was that, with low Doppler shift in behind a target, the TWS performance was poor. The long-range stern hemisphere performance trumpeted in the sales brochures was a pipe dream. Crews reverted to using the pulse radar which had been the norm in the Phantom, but the lack of development of the pulse radar immediately became evident. In concentrating on the TWS, the designers had neglected the pulse set and its performance now proved woefully lacking. The synthetic display was poor and the lock tenacity was fatally flawed. Losing lock in pulse mode when operating a Phantom radar was unheard of. With the Tornado F2, it was rare to achieve a lock on the first attempt, even when straight and level, and in air combat, it was problematic even with the enhanced pilot modes. A lock selection would be followed by nervous anticipation as the system considered whether to grant the request. Invariably, it hesitated or failed completely, leaving the navigator to try to rescue the situation. Such a deficiency seemed inconceivable, yet it took years to develop the pulse radar performance to an acceptable level. Although marginal improvements followed, I had finished flying before any real improvement was evident, and in my opinion, Foxhunter never matched the lock tenacity of the obsolescent AN/AWG 12, despite the passage of time.

TWS was to have been the major step forward for Foxhunter. Admittedly, the British plans were ambitious as even the original AN/APG 63 radar fitted to the F-15A Eagle was not able to operate in full 60/60 azimuth sweep and track tens of targets. Given the lapse in British capability in the air-to-air radar arena, to ask for such comprehensive capability over such a wide volume of airspace was asking a lot. It was to be many years and many upgrades later before the potential was realised. Nevertheless, when TWS worked, mainly in a benign air situation, it was indeed 'FM'.

One of the more amusing errors was in the implementation of the specification for one of the pilot air combat modes. The pilot could control a symbol in the head-up display which showed where the Sidewinder missile head was looking. If he could not bring the gunsight onto the target or the target was dropping infra-red flares, the pilot could take control of the Sidewinder seeker head and move it onto the target manually by moving the symbol in the HUD, thereby overriding the automatic functions. He would use a small knob on the pilot's hand controller on the left console known as the 'coolie's hat'. When the F2 entered service, pilots were concerned to find that the mode would not work. In a bizarre transposition of the specification, the Sidewinder symbol was controlled by the hand controller—

but the hand controller in the rear cockpit! Bizarrely, the navigator had control over a function which he could not even see, yet the implementation had never been challenged through the procurement process. Of course, navigators would never have frustrated a pilot's attempts to lock the Sidewinder missile to the target as that would have been immature and unprofessional....

As the improved 'W List' began to appear there was hope for progress. Unfortunately, this software load had been under development for some time and it was too late to include fixes for many of the early problems that had been identified, leading to further frustration. The responsiveness of the software update process was added to the list of concerns. Many of the issues that plagued 'Y List' were still evident despite changes to help crews to interpret the data. A 'B sweep'—a synthetic line which showed the azimuth scan of the radar—was introduced, giving an idea of where the radar scanner was pointing. It was felt that if the navigator could see the scan pattern, set handling may become more intuitive. A raw plot at the azimuth of a target plot was introduced to give a feel for what the radar was processing. A false target was unlikely to generate this raw return, and by cross checking, a navigator could decide if a target was real or false. Raw features were being added to a synthetic display and the navigator was being asked to overcome technical deficiencies but only by adding to workload. The 'attack store' was gone and some work had been done to provide better lock performance in the FMICW mode. Although the pulse lock had supposedly improved, there was little progress and former Phantom navigators continued to be frustrated by the step backwards.

The heart of the new weapon system was the software, and crews had to understand its complexities to appreciate failings. Each sub system had its own program to run the black boxes. The radar data processor, or RDP, ran the radar while the missile monitoring system, or MMS, controlled the weapons. In the background, the operational software, or OSW, coordinated top-level functions. Each of these loads had unfathomable designations which allowed the weapons instructors to develop a new language. Discussion of the merits of a 'W List' radar fitted with OFP 3-001, MMS PS4, and RDP Load 'umpty frap' left genuinely mystified crews believing the system had been designed by an engineer fluent in Egyptian hieroglyphics. Critically, for the first time, a new software load changed the displays in the cockpit and crews returning from ground appointments would be faced with different functions and modes which they were unable to operate without extensive retraining. Even at squadron level, a new software load had to be assimilated quickly and might demand new procedures.

The first radar standard that began to redress the deficiencies was known as 'Z List' and began appearing in 1988. Although it was the third standard for RAF crews, it was the fifth development standard, meaning some versions had not reached the front line. Even so, operational staffs had documented up to forty deficiencies against the original specification. With only slight progress, crews adopted short cuts to extract the best from a quirky weapon system while the manufacturer was taken to task over the deficiencies. Real problems were still evident, particularly against multiple targets. Given that the baseline capability was to be able to track twenty targets automatically in track-while-scan, the radar fell far short. Auto TWS would have overloaded the processors so navigators were still required to manually enter tracks. It was ill-advised to load more than four tracks as it was impossible to keep them 'associated'. Tracks of marginal interest were, invariably, left to run in memory, becoming irrelevant. Narrowing scan patterns in azimuth and elevation paradoxically seemed to do little to improve the tracking performance. Crucially, the data update rate was so slow that, when targets evaded, the crew was left with few clues as to which way they had turned; this was critical information to counter the defensive tactic. Inevitably, the radar failed to display the new heading, leaving the memorised tracks marching down the display towards the F3 crew. In reality, the memorised track might have no bearing on the true air picture and crews would be 'chasing ghosts'. As the chance of a reassociation lessened, the navigator would be forced to delete the track and begin the search process again, but by now with the target closer and degraded situation awareness. Screenshots of an early Foxhunter software standard show the problems the early crews faced.

As the problems became more public, the reputation of the RAF's new fighter began to suffer and uninformed and often cynical comment spiralled out of control. Commanders struggled with how much to release to try to manage perceptions.

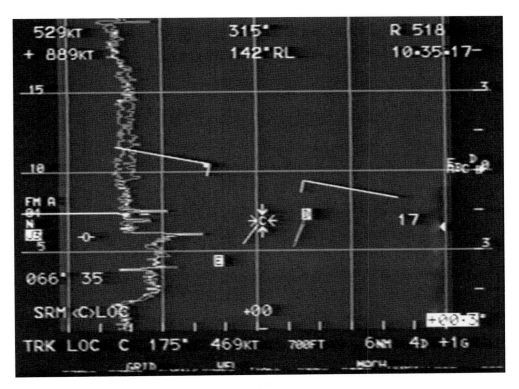

Locked to a target. (*UK MoD Crown Copyright, 1985*)

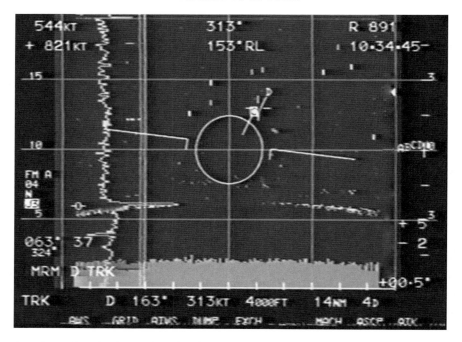

A noisy radar display at low level. Track C is in memory and only track D is associated. The navigator would want to lock to C as the nearest threat but the radar may not find it. There are multiple false plots on the scope, some of which might be real targets. (*UK MoD Crown Copyright, 1985*)

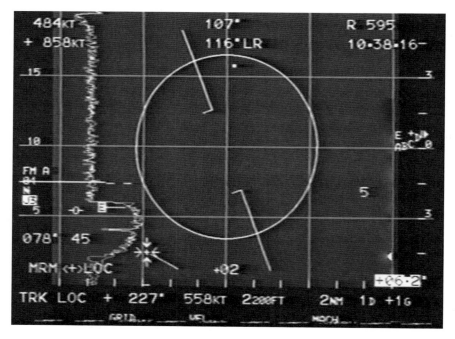

A close-range lock at low level to an opportunity target. (*UK MoD Crown Copyright, 1985*)

The air staffs were persuaded that action was needed and work to identify a 'Get Well Programme' led by the personnel of the Tornado F3 Operational Evaluation Unit began. As always, money was a key factor and commercial pressures meant that acknowledging who held responsibility for the problems slowed progress. The planned development programme would need to be modified and despite documented failures it took time to decide who would pay the bill. There was, however, the prospect of an order from an overseas customer and a reliable and effective Foxhunter radar was a pre-requisite if the sale was to go ahead. It provided a healthy impetus.

The first stage of any fix is to quantify the problems, and 'Trial Bunbury' was conceived to gather actual performance data in carefully controlled conditions to support corrective action. The trial began on the Operational Conversion Unit run by a staff officer from Group Headquarters, assisted by members of the weapons staff. A dedicated analysis area nicknamed 'The Bunbury Suite' was set up to allow the detailed assessment to proceed. Representative operational profiles were agreed and sorties were flown to gather data on how the radar performed in each environment. Each profile determined actual performance against the specification and a comprehensive picture emerged. A series of trial radar software loads were produced and tested, leading to a further array of confusing designations. A number of hugely dedicated aircrew and technicians, including a legendary radar specialist who was employed by the manufacturer and known as 'The Ferret', played tunes with the processors to try to improve the performance of the troubled radar. Some aspects could not be solved due to the constraints of the design, but eventually a solution was found which, although not perfect, produced a standard that showed enough promise to take forward to full development. A new contract was agreed jointly with BAE Systems and GEC Marconi, called the 395FD (Full Development) Contract, which provided the financial means to bring the radar up to specification. As with any procurement, it was to be some years before the definitive standard of radar would be delivered to the front line. It would be known as the 'Stage 2' radar.

One of the myths that emerged during the early days followed the fitment of radar reflectors in the Hawk target aircraft. The cynics took delight and stories developed that the Foxhunter performance was so poor that radar enhancement was needed so that Tornado crews could see the small Hawk targets on radar. The realty was that the OCU syllabus included intercepts against large bomber style targets. Typically a detection against a Bear or a Badger would be at 60 miles plus. The ideal was to use Canberras to replicate this threat, but often they were not available and a Hawk was substituted. Being a small fighter, the Hawk was a poor replication of this target, and would be detected much later. This meant that much of the long-distance intercept geometry could not be practised by the student crews. To solve this, research technicians produced a simple radar reflector which could, literally, be taped onto the head-up display of the Hawk which enhanced the radar return. The reflector cost pennies but magnified the returns significantly and meant that trainee crews had a much more representative target which they detected at a longer range against which to train. It was not, however, relevant to all phases of training, so during the air combat phase and the advanced radar phase when a fighter-sized target was nominated, the radar reflectors were not fitted. The irony was that detection performance had never been a major concern, yet the myth prevailed for years, proving that facts should never stand in the way of a good crewroom story.

While Trial 'Bunbury' identified the deficiencies and investigated potential fixes, operational staffs in MoD were tasked to produce a programme to rectify the problems. An interim standard emerged known as the 'Stage 1 radar', which finally gave a workable standard. In parallel, a 'Stage 1 Plus' standard was introduced onto a limited fleet of forty aircraft to support operations in the Gulf. In addition to the radar modifications, a number of ergonomic and performance modifications were fitted under 'Stage 1 Plus' to make the aircraft more operationally capable. These modifications were an entirely different initiative and I will describe the genesis later. 'Stage 1' proved to be a major improvement and for the first time crews began to realise the true potential of the weapon system, particularly if new missiles could be fielded. 'Stage 2' was planned to arrive in 1994 and would improve matters further still; by 1990 confidence was growing and a plan was emerging.

In concentrating on life in the cockpit, it would be remiss not to mention those on the ground who faced equally daunting challenges. With digital avionics came a 'box pulling' concept for maintenance. When a fault was diagnosed, a line replaceable unit was pulled and replaced with a serviceable unit. This meant that on the squadron where aircraft were housed in individual hardened aircraft shelters, the radar could be fixed reasonably quickly. Where jets operated from the main ramp such as on the OCU, operational security prevented work in full view of casual observers. They had to be towed back to a hangar and hooked up to test equipment leading to longer turnround times for rectification. With such constraints, groundcrew worked long into the night. Like the aircrew, radar technicians had to be trained on not only the new radar system but also the complex test equipment. Test equipment was only as good as the software that drove it. One of the crucial issues was keeping the test equipment up to date with the rapidly modified hardware. As Foxhunter matured, new radar standards were issued to the squadrons and it often took time to design and issue software updates for the test sets. This lag could adversely affect the ability of the groundcrew to produce serviceable radars to meet the flying programme. It was not only aircrew who were frustrated. Industry was pilloried over the Foxhunter saga, but despite some justified criticism, there were many unsung heroes who laboured tirelessly in the background, both in the factory and at the front line to try to fix the visible woes. Much effort, eventually successful, went into turning the fortunes of the Foxhunter around.

5

Saluting the Queen

As the introduction to service proceeded, Foxhunter was challenging the intellect of the navigators operating the system and the ingenuity of the engineers who struggled to install and maintain it. In parallel, more enjoyable tasks were emerging. With a brand new aircraft in service it was inevitable that the leadership would want to show it off in a high-profile way. An early accolade was the selection of No. 229 Operational Conversion Unit to represent the Royal Air Force by providing the flypast for Her Majesty the Queen's birthday celebration. The big day was to be 14 June 1986 and the unit was to put nine Tornado F2s overhead Buckingham Palace at 1300 local time on the dot. The formation was to be led by Wing Commander Rick Peacock-Edwards and Squadron Leader Stu Black in his back seat. There was only one potential flaw in the plan. The OCU had only ten flyable Tornado F2s on strength at the time. To succeed, all ten of the brand new fighters had to be serviceable on the day and at least nine of the ten aircraft had to remain serviceable throughout the sortie. The competition among the crews to be nominated to take part was keen. A flypast over Buckingham Palace seems such a serene event when viewed from the comfort of an armchair, watching the BBC coverage. Nothing could be further from the truth. To place nine aircraft in perfect formation overhead London at the precise second takes skill and accuracy of the highest order, and the implications of failure are obvious. The pressure varied massively among the participants. For the sortie leaders, both front seat and back seat, the responsibility was enormous. The lead pilot was in overall command and the obligation to be overhead at the appointed hour, 'on track; on time', rested with the lead navigator. For the deputy leaders, the pressures were similar, exacerbated by the fact that they may have to substitute for the leader at a moment's notice. For each pilot, only perfect formation flying would do, and he would spend a good deal of the sortie striving to maintain position and looking perfect from the ground. For the remaining seven navigators, we had the best seats in the house. Once joined in formation with the radars in standby, we had little to do other than keep our eyes peeled for conflictions and sit back and enjoy the experience. Nothing could go wrong!

The rehearsal schedule was complex, complicated by the fact that it was impossible to fly the whole route in advance as nine Tornados flying down The Mall ahead of the big event would not have gone unnoticed. In true military fashion, each rehearsal was a slow build up of each element of the plan, leading to a full rehearsal of all nine aircraft, albeit stopping short of an overflight of London. On 5 June, just the leader and deputy leader rehearsed the route, flying all the way to the initial point at Fairlop. At a later stage, the same crews were allowed to fly the full route in a search and rescue helicopter, all the way to Buckingham Palace. The next time they would see their 'target' would be on the day. On 6 June the formation was increased to four aircraft, culminating in a final rehearsal of all nine jets on 10 June 1986 which, surprisingly, passed without incident. The check in, taxi, take off, and joining procedures were rehearsed to make sure that everyone within the formation was aware of their role and responsibilities.

Planning had begun months in advance and started from the end game. In order to give Her Majesty an uninterrupted view as the formation approached, it would pass directly down The Mall on its run in to Buckingham Palace. Nine aircraft in close formation do not manoeuvre easily, so to achieve that precision pass, a straight line track was planned from a point to the north-east of London. A smart navigator takes a line from Buckingham Palace and extends it well out into the North Sea where the unwieldy formation can be assembled in safety. The speed to fly is carefully selected: too slow, and pilots would find difficulty in maintaining a comfortable formation position as the aircraft is less stable at slower speeds; too fast, and the formation is equally uncomfortable as the greater turbulence associated with higher speed flight leads to a bumpy ride. For the Tornado F2, 360 knots was a good compromise, allowing leeway either side to adjust the timing if necessary. It also had a significant advantage for the lead navigator in that flying a groundspeed of 360 knots meant that the formation covered 6 miles a minute. By working back along the planned route and identifying check features, he could ensure an accurate time over the palace. Despite the modern avionics of the Tornado F2, a map and stop watch still featured heavily in the execution. At the north easterly extent of the run-in track, well out over the North Sea, was a 'datum', or start point. Assuming that point was 120 miles from Central London determined that the formation would depart from the datum at 1240 local time to meet Her Majesty at 1300 local time. In order to guarantee the departure time, a timing racetrack with a two-minute outbound leg, a two-minute inbound leg, and a turn at each end of the racetrack, was established. The lead navigator could adjust his position within the racetrack to ensure he arrived overhead his start point at the correct run in time. If his timing was wrong, he could cut short the racetrack to adjust to the correct time. Fuel in a fast jet is not an inexhaustible commodity, so three or four timing racetracks are all a navigator can reasonably expect. Equally, there are no accolades for being precisely on time on the penultimate timing orbit, but then missing the final check time and departing early or late. With all this information in hand, working back from the datum time and taking into account the distance from RAF Coningsby, the formation leader could calculate a precise take-off time.

At this stage, with a basic plan agreed, the emphasis shifted to the lead pilot to plan the formation aspects. Although it may look impressive, a nine-ship formation is based on simple principles. Close formation on a fast jet squadron is based on a pair of aeroplanes. The lead pilot flies a steady heading allowing the wingman to join up and the final stages of the approach are flown gently, leaving vertical and lateral separation. Only when the aircraft are within feet of each other and the overtake is under control does the number 2 pilot move into a position where wings might overlap. At medium level the formation position is slightly below the lead aircraft and swept back in an echelon position. Each aircraft type has known formation references and certain small features on the airframe are aligned in order to position the wingman precisely and correctly. To fly a 'Vic' with three aircraft in close formation, a wingman will formate on each wing of the leader using those same references. If an echelon is extended beyond three aircraft it becomes more unstable. It takes time for a pilot to see the changes as an aircraft on which he is formating moves. Add three or four aircraft in a line and the changes take time leading to a ripple effect down the line. From the cockpit this appears like a whip in a hose as the oscillation passes down the line of aircraft. To fly a 'Box 4', the numbers 2 and 3 formate on each wing of the leader and the number 4 slots into the box position, flying a line astern position on the leader. The nine-ship is just a logical extension of the 'Box 4', achieved by adding further aircraft at each extreme. So within the formation, the three central aircraft are flying line astern, formating on the aircraft ahead, whereas the wingmen hold an echelon position on the aircraft inside and ahead of them in the formation.

The normal formation positions can be too close to make a nine-ship formation look good from the ground, so a 'whip' aircraft flies around the formation and visually checks the appearance from all aspects. Calls to individual pilots to fine tune their formation position allows them to fix the position in the mind's eye. Once 'whipped', failure to hold that reference position will lead to a scrappy and perhaps unbalanced formation.

Modern fighter jets are complex and problems in flight are not unknown. Abort procedures which allow the formation to break up safely are briefed and rehearsed before the event. For aircraft at the extremities of a nine-ship it is easy to depart as the pilot merely eases out and away from the formation and drops back. For the number 4 it is more problematic. The ninth aircraft flying in 'the box' needs to drop back, allowing space for the middle man to escape safely. Urgent problems that demand an immediate abort are rare but not impossible, so flying number 4 in the box can be a tense responsibility. Throughout the flight, it is vital that all the aircraft are in constant communication. Problems can occur, speeds can change, formation positions will change, so it is essential that the leader can talk to his formation at all times. Luckily, the Tornado F2 was fitted with a standby radio giving a back-up frequency to ensure that all the aircraft were in contact at all stages of the flight, even if the main radio failed. Given that only ten F2s were available, any minor problems with the airframes were categorised and compared against a 'No Go' list. While a minor avionics failure on the number 7 aircraft could be accepted, a major failure of the flight controls in the lead aircraft could not. Having a working radar was by no means essential for a flypast. The leader would be kept appraised of any failures throughout the flight and would decide if it constituted a 'No Go'.

The leader's plan was formulated and the preparation turned to the squadron engineers. The actual flypast was scheduled for the Saturday of Her Majesty's birthday on 14 June 1985. Whether by design of by accident, the date coincided with a Station Open Day at RAF Coningsby, so the airfield was to be taken over by thousands of enthusiasts who would watch the proceedings. The week leading up to the event was hectic as the training task did not abate and courses still had to progress 'up the line'. Grounding the aircraft for a week to prepare was simply not an option; the aircraft had to fly. With the 'No Go' list decided, a few minor snags could be carried on the day and providing the engines started and the main systems came on line, the aircraft would be part of the formation.

As the final briefing approached, there was a natural tension among the crews knowing that the whole nation's attention would be focussed on our efforts come 1 p.m. If the crews were tense, it paled into insignificance compared to the tension felt by the lead crew, on whose shoulders the full responsibility fell. As they worked through the briefing they repeated each aspect which had already been practised. Inevitably there were refinements. A NOTAM, or Notice to Airmen, had been issued which published the route the formation would take, detailing turning points, heights, speeds, and timings. This would highlight the event to other pilots and ensure that the formation would not be affected by other traffic—or so we thought. Most significantly, the route would pass very close to London Heathrow Airport and, for a few minutes, as the formation passed over the palace and before it turned back easterly, London departures would be delayed. Fortuitously, one of the biggest potential risks was that of poor weather, but the forecast for the route was excellent with blue skies and excellent visibility. A robust 'loser plan' was vital. Obviously, if the leader became unserviceable, the deputy leader would step in—no pressure there! The 'whip/photographic chase' would act as a spare and could slot into the formation in any role so the crew took copious notes of what was expected in case they became the last minute substitute. Ultimately, if less than nine aircraft arrived over the palace, a fall-back plan was briefed to modify the formation for eight or seven aircraft to ensure that it looked symmetrical from the ground. To be faced with that situation did not bear thinking about as the peer review would have been brutal.

Once the briefing was complete, the crews followed the usual pre-flight ritual. The flying clothing locker room was packed with bodies as crews collected lifejackets and helmets, climbed into G suits, and prepared for crew-in. Usually, an out-brief was conducted in the Ops Room to ensure that any last minute briefing points were covered by the Duty Authoriser. In this case, with eighteen aircrew competing for space, it would have been impossible to squeeze so many bodies into the confined area. For once, crews walked straight to their aircraft and only the leaders were out-briefed. Any updates would be passed over the radio. There was a palpable buzz as crews walked through the crowds which were already forming near to the aircraft. This in itself was unusual as normally there were no onlookers at this stage of a sortie. The ten Tornado F2s were lined up on the 'lazy' runway at Coningsby, well distant from the squadron accommodation, and it was rare to crew in under such scrutiny. The engineers were already at the jets making the final preparations and the noise of the Houchin external power sets was already ringing out. The aircraft had been positioned in formation order with the leader to the left. Being number 7, my own aircraft, ZD940 'Alpha Tango', was towards the end of the line up. Leader's perks meant that he had chosen one of the most accurate inertial navigation systems; fortuitously the tail code was 'AQ' and was nicknamed 'Queenie' for the day. Given that the aircraft had been in service for less than a year, and that there were only ten serviceable aircraft available, the sight of the line up was truly impressive and was a huge credit to the engineers and groundcrew.

The start-up was a well-drilled process and the crews ran through their checks methodically. A formation check in time had been nominated and as the time approached, each aircraft slowly checked in on frequency with a 'Ready' call. Whether the tension dissipated or heightened as the leader acknowledged each call was debatable, but as the final aircraft checked in there was a note of relief evident in the his acknowledgement.

At the appointed minute: 'Windsor Check' ... 'Windsor 2, 3, 4, 5, 6, 7, 8, 9, 10.' Staccato but perfect. All the jets were serviceable. 'Windsor Taxi' ... 'Windsor Formation taxi for Runway 26.' The sortie was underway.

The leader made his way towards the threshold of the runway, followed by the rest of the formation as the crews readied their aircraft for departure. Getting ten aircraft into the sky in a short time is demanding. Unlike the Red Arrows, squadron crews do not roll with nine aircraft in close formation on the runway at the same time. The thrust from a jet engine at take-off power is fierce and the risk of damaging the engines by throwing debris into the intakes is high. The leader had briefed three aircraft would line up in echelon with a large gap between flights of three. Each aircraft would roll down the runway at ten seconds' spacing, meaning that it would be nearly two minutes after the leader had pushed his throttles open before the last aircraft rolled. Luckily Coningsby was on the westerly runway so after take off the aircraft would turn back onto an easterly heading to make their way to the rendezvous over the Wash. As the leader extended slightly upwind, the remainder of the formation arced the turn, pulling inside to close the distance. By the time the leader had made his way across Lincolnshire and reached Skegness, the stragglers were closing into a loose Diamond Nine formation ready for the 'whipping-in'.

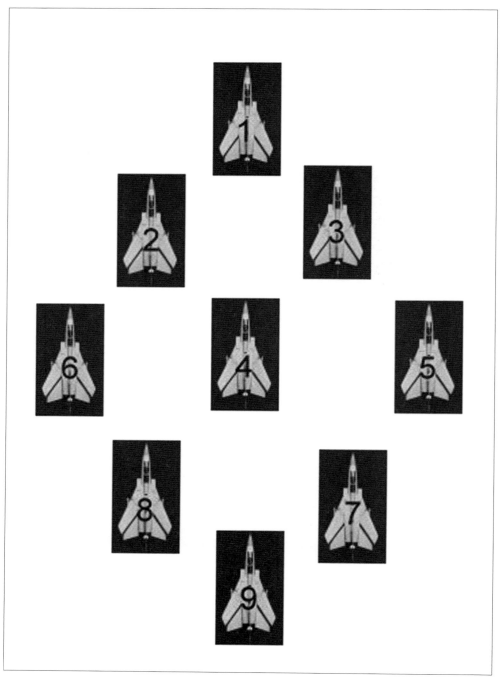

The Diamond Nine numbering.

Strapped in and ready for departure.

The formation joins up.

Joined up over Lincolnshire.

Flying close formation on another aircraft is demanding and requires ultimate concentration. Literally a moment's inattention can lead to a collision. Flying formations of four aircraft is extremely demanding. Flying formations of nine aircraft requires the utmost concentration and is only attempted for short periods, ideally straight and level or in a gentle turn. The apparently effortless precision of the Red Arrows takes much skill and training and the days of nine Lightnings flying nine-ship loops at Farnborough are long gone. Using the known references, there are minor differences in the way each pilot interprets them, so it was vital to check the formation symmetry. This was the role of the 'Whip', so once called into close by the leader, he flew around the formation checking spacing between the jets at all aspects. What looked good from the air might not necessarily look good from the ground so the variations and viewing angles were explored. Small corrections were passed to some pilots, allowing them to adjust position. Once the 'Whip' was happy, a few circuits of the holding pattern would ensure that the formation could hold the new positions and that they were imprinted in the pilot's brains. At that stage, the 'Whip' navigator was charged with capturing the event for posterity and his role switched to official cameraman.

It was about now when the first problem arose as the number 6 crew declared their aircraft unserviceable. As the broken jet returned to Coningsby the 'Whip' finished his task and adopted his new role as part of the formation. Windsor was down to nine and there was no more flexibility. Another failure did not bear thinking about.

By this time, the departure time from the datum was burned in the mind of every navigator in the formation, and none more so than the back seat of the lead aircraft as the digital read out in the cockpit wound down towards datum time. Luckily, the F2 had only a single inertial navigation platform and, with variations in the accuracy, there was no guarantee which was the most accurate system at this stage. Even so, a few comparisons were made on the standby radios. The only 'real' time which was relevant was the time on the trusty aircrew wrist watch of the lead navigator. The timings would be refined with good old-fashioned visual checks over positions on the ground as the formation approached London. There was a feeling of relief throughout the formation as it finally set heading for The Mall. The holding pattern had been flown at medium level, and once established on heading, the formation relaxed into a looser diamond. Although a few spectators over Suffolk and Essex would have been disappointed, it would have been impossible to hold a tight close formation for the tens of minutes it would take to cross the East Anglian countryside. Switching frequency from the fighter control agency to Eastern Radar and eventually to London Military, the leader began to descend to a lower level. The track on the low flying map identified cross track features such as motorways, which would give a progress check on the critical overhead time for the palace. Ironically, despite the complex navigation features built into the Tornado F2, it was still a case of following that crucial line on a map, using a stopwatch to guarantee a 'to the second' arrival overhead. The advent of GPS systems and twin inertial platforms improved the capability over the years, but in its infancy, the F2 navigator still relied on the fundamentals for precision.

The final navigation fix was to be overhead Boreham Wood, after which it became much more difficult to adjust the timing. At this stage everyone had relaxed into the routine and thought nothing could go wrong, but we were about to be tested. Suddenly, one of the aircraft on the southern side of the formation called a visual contact at close range. The pilot of a Cessna had decided to take a closer look but, in doing so, had put himself at risk of a collision. The formation turned away from the confliction to avoid the light aircraft, but with nine aircraft, this is not done easily. As the pilots fought to hold position in the tight turn it proved impossible for some and they fell out of formation. Once clear of the errant Cessna, the leader resumed heading surrounded by a ragged collection of Tornado F2s jockeying for position. Not only was the formation off track, the lead navigator's timings had been compromised as the turn had cost time—only seconds, but those seconds were critical. The cardinal rule was that the formation should approach directly down The Mall and pass overhead precisely on time, but this had been jeopardised by the intervention of the light aircraft pilot. To this day I have no idea how the leader recovered the situation, but as The Thames came into view, the formation was back together. The Mall was clearly visible ahead of the formation and the timing was perfect. It was the ultimate recovery and a credit to the skills of the lead crew and some very snappy formation flying by the pilots. The pictures I captured only moments before 1300 show no signs of the mayhem that had immediately preceded them.

Sadly the actual flypast was something of an anti-climax. The lead navigator had nailed the timing and the Diamond Nine formation of Tornado F2s flew over

Windsor formation approaches London. (*Bob Burden*)

Windsor formation runs in. (*Bob Burden*)

Windsor formation over London.

Buckingham Palace at 1300 local time on the dot. For the pilots, the moment was marked by intense concentration, making sure that the spacing and positioning within the 'Box 9' was perfect. For the navigators, there was little to do but enjoy the thrill of flying over London at 1,000 feet in close formation. The palace was all but invisible as it was directly below the belly of the lead aircraft so we had to make do with a perfect view of the Royal Parks. The inevitable countdown to the overhead in the lead aircraft was followed by a simple call from the leader: 'Coming Right'.

An uncharacteristically quiet London Heathrow was just visible in the near distance as the formation turned back to the north-east for recovery to base. All take offs and landings had been suspended for those few minutes to allow the formation unimpeded passage through the London Zone.

On arrival back at Coningsby there was to be no rest for the pilots. The formation had been advertised as the principal event in the Open Day programme. A sequence of nine-ship flypasts over the airfield for the benefit of the Open Day crowd provided a spectacular debut for the Tornado F2 in its embryonic career. After the nine-ship flypast, five F2s landed while the remaining four-ship returned to a tactical towline to refuel from a VC10 tanker. Shortly afterwards, the smaller formation returned to give a further display for the public. Once the final F2 had shut down there was very little debriefing. What I can safely say is that if the pilot of the errant Cessna had been present, he would have been unlikely to survive the encounter with eighteen very angry Tornado F2 pilots and navigators!

The event to mark Her Majesty's 60th birthday was captured on a first day cover, and each of the crews received one to mark the occasion. Each cover was flown in the lead aircraft flown by Wing Commander Rick Peacock-Edwards and Squadron Leader Stu Black.

There is no finer experience for an Air Force officer than to salute Her Majesty the Queen from the cockpit of a fast jet overhead Buckingham Palace.

6

Exercises Swift Sword, Radlett, and Operation Buhl

One of the major events for the newly formed No. 229 Operational Conversion Unit, or more correctly its shadow guise of No. 65 (Reserve) Squadron, was to take part in the inaugural Exercise Saif Sareea 86 (Swift Sword) in Oman and, subsequently, Operation Buhl in Jordan and Exercise Radlett in the Gulf. The first squadron, No. 29 (Fighter) Squadron, had not yet formed, so if the Tornado F3 was to take part in the infrequent but important event, No. 65 (R) Squadron would have to pick up the commitment.

A biennial exercise known as Exercise Magic Carpet had been held in the Kingdom of Oman supported by the Phantom force for some years. Exercise Swift Sword was to be much larger and a joint exercise including the Royal Navy and the Army. The Omanis had traditionally bought British fighters and fighter bombers and, at that time, were operating a dual fleet of Jaguars and aging Hunters. The aircraft were flown by a mix of Omani nationals and British pilots, some of whom were secondees paid under commercial contracts while others worked under loan service arrangements. The Jaguars were based at the airfield at Masirah located on an island on the east coast of the Arabian Gulf while the Hunters operated from Thumrait in the far south of the country, close to the city of Salalah and the southern border with Yemen.

The exercise was planned for November 1986 and was led by Headquarters No. 1 Group, which at that time commanded the RAF ground attack forces with the senior air staff officer, a One Star Air Commodore, nominated as the Task Force Commander. A fictional country looking very similar to Oman was being threatened by a hostile nation equipped with high technology defence forces. The UK had offered expeditionary support to defend the country and would set up a Joint Headquarters at the airbase at Masirah. The Army would deploy airborne forces, the Navy would take part in combined exercises with a US Navy Carrier Battle Group operating off the coast, and the fast jets would deploy to Masirah with support forces. The refuelling tankers would be based outside the capital Seeb in the north and would give the Omani Jaguar pilots some rare air-to-air

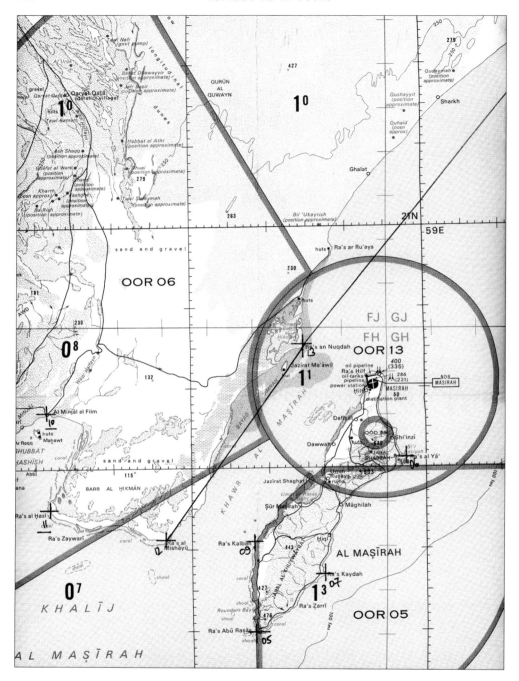

A map of the airspace around Masirah airbase. (*UK MoD Crown Copyright, 1986, Andrew Lister-Tomlinson*)

refuelling training. The Omani aircraft would act as the 'enemy', but would also join combat air patrols for mixed fighter operations with the Tornado F3s. US Navy fighter bombers were also expected to fly in an offensive role and we could expect to see 'hostile' A-6 intruders, F-18s, and EA-6B Prowlers. Events a few years later were to make the exercise scenario chillingly familiar, but when Saddam invaded Kuwait it was to be on a much larger scale. With hindsight, although the Iran–Iraq war was raging and would not end until 1988, perhaps planners were already attuned to the idea that his intentions were less than friendly towards his neighbours.

The exercise planning was hugely complex and with such a sizeable force to be deployed it took many months. Regular progress meetings slowly defined the flying task, producing the typical logistics nightmare which accompanied an overseas deployment. An 'on site review' always preceded a major detachment so key planners from each unit climbed aboard a C-130 transport and flew the huge distance between the UK and Oman in order to inspect the local facilities. After boarding the aircraft at RAF Lyneham bound for the Middle East, an overnight stop in Cyprus and another noisy flight aboard the C-130 saw us landing at Masirah. At that stage the party split to investigate individual areas of interest, which for me involved checking operational and support facilities and ensuring that our Tornados could operate efficiently and, more importantly, safely. I needed maps of the local areas, briefings on procedures, a visit to the operations complex, and a look at the dispersals. How and where we would operate on the nominated base was decided and the detailed engineering challenges of operating from an unfamiliar location were considered; with a strong British influence on how the Omanis operated, many aspects were immediately familiar. Even so, there was an old adage 'Don't Assume, Check', and this exercise was to be no exception to the rule. It was vital to ensure that operational procedures that appeared the same on the surface really were the same when implemented. Two days of high intensity discussions elicited a raft of fine detail to move the plans forward.

Although the time on the ground was limited, the visit coincided with spawning time for the giant turtles. In the evening, with business done for the day, it gave a welcome diversion from the high-tempo preparations. Thousands of sea turtles migrate annually from around the Arabian Gulf, the Red Sea, and Somalia, to lay their eggs on the beaches of Masirah Island. Green turtles migrate but the Loggerhead and Olive Ridley turtles nest on the island. The visitors only come ashore at certain times of the year, and the coastline at Masirah is suddenly littered with the huge creatures. A local guide took us down to the beach and we spent a fascinating hour watching as these huge but gentle creatures lumbered up the sand to lay their eggs. After digging a shallow hole in which they laid their eggs, they carefully covered them over before making the short trek back to the water. Once hatched, the young turtles make the short trek back to the ocean to begin their own journey. It was a truly amazing sight and a refreshing contrast to the 'warlike' preparations.

With masses of paperwork in hand, the long trip home in the C-130 along the reciprocal route somehow seemed even longer. This was a prelude to what would be the longest trip I would ever undertake in a fast jet aircraft as we deployed for the exercise. The vast cargo bay of the C-130 was, surprisingly, more luxurious than my transport when I next flew the route.

Back in UK there were challenges to overcome. In order to deploy a mixed detachment of Tornado GR1 bombers and our own F3 fighters, a complex air-to-air refuelling plan was required. To cover the huge distances between the UK and Oman, not only VC10s would be involved, but the Tristar strategic tanker that had recently been introduced to service in the RAF would take part for the first time. Planners would use the exercise to experiment with the use of this new capability. Although it had a massive fuel giveaway, it had only two refuelling baskets. Efforts to fit wing pods had failed and its single fuselage-mounted hydraulic drogue unit could only trail a single hose at any one time. This left it vulnerable to damage and there was potential for vast amounts of fuel to be trapped onboard the Tristar, unable to be offloaded because the basket had been damaged by over-zealous prodding. Even with its massive giveaway, the Tristar would need to be supplemented by VC10 tankers based along the route in Sicily, which would then continue to Masirah to take part in the exercise. Only recently introduced to service, the Tornado F3 was not yet cleared to tank from the Tristar, so a rapid programme to issue a clearance was initiated.

Once in Masirah, it would be the first time the squadron had flown against the Hunter, so a comprehensive work-up would be needed. Ostensibly, the Hunter was a simple aircraft with no radar and armed only with stern aspect AIM-9P Sidewinders. In fact, it was a highly manoeuvrable aircraft and in the clear air of the Gulf it was still a formidable opponent, despite its age. The Jaguar was more familiar as it was a regular opponent in the UK. As well as combat air patrols or CAPs, we could potentially be tasked to provide escort for the bomber force as well as operating as mixed pairs of fighters on CAP, leading Omani aircraft into the fight. To prepare, Jaguar and Tornado GR1 sorties were easily arranged, but finding Hunters was more of a challenge. Our own aggressor squadron, in the guise of No. 45 Squadron at Wittering, had flown Hunters but had disbanded many years before. The Buccaneer force had a few two-seat Hunters which were used for dual checks and the Navy Fleet Requirements Air Direction Unit, or FRADU, still operated the type. With some hasty phone calls, a number of willing squadron programmers agreed to help and soon a plan took shape. The work-up schedule was a welcome break from the normal conversion flying on the Operational Conversion Unit. As the phase unfolded, escort missions were rehearsed in which the F3s protected the Jaguars when opposed by the Hunter. This scenario expanded with combined packages of Jaguars and Tornado GR1s flown against Phantoms acting as 'Red Air'. Although not planned to take part in Oman, given the Hunter's lack of air intercept radar, the Phantom crews assisted the Hunter pilots to find the 'package' in the more inclement British weather. The tactical training progressed well and the crews became well versed in the techniques which would be needed on arrival in theatre.

At that stage, efforts turned to tanker qualification, particularly as the deployment would include night flying. The brief testing which had been done by test pilots and navigators at Boscombe Down was validated and the Tristar proved to be an excellent tanker with few vices. One of the unknowns was whether there was sufficient engine oil aboard the F3 to complete the planned ten-hour-plus deployment sortie. Oil consumption checks would be needed to verify usage and involved a long, and at times boring, transit behind a Tristar tanker. Prodding by day before prodding by night, at the end of the four-hour-thirty-five-minute mission we had seen enough of a Tristar's backside to last a lifetime. This epic was followed a few nights later by a further sortie to re-qualify on the VC10 tanker at night. The VC10 was the workhorse of the tanker force, but unlike the Tristar, it was familiar and this was to be one of the easier qualifications. In the event, the long hours spent behind the tankers were nothing compared to what was to come.

As the deployment date neared, a vital element of the VIP demonstration which would occur on the day after arrival had yet to be rehearsed. The task force was to demonstrate the ability to escort a C-130 force during a parachute insertion, and therefore a C-130 transport aircraft was secured to prepare for the key event. Launching from its base at RAF Lyneham in Wiltshire, the C-130 flew to the Leominster area to join each of the aircraft types participating in the demonstration. A full dress rehearsal of the profile using similar tracks and timings to the ones I had chosen for the real event in Oman was practised. Remarkably, all went perfectly and the sequence seemed viable. The next time it would run would be in front of the Sultan of Oman.

A full dress rehearsal for the actual deployment sortie followed with a further day-into-night profile in which the Tornado GR1s from Marham joined the F3s. The Tristar and VC10 tankers completed their own rehearsal of tanker-to-tanker transfers and proved the procedures which they would use on the day. The sortie of four hours ten minutes daytime flying ended with one hour twenty-five minutes at night, culminating in a landing at RAF Marham to attend a final coordination meeting. The back-aching sortie was to be just half the duration of the real event. The debrief brought together the GR1 crews and the F3 crews who would be taking part for the first time. As each brick was slowly added, we began to feel more confident that the complex plan was viable.

Some would think that a VIP exercise staged half way across the world using aircraft and bases which had never before been used might be enough of a challenge. Such was the mayhem of the introduction to service of the Tornado F3 that the OCU was tasked in parallel to complete an Armament Practice Camp at the RAF base at Akrotiri in Cyprus. The remainder of the squadron had already deployed to the Mediterranean and would remain in Cyprus for a month, leaving an engineering party at RAF Coningsby to support Swift Sword. Even though the high-profile exercise in Oman was imminent, the squadron was not immune from the NATO requirement to qualify crews in air-to-air gunnery techniques. Without this qualification the crews and aircraft could not be declared combat ready. During the week prior, the crews nominated for Swift Sword flew down to Akrotiri on the regular trooping flight to fly against the banner in the deployed Tornado F3s leaving engineers at base preparing for the major exercise. In the short time available, the crews completed the academic, limited operational, and operational shoots to achieve Allied Command Europe (ACE) qualification. At the same time, preparation to run the first squadron conversion course was moving along at a steady pace, almost in the background. Training was still the primary role and final efforts to validate the syllabus were in train, but delayed declarations were political dynamite.

Optimism that the return from Cyprus would leave a few clear days in which to prepare for the mission faded when ZE166, the principal aircraft and my mount for the trip, developed problems. The oil usage on this jet had been verified so it was vital that it remained as the primary choice if possible. After some heroic engineering efforts, the jet was declared serviceable and we flew an air test on 21 November, just days before the event. It passed and the preparation moved into the final stages.

The deployment was planned for 24 November 1986. The Boss, Wing Commander Rick Peacock-Edwards, and I were to lead the deployment with my normal pilot and his navigator Bob Burden in the number 2 aircraft. On arrival, a flypast at Masirah airbase was scheduled for 1300 local time. By working back from the time on task it became apparent that the take-off time would be late in the evening of the preceding day. We would launch from RAF Coningsby at 2200 local time and it would be pitch black. The long sortie would involve periods of boring route flying alongside the tankers at a time when our bodies would be more interested in sleeping than flying in close formation on a tanker. We were advised to establish a sleeping pattern over the preceding days—hugely popular with our families who would be left behind—and we became nocturnal. Staying awake on the night would be a problem and the concept of alternating 'uppers' and sleeping pills became reality. I began to feel enormous sympathy for airline pilots who must face this phenomenon regularly.

The pre-mission briefing had been held in advance so, on the night, it was a case of a few vital reminders and a weather update for the route. Our groundcrew would be on the ground in Masirah when we arrived and would accept the jets. Akrotiri was available as a bolthole *en route* and our detachment would be on readiness to provide support to fix the jets if they misbehaved. We had a spare aircraft on standby in Cyprus ready to launch if one of the primary F3s was unserviceable during the mission. Spare F3s were nominated at Coningsby and we would switch aircraft if we had problems on start. A further spare would launch and be prepared to continue down route if either of the nominated aircraft should become unserviceable once airborne. All bases were covered and a complex contingency plan stored in the memory banks.

During the planning I had spent many hours on the Cassette Preparation Ground Station translating the air-to-air refuelling plan into data that the Tornado main computer could understand. The navigation waypoints, TACAN beacons,

```
/NVPT        AKR - GULF
NVPT 01      34D35.0N 032D59.0E  AKR
NVPT 02      33D52.0N 032D04.0E  APLON
NVPT 03      33D06.0N 030D57.0E  RASDA
NVPT 04      32D02.0N 031D04.0E  MUAD
NVPT 05      31D31.7N 031D07.2E  BALTIM
NVPT 06      30D04.0N 031D11.0E  GMB
NVPT 07      28D59.0N 031D45.0E  RASNI
NVPT 08      28D02.0N 032D03.0E  SUMRU
NVPT 09      27D18.0N 032D17.0E  NABED
NVPT 10      25D45.1N 032D46.0E  LUXOR
NVPT 11      26D05.0N 035D44.0E  IMRAD
NVPT 12      27D07.9N 044D43.3E  ALKIR
NVPT 13      26D56.5N 046D23.4E  SIBLI
NVPT 14      26D44.3N 048D00.4E  SILNO
NVPT 15      26D15.5N 050D39.3E  BAY
NVPT 16      26D30.0N 051D20.0E  MOTTA
NVPT 17      25D32.9N 052D53.8E  SORPO
NVPT 18      25D14.0N 053D22.2E  SHAIF
NVPT 19      24D26.8N 054D38.8E  A DHA
NVPT 20      24D51.2N 054D57.6E  MAIDA
NVPT 21      25D15.8N 053D42.1E  DOLBA
NVPT 22      25D45.9N 053D04.4E  BELSO
NVPT 23      26D55.6N 050D10.4E  AVLON
NVPT 24      28D01.5N 049D22.2E  SELEG
NVPT 25      26D55.6N 050D10.4E  ALVON
NVPT 26      25D46.0N 051D06.0E  DELSA
NVPT 27      25D01.5N 052D30.3E  BUNDU
NVPT 28      24D51.7N 053D07.3E  BILO
NVPT 29      24D35.0N 054D10.1E  BATREN R.P.
AFB  31      34D35.0N 032D59.0E  AKR 52
AFB  32      30D07.0N 031D24.0E  CAI 53
AFB  33      25D40.0N 032D42.0E  LUX 54
AFB  34      24D33.0N 039D42.0E  MAD --
AFB  35      24D58.0N 046D42.0E  RIY --
AFB  36      26D16.0N 050D09.0E  DHA 58
AFB  37      26D16.0N 050D38.0E  BAH 59
AFB  38      24D26.0N 054D39.0E  AUH 60
AFB  39      25D20.0N 055D31.0E  SHA --
AFB  40      25D15.0N 055D22.0E  DUB --
AFB  41      24D26.0N 054D28.0E  BAT 61
AFB  42      25D16.0N 051D34.0E  DOH 63
AFB  43      29D13.0N 047D58.0E  KUW 64
TACN 52      34D34.8N 032D57.8E  AKR 107 02E
TACN 53      30D09.0N 031D25.0E  CAI 072 02E
TACN 54      25D45.1N 032D46.0E  LXR 096 03E
TACN 55      26D10.7N 036D29.3E  WEJ 086 02E
TACN 56      26D26.0N 039D16.1E  HLF 112 03E
TACN 57      27D25.5N 041D41.0E  HIL 082 03E
TACN 58      26D15.6N 050D08.0E  DHA 074 02E
TACN 59      26D15.5N 050D39.3E  BAH 100 02E
TACN 60      24D26.8N 054D38.8E  AUH 077 01E
TACN 61      24D25.9N 054D28.0E  VAD 087 01E
TACN 62      25D19.7N 055D31.2E  SHJ 070 01E
TACN 63      25D16.0N 051D34.0E  DOH 071 02E
TACN 64      29D13.1N 047D58.0E  KUA 102 03E
/ORD
NVPT ALOC    01  22  23  --  --  --  --
AFB  ALOC    35  40  39
TNK  ALOC    T5  T1
MEZ  ALOC    M-  M-
/AIR
TNK  T5      26D18.0N 037D34.0E 082D 120NM25000FT
TNK  T1      26D52.0N 046D55.0E 095D 056NM25000FT
/RTE
RTE          01  02  03  04  05  06  07
```

Navigation data from the cassette preparation ground station. (*UK MoD Crown Copyright, 1986*) air force bases, and tanker towlines were programmed into the system, loaded onto mission tapes, and printed out as kneeboard inserts to carry in the cockpit. Maps were drawn showing routes, diversions, tanker brackets, timing marks, and diversion fuel calculations, and would be carried in the aircraft as a backup. The mission data was pre-loaded in the deploying aircraft.

Despite the new 'all singing, all dancing' tactical displays, navigators in the early days still resorted to tried and trusted manual techniques for long routes. One navigator cut out the legend from the front of a large-scale topographical map. The small graphic showed the coverage of the chart between the Mediterranean and Masirah, was about 2 inches long and covered thousands of miles. He drew a line from one side of the tiny chart to the other and presented it to his pilot. Leave the rest to me, he announced.

It was vital to have a 'Loser Plan' and aircraft faults were categorised by severity. Some critical failures such as engine failures were easy to decide upon and were simply 'show stoppers'. Others, such as avionics failures may or may not be critical depending on the phase of the mission. We had a plan for which defects were acceptable and which would demand a diversion, and this would guide our contingency thinking as we pressed down route.

Walking to the jets, a shot of adrenalin helped out. After all the preparation, the day—or night—was finally here. I do not recall whether there were any issues on start up as my thoughts were firmly on the rendezvous and join up, but we launched in our planned aircraft, ZE166, exactly on time.

The join was to be a complex affair as the initial group comprising a Tristar, two VC10s, four Tornado GR1s, and our own pair of F3s, formed up. The additional VC10s, operating from a base in Sicily, would join us over the Eastern Mediterranean. After take off, we headed for the rendezvous point at 54 degrees north, 2 degrees east, well out over the North Sea before setting track for Dover. Knowing that we were to head south and east it felt strange to be heading off in a north-easterly direction at first. There was logic in the plan, however, in that the tanker leader wanted all the 'chicks' onboard before crossing the Flight Information Region boundary into French airspace. The short sea leg in the UK would allow replacement aircraft to join the formation in the event of aircraft becoming unserviceable. With help from the control and reporting centre at Neatishead, I found the tankers on radar and we had an uneventful join, pulling alongside the huge Tristar tanker with a certain feeling of relief. Shortly afterwards, the Tornado GR1s from RAF Marham also pulled alongside and, once in formation, we transferred to our tactical transit frequency. From here the lead tanker captain would talk to the air traffic control agencies and coordinate the passage of the whole formation. Eight aircraft had become a single entity and we would merely hear updates of which agency and which frequency he was using as we progressed down route. Our first refuelling bracket was in UK airspace. That way, if there were any problems with fuel transfer they would be identified early and contingency plans could be put in place. All went to plan and all six Tornados were topped to full before leaving 'Blighty'. As we headed south over

France, the first VC10 topped off the Tristar's fuel tanks before returning to RAF Brize Norton. The second VC10 then gave the fighters more fuel during a second tanker bracket just south of Rambouillet in France before returning to the UK. The formation continued south past Lyon, Nice, and Alghero in Corsica, and in the early hours of the morning we received a top up from the Tristar between Bular and Trapani in Sicily.

At this stage the three VC10s operating from Sicily were scheduled to launch and we were to rendezvous overhead the island for our final tanking bracket in the Mediterranean. These were the VC10s which would continue down route, but using these aircraft had another advantage. The Tristar was fitted with two baskets in a single hose drogue unit in the rear fuselage. We could live with damage to one basket and still use the spare. Damage to both meant the fuel was trapped onboard the huge tanker. By using the VC10s, that risk of damage, which could easily occur at night over the turbulent Mediterranean, was minimised. In a single prod, large amounts of fuel could be transferred from one tanker to another, giving flexibility to the fuel plan.

As we approached the refuelling bracket, the medium-level cloud began to thicken and by the time we heard the VC10s check in on frequency it was positively murky. The rendezvous involved a head-on intercept controlled from within the tanker formation, using direction-finding equipment and ranges from the TACAN navigation equipment. For fighter aircrew used to controlling intercepts using air intercept radar, this seemed like an imprecise art. The two formations closed inexorably, with our own formation following the planned route approaching the VC10s on a reciprocal heading. The navigator in the Tristar would call a turn at an appropriate range, at which time the VC10 formation—three large tankers in quite close trail formation—would turn about and match our heading. In loose formation on the Tristar I watched the three tankers approach on my radar. The airspace around was otherwise clear of traffic as you would be expected at 2 a.m. on a dark night over the Mediterranean Sea. If the join went to plan they would roll out 2 miles ahead to allow the Tristar and 'chicks' to close. At the point at which I would have called the turn there was a marked silence and a few uncomfortable seconds followed; and seconds were critical at these closing speeds. The call to turn came late and by the time the VC10s were half way around the turn they were pointing directly at our formation a mere 1,000 feet below and looking uncomfortably close. I called the incoming tankers to the rest of the formation, and despite knowing that we had height separation I was not surprised to see the other Tornados around me ease up involuntarily as the tankers flashed past below, their navigation lights winking through the murk. They rolled out some miles abeam and slightly ahead but, luckily, visible on radar. After a few reassuring calls to establish visual contact they pulled alongside and joined the formation. It could not be classed as a textbook join, and had that been one of my intercepts, I would have received some healthy banter from my peers. It was, however, a crucial manoeuvre because had we failed to rendezvous, we had insufficient fuel to make it to Oman. The repercussions of a mid-air collision were even more worrying to consider, but the heights had been carefully briefed. It just looked close!

Safely aboard, as the fast jets filled to full from one VC10, the tankers redistributed their fuel among themselves. It is surprising how you can forgive a mistake when the offender gives you his precious fuel for free. The next refuelling would be some hours later over Saudi airspace. The GR1s were operating in their normal combat fit carrying 1,500-litre external fuel tanks on the inboard pylons and a Skyshadow ECM pod and a BOZ chaff pod on the outboard pylons. In this heavy fit they struggled to maintain 27,000 feet and remain plugged in as the tanks filled to full. We could see the odd dab of reheat as the bomber pilots worked hard to stay in contact. In contrast, we had no external tanks or defensive aids, and in a clean F3 we were comfortable at that height. If we had worked hard so far, our colleagues in the grey and green jets were working harder.

My next challenge then presented itself as I had to carry out a previously untried procedure in the Tornado F3. The programmable navigation and tactical mission data was normally loaded using a cassette tape on the ground before flight. During this procedure the TV tabs were blank, but after a short time the main computer rebooted with the new mission-specific information installed. Under normal conditions, enough data was loaded for the whole sortie and minor amendments could be made in flight using the keypad on the TV tab. The tiny main computer could hold the route data for the UK to Cyprus but no more, so sitting in the dark at 27,000 feet I would have to reload the mission data for the second half of the route. I pushed that small plastic cassette tape into the loading port with a great deal of trepidation. My first worry was that it may not have loaded correctly on the preparation station at Coningsby and, if so, the procedure would abort. My second worry was that either the data loader or the tape would throw a 'wobbly' and it was not unknown for the magnetic tape to be eaten alive by the mechanism. In the event of a failure, I would spend the next thirty minutes typing on the cumbersome keyboard, loading the data manually. I primed my pilot, rotated the knob marked 'data entry', and hit the switch marked 'Start'—the screens went blank. The cockpit suddenly seemed a lonelier place, and although the data entry process took only a few minutes, it seemed like hours. My relief was tangible when the screens burst back into life and the new data was displayed in glorious green. Next stop, Masirah.

I had flown to Akrotiri many times and the navigation points had a familiar ring, but as we headed south over Egypt they began to sound much more mysterious. As we passed Baltim, Luxor, and Shaif, dawn had broken and the Egyptian Pyramids, easily visible from our cruising height, gave way to the Saudi desert landscape, dotted with irrigated crop circles. The fifth tanker bracket was flown in glorious sunlight at about 37 degrees East, between the exotic sounding beacons of Sibli and Silvo. The tankers had descended to 25,000 feet which gave the GR1s a little more performance in hand, and life became easier. After a final top off from the Tristar at 47 degrees East, we prepared to be cut loose. Once in contact with the Omani air traffic agency we accelerated ahead and set course for Masirah, expecting to be joined by Jaguars from the host base to lead us in. The arrival in the circuit was to be in individual formations—the Jaguars followed by the F3s, followed by the GR1s—and after the flypast the formations would break into the circuit to land. The pilots were extremely tired after the long transit and heroism was undoubtedly constrained by realism. The Omani Air Force was renowned for its low-flying expertise and their pilots were fresh and rested. Flypasts over the airfield were renowned and a height of 10 feet above the ground was not unheard of. For that reason, one of the major briefing points from our leader many hours before had been to remain above the Jaguars. True to form, those who saw the arrival from the ground confirmed that the locals were spectacular and the Brits a little more restrained.

The sortie lasted ten hours fifteen minutes, strapped to a Martin Baker ejection seat throughout with little room to wriggle. Breakfast had been a small sandwich and my fluid intake had been carefully controlled to avoid having to use the 'piddle pack', which we all carried. Somehow the passenger in the Tristar waving his breakfast tray in the window of the tanker hadn't seemed funny as we passed over Egypt. Of that time, four hours forty-five minutes was at night and the sun had risen for the final five hours thirty minutes. We flew over Masirah at 1300 local on the dot, and were met by the Joint Force Commander and the Base Commander. The F3s manoeuvred onto the first two slots, followed by the GR1s on the remaining armament slots. The moment the F3s closed down, the groundcrew began to service the aircraft and as we climbed from the cockpit it was good to stretch my limbs in the afternoon sun.

Oils replenished and turnround complete, new crews accepted the aircraft and within minutes of landing, the engines spooled up again and the F3s launched on a sortie. For real, the aircraft would have deployed carrying a full missile load, and this was to demonstrate that they could have mounted a combat air patrol immediately on arrival.

On the day following our arrival we were to fly the demonstration sortie for the Sultan of Oman and his entourage. The fifteen-minute demonstration was to include a low-level parachute drop by the Parachute Brigade, and both the F3s and the GR1s would participate. We could call upon two Omani Hunters as 'opposing forces'. With such limited assets it would be a challenge to maintain interest if the crowd saw only the occasional fly through from each of the participants, so a little choreography was needed. I set up an initial point (IP) some 10 miles from the dais where the Sultan would be seated. Within the time slot it would be possible for the F3s to return to the IP and be involved in each part of the demonstration. The script had friendly forces attacking a desert airstrip, and after a suppression attack by the GR1s, the C-130s would drop airborne forces to secure the airfield. During the insertion the airfield would be attacked by hostile Hunters which would be chased off by the defending F3s.

The time on task was to be 1300 local time for the opening run, but as we started up our wingman developed a problem and we taxied with four Tornado GR4s, but only a single Tornado F3. The leg to the desert strip was uneventful

A Royal Omani Air Force
Jaguar breaks into the circuit at
Masirah airbase. (*Bob Burden*)

The Tornado F3 crews arrive after a ten-hour-fifteen-minute mission. (*UK MoD Crown Copyright, 1986*)

The Tornado F3 crews are greeted by the Masirah Base Commander and the Joint Force Commander on arrival. (*UK MoD Crown Copyright, 1986*)

The Tornado operating area at Masirah airbase. (*Bob Burden*)

The Royal Omani Air Force squadron buildings. Artwork survives from RAF days.

and at the precise second, the Tornado GR4s made a high-speed pass over the top with our own Tornado F3 in close escort. The Hercules parachute drop would be a set-piece event, flown by eight C-130 crews with the final Hercules containing local Omani paratroops. We would spice up the show by providing a pair of Tornado F3s in close escort above the stream—if our wingman showed up. As soon as the GR1s had flown through, we returned to the initial point at high speed, picking up the inbound transport aircraft on radar. The drop was planned at 180 knots as any faster would risk injury to the parachutists. For that reason, there was no way we could stay in any type of close formation position, so we set up a weave manoeuvre overhead the stream as it ran in. The slowest speed at which we could safely manoeuvre was 250 knots and to do that we would need manoeuvre flap and slats and full reheat for much of the pass. As the lead aircraft slowed to his target speed, he let down to the drop height which was only 1,000 feet above the ground. We were well towards the rear of the stream but because of our greater speed, slowly crept up the line. I had talked my pilot onto a visual acquisition as we joined, and he was holding our aircraft in a tight weave just 500 feet above the lumbering transports. It must have looked quite impressive from the ground, particularly with the eight massive C-130s just below us, even if it wasn't the epitome of good air defence tactics. In a real engagement we would have been massively vulnerable at such a slow speed, but for the demonstration it would look good. As we crossed the airfield boundary I could see the parachutists streaming from the ramps of the transport aircraft. By then I was keeping track of the time and the whereabouts of the rest of the stream and had the perfect view of the drop as my F3 turned tightly above them. Watching the parachutes billowing into the airflow was reminiscent of Arnhem in the desert. I could only imagine the thoughts going through the minds of the parachutists. Not only did they have the challenge of a low-level drop, but what must have seemed like World War 3 was going on just a scant 500 feet above their heads. More relevant, the noise must have been truly ear shattering. As we reached the airfield we pulled off into a high looping turn and set off again for the initial point for the final run. At this stage our errant wingman had joined and we ran out as a pair. Again picking up our 'opponents' on radar, we turned tight in behind the Hunters and set up in a short trail with an F3 on each Hunter. The Hunter pilots proved to be the most accommodating 'bad guys' in history and, as they made an aggressive pass over the parachutists on the ground simulating a strafing run, they obligingly allowed us to sit firmly in their 6 o'clock in a guns tracking position. It must have been a real crowd pleaser because the Sultan, apparently, asked how many F3s had deployed for the exercise. We had returned so often that he assumed each pass was a different formation. This was the last time during the exercise that the Hunter pilots would be quite so accommodating.

One of the less attractive tasks as project officer was to produce the unit Operation Order, the authority to take part. Exercise Saif Sareea was an Out of Area Joint Forces Field Training Exercise. The Joint Task Force would operate from a combined UK/Omani Joint Force Headquarters at Masirah and would also act as a forward mounting base. An airhead would be established at a desert airstrip at Al Mahatta. The aim of the exercise was to demonstrate the UK's capability for rapid strategic out-of-area operations and to practice combined operations with the host nation. As well as our own air forces, Oman would provide up to twenty-four Jaguars from Nos 8 and 20 Squadrons, twelve Hunters, three C-130s, and ten support helicopters. HMS *Illustrious*, with its three Sea King airborne early warning helicopters and fifteen support helicopters, would join a naval task force. Our tactical callsigns were Scorcher and Birch formations and the GR1s were Vandal formation.

After the extensive preparation and the long transit flight, closely followed by the hectic demonstration sortie, the exercise was almost an anti-climax. Operating from Masirah, the Tornados held up well during the three days of flying. The early sorties saw dissimilar air combat pitted against the Jaguars of the Omani Air Force. The Omanis were keen not only to work with us but to explore the capability of the aircraft as an order was in the offing. In Omani service the Jaguar was unencumbered with the external fuel tanks and electronic countermeasure pods typical of British Jaguars. This improved performance somewhat, although with its lack of power and high wing loading, it could never be described as agile. Flying against the Jaguar, the beyond-visual-range capability of the Skyflash plus the better turn performance at all altitudes really made it a no-contest. The Jaguar was a superb bomber but was sadly lacking as a fighter. Operating together, we explored mixed fighter force tactics with the less agile fighter bomber. Armed with two AIM-9P Sidewinders, we provided a voice commentary to the Jaguar pilot as we prosecuted an intercept. A Jaguar would sit in loose formation on each F3 as the formation vectored towards the incoming raid. After launching Skyflash missiles, the F3 navigators would provide a visual commentary to the Jaguar pilots to talk them into a visual contact. After gaining 'Tally' (fighter speak for visual contact with the enemy), the Jaguars would engage the Hunters to attempt further missile shots.

A merge with two Tornado F3s leading two Jaguars against four Hunters over the desert landscape proved extremely demanding as the nimble Hunter was a worthy opponent. Although the Omanis had operated this aging British fighter since 1975, it still performed well. Two AIM-9P Sidewinders had been fitted on underwing pylons mounted inboard of the external fuel tanks. Old-style bomb racks could be mounted towards the wing tips to carry unguided rockets and bombs. For the exercise, only missile pylons were fitted and, in that configuration, the Hunter and the F3 were well matched in pure airframe performance. Without a radar warning receiver, the Hunter pilot could only guess when a Skyflash had been launched, so their tactics could be rudimentary without ground control. Despite often achieving a kill even before seeing the Hunter, we pressed to the merge, keen to compare performance. In pure handling terms, we could call it an even match. The turn performance was close, but the Tornado enjoyed much more power using reheat. The decider was the massive improvement in weapons technology which had occurred over the years. Compared to the Hunter's AIM-9P Sidewinder, which still relied on being fired within 60 degrees of the tail, the F3 had a huge advantage. With the enhanced weapon system and the all-aspect AIM-9L Sidewinder, a well-flown F3 was able to claim a shot in most circumstances. Ironically, both the Jaguars and the Hunters were equipped with AN/ALE40 chaff and flare dispensers, which was more than we could boast in the Tornado F3 force in the early years. At that time, our own AIM-9Ls were vulnerable to infra-red countermeasures, so maybe the fight was more even than it appeared at first sight. An accurately dispensed flare programme would have negated any AIM-9L shot we took.

One of the planning issues had been to delineate between normal day tactics events and air combat. In the former there are clearly defined roles. A fighter (the attacker) tries to progress to a missile shot or gun shot against the defender who, in turn, evades, trying to prevent the attacker getting into a tracking solution. In air combat, both are aggressive from the outset. Any participant can take a shot at any time and will manoeuvre to the maximum limits to do so. The Operation Order was crafted carefully to define the attacker and the defender. The reality was that once the horns were out and crews entered a turning fight, the division would become blurred. When a defender who is making angles on his attacker suddenly finds that he has the opportunity for a missile shot, no self-respecting fighter pilot, or indeed bomber pilot, would ever pass on that opportunity! The flying was enjoyable.

The operating area consisted of the majority of the overland mass of Oman, stretching from the Yemeni border in the South to the Gulf of Oman on the northern coast. The attacking forces would approach from the northern coastline and route in a southerly direction overland. Blue forces would establish combat air patrols in areas where low-level targets would be detected, despite the hilly terrain of the hinterland. Navigation points showed a rudimentary depiction of the coastline on the tactical plan display, with other points showing combat air patrol datums or entry points into the fighter areas of responsibility, or FAORs. A number of reporting 'bullseyes' were given the names of Teem, Fanta, and Softy. Others attracted the names crush, Pepsi, and Coca Cola. This should have been a clue that this was to be a dry exercise; Batemans, Tetleys, and Greene King were not mentioned.

There were only two rules in the Omani Flying Order Book and these were 'Don't fly over the Sultan's palace' and 'Don't screw up'. As the palace was in the northern city of Seeb, we were relatively sure of not falling foul of rule number one. We were also keen to ensure that we complied with rule number two.

During every exercise lessons are learned, and this was no exception.

Lesson One: In VFR [visual flying rules] you may not need a radar.
A medium-level combat air patrol was flown at 15,000 feet, dropping to lower levels to engage a target. The Hunters flew formations split in height with only one pilot flying at low level to attract attention. As the F3 manoeuvred for a shot, the wingman flying in the upper air would descend from above and engage. It should have been possible to negate this tactic with an effective radar search but it could be remarkably effective if flown well. The lack of radar was only a minor disadvantage to the Hunter pilot as, with the tremendous visibility, visual detection ranges were enormous. Set against the sandy desert, the light air defence grey colour of the Tornado F3 stood out like the proverbial 'sore thumb'. Lessons are learned quickly and within hours we were watching for 'The Hun in the Sun' to prevent the Hunter dropping into our six o'clock from tens of thousands of feet above like an 'avenging angel'. With visually aimed Sidewinders in clear air, the Hunter was remarkably effective, although in adverse European weather it would have been a different story. With practice, we began to return the favour on more than one occasion.

Lesson Two: Don't fly below an Omani Jaguar!
As we had learned on arrival, the displays of low flying skill were legendary, particularly from the British loan service pilots. We watched Jaguar formations recover to the airfield and, as they approached the parking ramp, a sand trail was blown up in the desert dust. At the head of the trail was a Jaguar. Jokingly, pilots boasted that they would pull up over the 4-inch concrete lip of the ramp, but the reality was not too far removed. Amazingly, there were few accidents and the only exception I recall was when a Jaguar struck the metal railings of a range control building with its wingtip. Remarkably, the aircraft recovered to base safely, although the pilot was relieved from duty for transgressing rule number two.

Above left: A Royal Omani Air Force Jaguar flies low over the Omani coastline. (*Bob Burden*)

Above right: A No. 65 Squadron Tornado F3 flies low over the Omani desert in 67 wing. (*Bob Burden*)

There were many other lessons learned during those few days which set a good grounding for future Tornado deployments to the Gulf. I learned an old lesson yet again. With Omani aircraft acting as both fighters and enemy forces, identification was problematic. We had to pay close attention to the roles of each aircraft type on each day. Critical was the electronic code from the IFF system (identification, friend or foe) which each aircraft transmitted for identification purposes. We had been sent to man a combat air patrol over the highlands in the centre of the country and it had been relatively quiet when a contact appeared on the Foxhunter radar. I popped it into track-while-scan and it formed a track running at high speed towards us. After taking a closing vector I hit the IFF interrogator which was programmed with the exercise codes. This electronic box pinged the target and read its electronic response comparing it with the codes of the day. There was no response from the target which should have switched from track A to track 1 on my display if it was friendly. I called the contact to the fighter controller and added 'showing hostile'. At the word 'hostile', our fighter controller immediately cleared us to engage. After sweetening the shot, as the target came inside missile parameters, my pilot pulled the trigger and the simulated Skyflash missile sped off to its target destroying the 'bogey' seconds later. As we pulled off and dropped a wing we saw one of our own GR1s, which were acting as friendly forces that day, flash down the side many thousands of feet below. We had engaged one of our own aircraft! This is known as a 'blue on blue' engagement and has since become all too familiar on media reports.

Why did it happen? I checked my own codes at the time and I was sure I had selected the correct switches. The GR1 navigator may have set the wrong code or missed the time at which the codes were changed leaving the old code set. The controller should have taken more care to confirm his own definitions of a hostile aircraft. Now, did I really have the right codes in my interrogator and had I set that switch correctly? Whoever was at fault, it proved a point in a training environment. Procedures have since changed and equipment is more robust, but the problem was to take on more prominence during later Gulf operations and have a much more tragic outcome when a Tornado GR4 was destroyed by an American Patriot missile. Despite huge leaps in identification technology since the 1980s, it has been proved over and over that, in the heat of battle, mistakes can and will be made.

Once stood down from exercise flying in the UK, we would retire to the aircrew briefing facility where we would sleep in metal bunk beds in a darkened dormitory. For this exercise we retired to the small accommodation huts on the domestic site where the attraction of some winter sun was far too good to turn down. I confess to feeling a little guilty at the time as the aircrew were allocated accommodation blocks whereas the majority of the detachment was housed in a tented city which sprung up on the airfield. After the flying day, an array of extremely suspect shorts replaced flying suits for a touch of sunbathing. It could be tough on exercise at times.

Although Oman was not a dry country, it had been decreed that the exercise would be a non-drinking event with alcohol banned during the exercise period. Imagine our delight when invited to the Station Commander's house for the final social event, we found a lavish bar and some wonderful local delicacies. It took a little explaining the following morning when our groundcrew noticed a few slightly red eyeballs as we reported for duty.

Such was the complexity of Exercise Saif Sareea, it would not be repeated again until 2001.

The return deployment proved to be less taxing. The gunnery detachment was still underway at RAF Akrotiri in Cyprus and a single leg from Masirah to Cyprus on 1 December 1986 took a much more gentlemanly five hours fifty minutes. After an overnight stop we were straight into our second commitment which was a short visit to Jordan, known as Operation Buhl. This time we were not to be accompanied by tankers so I would have to earn my keep as the navigation would be my responsibility. Operation Buhl was to be another demonstration visit as the Jordanian Air Force had expressed an interest in the Tornado F3 as a possible replacement for its aging Mirage F1 fighters. We were to visit Azraq, or more correctly, Shaheed Mwaffaq airbase to fly against the Jordanian Air Force and demonstrate the aircraft's capability. It was a difficult experience flying into Azraq because, given the history of Middle Eastern conflict, Arab nations were reluctant to publish information about their military bases for fear of attack. Essential information to allow us to flight plan our visit had to be teased from our Air Attaché in Amman and relayed through diplomatic channels. This was all very odd to simple flyers. The airbase sits adjacent to a main highway. Head east and the next stop is Baghdad; head south and the road leads to Saudi Arabia. For me this was unfamiliar territory. There were some interesting restrictions in the Flight Information Handbook which we chose to observe on our initial approach. Low-level operations below 11,000 feet were discouraged apart from landing at our destination. Additionally, speed restrictions below that height ensured that any approaching aircraft looked docile to a surface-to-air missile battery, of which there were many. We were keen to comply and kept our approach speed below the published criteria. The Middle East was, as always, a hotbed of politics, but in this instance the politics had a very real consequence.

We were to be accompanied by a pair of Tornado GR1s, although we would arrive at Azraq independently. As I planned the route, attempting to seek clearance through either Lebanon or Israel seemed fraught with difficulties. For some reason a flight of fighter jets attracts much more attention than an airliner. I compromised by planning a track south from Akrotiri to a reporting point on the Egyptian coast and on to Aqaba which avoided penetrating Israeli airspace. We returned back north, by then in Jordanian airspace, heading for the remote base. This seemed by far the friendlier option with a formation of fighter jets. Our Embassy staff in Cairo greased the wheels of diplomacy and the plan was approved. Despite the extended routing, Azraq was within unrefuelled range. As we made our approach I could not fail to notice a highway strip situated close by to the airfield. Equipped with obvious parking areas and a long straight stretch of road which would act as a runway, it reminded me of the highway strips I had seen on the autobahns of Germany during the Cold War. It was interesting to see that our hosts intended to continue to operate if the main base was damaged. Luckily, as we arrived at initials we were cleared to increase speed and make a respectable run in and break at the airfield. It would have been slightly sad to make our approach at 250 knots from a straight in approach to land as this was not the impression we hoped to convey. We touched down on the long 10,000-foot runway and taxied the F3s to the nominated dispersal alongside the hangars, where we were met by personnel from the resident Mirage squadron who proved to be genial hosts throughout our short stay. The C-130 landed shortly after us and disgorged our groundcrew who wrapped up the jets for the night.

Azraq is located east of Amman in northern Jordan, an hour's drive from the capital city along a wide open desert road. We were hosted on our first night by the Air Attaché who explained local customs and culture and things to do—and as importantly what not to do! After a brief reception it was back to the hotel to prepare for the sorties for the following day.

It was to be an intense, albeit brief, professional encounter with our hosts. A short session of low-level intercepts against Northrop F-5s culminated in two dissimilar air combat splits against the resident Mirage F1s—two F3s versus two Mirage F1s. It was clear that our hosts were interested to see how Foxhunter coped in the low-level environment. Amazingly it worked perfectly, much to our surprise and relief as it was still early days for the temperamental system. Equally, the Mirage pilots wanted to see first-hand whether we entered the fray with Skyflash missiles in the air, before evaluating the performance of their own fighter against the F3 in a turning fight. Luckily, they came down into the lower airspace where we were most comfortable because, had they dragged us into the upper air, there would have been far less post-merge manoeuvring. Not unexpectedly, there was some trepidation as the 'Z' List standard of Foxhunter was not performing entirely as promised at that time. A more welcome phenomenon was that, like its predecessor the AN/AWG 11/12, Foxhunter seemed to enjoy its holiday in the sun. In the clearer atmosphere of the Middle East it seemed to perform much better and certainly remained serviceable much longer. Maybe those wet days sitting on the dispersals at Coningsby were part of the problem? In the event, we acquitted ourselves well, taking shots against both the F-5s and the Mirages, and were able to validate the shots. We came away feeling satisfied. Whether it impressed our hosts or not we never knew, but they certainly asked some penetrating questions and seemed well briefed.

After the flying came a positive treat. Unannounced, we heard that a Royal visitor had arrived on base. A gleaming white Boeing 727 with its red and gold cheat line taxied onto the dispersal belonging to no other than His Majesty King Hussein of Jordan. It was well known that, as a qualified pilot, the King flew his own jet on his travels and regularly visited his squadrons. He walked across to the squadron building immediately at ease with his people where we had assembled in an impromptu receiving line. He shook our hands, adding a few kind words and offering each of us a small gift as a token of friendship. A tiny man, what he lacked in stature he made up for in charisma. His pilots clearly adored him and I could not help but feel a huge sense of respect for this charming and fascinating leader. After a cup of tea he climbed back into his jet and was gone.

RAF aircraft on the ramp at Azraq airbase alongside a Jordanian Air Force Mirage F1 fighter.

Following the busy flying day our genial hosts had planned a day of rest. A trip to the Dead Sea including a lunch at a seaside restaurant was a welcome diversion from the tempo of the trek around the Middle East. What flying detachment would be complete without a camel race on the shores of the Dead Sea and the obligatory picture, floating in the salty water reading a newspaper?

Slightly saddle sore, the departure was a relatively muted affair as we headed back to Akrotiri in separate formations, the Tornado GR1s leading some thirty minutes ahead of us. The C-130s followed, leaving the groundcrew to see us off and to troubleshoot any snags on start up. After the obligatory flypast at Azraq we set a southerly heading to skirt around Israeli airspace via the Sinai Peninsula before running back north into Akrotiri. On 9 December it was all over and, once again, I was tucked in behind a VC10 tanker on the way back along the Mediterranean, homeward bound.

By 15 December I thought that the fanfare of introducing a new aircraft was over. The first true squadron conversion course was imminent. I flew a basic radar phase 1 sortie converting one of the pilots on No. 3 Squadron Conversion Course for his instructor work-up. Within weeks he would be cleared to instruct and the core of the Operational Conversion Unit staff would begin training new crews to man the Tornado F3 force. After a huge debrief at Marham on 18 December, Christmas beckoned and Exercise Swift Sword was a memory—or so we thought.

There was to be one final effort before the OCU returned to its primary task. During January and February the first No. 29 Squadron crews began training. The Air Officer Commanding No. 11 Group had already converted to the aircraft, the station executives were converted to type, and the Operational Evaluation Unit had formed. There was to be one last sales push and, given our demonstrated ability to plan Gulf deployments at the drop of a hat and the fact that the experience still lay with the OCU, we were again selected for the honour. I was reassigned as the project officer for Exercise Radlett, which was to be a tour of the Gulf region. Four Tornado F3s supported by a Tristar tanker and a C-130 transport aircraft were tasked to visit Kuwait, Bahrain, Qatar, and Abu Dhabi. It would be a whistle-stop tour over ten days, stopping only briefly at each venue. The core of the tour would be to mount an aerobatic display by the Tornado F3 demonstration pilot at each airfield. As his regular navigator was remaining in the UK during the deployment, I was seconded to act as the display navigator for the short stint.

Just before departure, the Kuwaiti visit was cancelled. The Iran–Iraq War was still raging and Kuwait's position close to the shared border was near to an area of intense fighting. Arming the aircraft for self-protection was considered, but it seemed provocative to send Tornado F3 fighters close to a war zone and caution prevailed. This reticence was to prove prophetic when on 17 May 1987 Iraqi Mirages attacked the USS *Stark* lying off the Kuwaiti coast, firing two Exocet missiles, causing major damage, killing thirty-seven of the crew and injuring twenty-one others. Relationships with Iraq became strained and this exchange proved to be the opening shots of what would lead to Saddam Hussein invading Kuwait in 1990.

There would be none of the epic voyages of Swift Sword and shorter legs were planned. On 6 March 1987, I found myself, yet again, plugged in behind a Tristar tanker on the way back to RAF Akrotiri in Cyprus with another four hours fifty minutes added to the log book. After a short layover we pressed on to the joint civilian/military base in Bahrain. The airfield at Muharraq just outside the capital of Manama would be familiar to many old timers in the RAF. It was known as RAF Muharraq from 1943 until independence in 1971 and was home to detachments of Hawker Hunters for many years. This was to be our first venue and we touched down in bright sunshine. Although a joint military/civilian airfield, military traffic was light and restricted mainly to an occasional US Navy Lockheed P3 maritime patrol aircraft. Flying an aerobatic display at such a venue was a bizarre experience. To arrive at an international airport, which within hours was closed to all traffic, and conduct a ten-minute display down the main runway in full afterburner was surreal.

On 11 March we climbed into the jets yet again having filed a flight plan for an unaccompanied hop across the short stretch of water between Bahrain and Qatar. In a strange twist it had become apparent that the two Arab countries were not on the best terms. Normally when transiting between two countries the radar unit of the departure country coordinates the departure track with the destination country and the formation is cleared into the airspace as per flight plan. Apparently, the two countries were so estranged that there was no direct link between the air traffic agencies. The direct track from Bahrain International to Doha International in Qatar was virtually due east. In order not to appear in any way hostile, we were advised to route in a northerly direction and to make a blind call to the air traffic agency in Doha as we approached their airspace. A turn east and a further turn back to the south would take us to our destination but a trip which may have taken fifteen minutes became thirty minutes due to the choreography. As we made contact and gave our position report, all seemed well. I confess to feeling a little concerned when my radar homing and warning receiver lit up with the signal from a Cyrano IV air intercept radar. We had not been briefed to expect a reception committee but I soon had a pair of aircraft displayed in track-while-scan and they were on an intercept course. We called the contacts and received more reassuring noises from the ATC controller. Sure enough, the Cyrano belonged to a Mirage F1 fighter of the Qatari Air Force which was accompanied by an Alpha Jet. The desert camouflage looked stunning against the blue waters of the Gulf as they pulled alongside into close formation making cheery gestures. Their intentions were clearly friendly and nothing to do with our circuitous route from the north. They escorted us virtually all the way to our destination of Doha International, descending to low level before breaking off and making individual approaches. This was a great relief given our blatant lack of weapons and the apparent breakdown in communication between Manama and Doha. After an aerobatic display at Doha International airport, but disappointingly little contact with our peers on the flying squadron, the next day we flew on to Abu Dhabi Bateen airport for yet another display before heading back behind the Tristar to RAF Coningsby via Akrotiri.

This time it really was the end of the demonstration tours and the following morning after arriving home I briefed an advanced radar phase sortie back on the OCU at Coningsby as we continued to push squadron crews through the conversion course. It is a matter of record that none of this effort turned into orders for the Tornado F3. Oman looked seriously at an acquisition and ordered eight F3s but this was cancelled before delivery. No order was forthcoming from Jordan and a planned order for Mirage 2000s was cancelled. Given the well-publicised deficiencies of the Foxhunter radar at that time, perhaps this was no surprise. On a positive note, the order for twelve Typhoons and eight Hawks signed by the Omani Government in December 2012 reinvigorated the long tradition of cooperation between the two nations.

Following the early deployments by the OCU, in 1988, No. 29 (F) Squadron were to generate another first during Exercise Golden Eagle. Four Tornado F3s from the squadron supported by Tristar tankers embarked on an epic detachment during which the jets would circumnavigate the globe. In an eight-week detachment, the aircraft deployed to Butterworth in Malaysia via Seeb in Oman to take part in a five-nation Integrated Air Defence System exercise. Short visits to Thailand and Singapore were made before continuing to Australia to participate in the bicentennial celebrations. Returning via the exotic locations of Pago Pago and Hawaii, the aircraft dropped in to Travis Air Force Base before taking part at an airshow in Harrisburg, Virginia, in the USA, and making the final transatlantic hop to return to RAF Coningsby. The aircraft and crews flew around the world in sixty-eight days. Whatever its problems with the mission avionics, the Tornado was proving itself to be remarkably robust in its ability to deploy overseas over long distances. This was to be a vital capability within a few short years as events in the Gulf region began to take on added significance and the detachment in the South Atlantic continued.

What I was yet to find out was that with my imminent promotion, I would be the first current Tornado F3 aircrew member to be pulled from flying and given a ground appointment. On 15 April 1987 I flew a sortie which was to be my last before temporarily hanging up my flying boots and heading off to the Ministry of Defence for a ground tour. I was devastated at the news, despite my impending promotion. I wondered whether there really was life after flying.

7

The First Gulf War

I arrived in the Ministry of Defence feeling very depressed. I had left the cockpit after flying just over 200 hours in the Tornado F2 and F3 and was looking at a three-year 'jail stretch' before I got back to flying. It seemed like an eternity but I was quickly grounded, in more ways than one, when I realised what a complicated system I would have to operate under. I also had a lot to learn, not least of which was how to find my way around the labyrinth which was the MoD Main Building. The office I joined had the grand title of Operational Requirements (Air) 32 and I was to become OR32a (Air). Although it was a 'joint' appointment, meaning that it was a tri-service, or 'purple' post, the four in the office were all RAF officers reporting through an RAF Group Captain to an RAF Air Commodore. It all seemed very 'Light Blue' to me but who was I to complain at this stage? The new Boss was an experienced air electronics officer who had flown throughout his career on Vulcans and Nimrods and had a slightly jaundiced view of the fast jet community. I was replacing a hugely experienced squadron leader pilot who had been promoted and was leaving to become a squadron commander. He had clearly excelled in the role and was a hard act to follow.

My first week was a tour around British industry to hear proposals for the embryonic Eurofighter Defensive Aids Sub-System, or EFADASS, for which I was to be responsible. The presentations were attended by representatives of the other three nations involved in the project with each being delivered in perfect 'Venusian' using terms such as 'scanning superhets', 'bragg cells', 'distributed architecture', and other hieroglyphics with which I was to become intimately familiar. I was awed by the complexity, nervous about the politics, and positively scared by the risk of saying something out of turn which might give one company an advantage over another. It was a baptism of fire after the cosy confines of the squadron crewroom. Handover complete, my predecessor left me to my own devices and returned to his cockpit. I also inherited the new electronic warfare suite for the Harrier GR5, a missile warning system for the Harrier GR5 and Tornado GR1, a number of legacy projects, and the huge responsibility to turn the EFADASS European Staff Requirement for Development, which had just been agreed, into a specification. The final responsibility was to become the division expert on 'stealth'. I had heard the term but at that stage I would have happily confessed to total ignorance, yet it was to feature large as the Gulf War erupted. Ironically, the chaff and flare dispenser fit for the Tornado F3 which I had most recently flown was not one of my responsibilities on the fast-jet desk. That project was being run by another desk officer and I had very little sight of the detail, although that would change during my later tour in MoD. In the meantime, I had plenty to keep me occupied.

An operational requirements officer was responsible for setting out the Air Staff Requirement for any equipment that was needed. Each enhancement went into the melting pot with other potential defence projects and, if approved, was funded for project definition and then full development. After the requirement was agreed it was handed to the MoD Procurement Executive, which was comprised largely of civilians, to write a specification. Expert and specialist help from the Royal Aircraft Establishment at Farnborough aided the process before the specifications were issued to industry, after which individual companies would write proposals. MoD (PE) would evaluate these bids and select a contractor to take the design to full development. Progress meetings were held, leading eventually to prototypes before initial production was approved and a trial installation was tested. This convoluted process took years and was closely monitored by the operational requirements staff officer to ensure the requirement was not diluted.

The biggest challenge was that the requirements officer could not say 'I want a Concorde'. He had to ask for a supersonic aircraft which carries lots of passengers and flies a long way.

There was an old joke on the front line showing how the staffing process distorted the operational requirement.

In the beginning there was a requirement for a 'widget'.

And then came the specification and the specification was without form.

And a 'widgy' was produced by the company after much consultation with well meaning idiots and it was completely without substance.

The requirements officer checked the 'widgy' against his requirement for a 'widget' and told the Head of Operational Requirements: 'It's a crock of shit and it stinks!'

The Head of Operational Requirements then told his peers: 'It is a pail of dung and none may abide by the odour.'

His peers told the Head of Defence Procurement: 'It's a container of excrement and it is very strong such that none may smell it.'

The Head of Defence Procurement then told the Defence Board: 'It is a vessel of fertilizer and none may abide by its strength. It contains that which aids growth and it is very strong.'

The Defence Board decides that the 'widgy' is so good it must be delivered into service as soon as possible, saying: 'It promotes growth and it is very powerful. It will help us smite our foes. Pay the company huge sums of money and we should rejoice.'

And the Service Headquarters received the 'widgy' and passed it to the Evaluation Unit for testing and said: 'Tell us what you think of this fine "widgy".'

The Evaluation Unit flies the 'widgy' and says 'Where is the "widget"? This "widgy" is a crock of shit and it stinks!'

And this is how shit happens.

The whole process was complex and for aircraft or major systems it could take many years from writing the requirement to installation on an airframe and completion of operational testing. This was particularly relevant to electronic warfare systems as, by nature, they had to be responsive to current threats. MoD (PE) project managers wanted a tight specification which they could deliver to a budget. If a jammer was intended to jam a Soviet SA-6, but by the time it was fitted to an aircraft the SA-6 had been replaced by the SA-11, the jammer might be of little use to the crew in the cockpit. For that reason, contractors would accuse the requirements officer of changing the goalposts and Operational Requirements would accuse the contractor of being inflexible. The MoD (PE) Manager would simply say that he had delivered to specification and that the money was spent. The reality was the threat had changed over the time of the protracted procurement. The biggest frustration was that an MoD project manager had no responsibility to prove that equipment worked. Providing it was delivered on time and cleared for switch on, the average programme manager might feel his work was done. Presuming the jammer did not turn the aircraft upside down when it transmitted and it was safe to use, many programme managers had little interest when told that it was ineffective against the threat it was intended to protect against. It would be for others to prove operational effectiveness, yet they might not have control of the budget, explaining why many 'get well' programmes were needed for MoD projects. Unlike the system in the USA where operational capability must be formally demonstrated, there was no such test in the UK, although improvements have since been made. The end user was neglected for too many years and funding was often exhausted before operational capability had been proven. By the time deficiencies were documented by the operational community, lawyers had spoken and the contractor could, invariably, demand large sums of money to rectify problems, if indeed additional funds could be found at all.

In the case of the Tornado F3, with the impending Gulf War, problems had already been identified and a 'get well' package was already in train. The aircraft had earned a shocking reputation and most uninformed commentators had decided it was a 'basket case'. Typhoon was coming in ten years or so and would solve the problem so the F3 could be left to 'wither on the vine', or so the story went. It felt as if only the specialists in the aircraft offices were determined to rectify the problems. As a recent operator, the lack of defensive aids was a great concern, although the radar homing and warning receiver, or RHWR, had already been delivered and was slowly being fitted. Although reasonably early in the aircraft's service life, the programme was running well behind the introduction to service. The RHWR hardware had worked reasonably well at inception, but the software took many years to develop to its full potential. The only other defensive equipment envisaged at the outset was for a chaff and flare system and a staff requirement had been approved to fit dispensers and design new flares. There was no active jammer anywhere on the horizon at that early stage.

As I learned my new 'staff language' and digested the alien culture of electronic warfare I became more confident in the role and spent time learning from experienced colleagues. There were tales of contingency programmes implemented during the Falklands campaign, including an airborne jammer, known as 'Blue Eric', which had been fitted to the Harrier GR3. There are varying assessments of how successful the jammer proved to be, but what was indisputable was that it had been a masterpiece of execution as it had been taken from concept to fitment in a few short weeks. This set me thinking about how I would tackle such a contingency plan should the need arise. In those days the UK defence posture was centred on the Cold War threat, and overseas interventions were few. The most ambitious I recall was the slightly gung ho 'show of presence' in Lebanon under the guise of Operation Pulsator. During this time Buccaneer crews escorted by Phantoms operating from RAF Akrotiri in Cyprus mounted missions over Beirut to support British interests. Apart from the risk of Syrian intervention during ingress to the target and the constant worry of an inadvertent tussle with the Israelis, there seemed little chance of an air-to-air engagement. The Air Staff might have been in danger of becoming complacent.

The Phantom had been fitted with the AN/ALE 40 chaff and flare system but with it approaching the end of its service life, there was little chance of any serious new money being approved. The Phantom had entered what was euphemistically known as 'planning blight', which restricted funds for improvements. With that in mind, my contingency plan concentrated on the 'brand new' Tornado F3 which had only just entered service. Any contingency plan had to be achievable and affordable if it was to pass muster. I would need an interim chaff and flare dispenser system should the need arise pending introduction of the formal modification.

Chaff was one of the earliest radar countermeasures developed during the Second World War; strips of tin foil were deployed into the airflow to confuse enemy radars by producing a response on a radar screen which appeared like the real target. Modern chaff is metallised glass fibre but the principle remains the same. Flares are cocktails of chemicals which ignite when deployed, replicating the heat signature of the host aircraft. Both countermeasures are housed in metal cartridges within a dispenser and ejected into the airflow by the crew using a button in the cockpit. Sequences are devised to protect the aircraft against the typical threats it might meet. Once a countermeasure is deployed, the threat missile seeker sees the false target and, if the designers and developers have been smart, the missile is decoyed away from the host aircraft.

Also on my shopping list was, ideally, an active jammer, although that was a more complex problem as there were additional factors such as interoperability with the radar and radar warning receiver to consider. Shortly after my arrival I lobbied to fit an active jammer to the Tornado F3, but the idea was rejected outright with lack of funding given as the reason. Jammers for ground attack aircraft were generally accepted as essential, but even the electronic warfare community was less willing to recognise a need for a jammer on an air defence platform, although that view had already changed in the case of the Eurofighter Typhoon. This lack of foresight was to resurface during Operation Deny Flight in 1993.

A final option was to modify the radar cross section of the Tornado, which was quite large for a fighter. We had been experimenting with using radar absorbent material to reduce the radar echo and had plans to fit these tiles to a trials aircraft to evaluate the protection. Funds had been identified to develop the material but not to run the evaluation.

The greatest risk as tensions rose in the Gulf region was procurement delays. Although the defensive aid programmes for the F3 were moving forward, the systems were being procured separately under individual staff requirements. Separate specifications had been written for the Radar Homing and Warning Receiver and the chaff and flare system. The chaff/flare system which was to be fitted had been set down under its own Staff Requirement and had experienced a rough ride through the staffing procedure. The contract had been placed with separate companies with a chaff dispenser and a defensive aids controller procured from a Swedish company, Celcius Tech, who produced excellent countermeasures equipment. The contract for the flare dispenser had been given to Vinten, a UK manufacturer which produced equally effective equipment, but overall system integration responsibility was vested in BAE Systems as the aircraft designer. The chaff dispenser was to be the 'BOL'—an innovative design that incorporated the chaff dispense mechanism into a modified missile launcher. The large coolant bottle for the Sidewinder was replaced with a smaller bottle and the dispense hardware was fitted into the space that was freed up. Each launcher—and four could be carried on the stub pylons while still carrying a missile—could carry a respectable 160 packets of chaff. When the button was pressed in either cockpit, each chaff packet was mechanically flipped into the airflow behind the aircraft. Once deployed, the chaff bloomed into a chaff cloud. As a savings measure, however, each F3 was only to be fitted with two BOL launchers, although they could be fitted to any of the four SRAAM missile pylons under the wing. The two flare dispensers would be installed on the lower engine bay doors at the aft of the fuselage, pointing directly astern. Each dispenser carried a larger 55-mm flare in eight circular housings. In order to increase the payload it had been determined that a double shot could be fitted into each flare cartridge giving sixteen shots per dispenser, thirty-two shots in total. Both systems were controlled by a cockpit controller fitted in the rear cockpit known as the 'BOP'. Crucially, however, the in service date was 1992.

As the risk of conflict in the Gulf increased I often pulled up my contingency plan and dusted it off. I looked at the various options and worked out progress on the formal modification programmes to gauge when they might be available in similar timescales to the contingency items. Slowly the timescales narrowed but they were never to narrow sufficiently and some programmes could never be available in short contingency timescales. The Joint Tactical Information Distribution System, or JTIDS, was a long-term development and would not appear until the mid-1990s. Equally, the new generation of weapons would not appear until the mid-to-late 1990s. The Advanced Short Range Air-To-Air Missile (ASRAAM) would arrive first, followed hopefully by the Advanced Medium Range Air-To-Air Missile (AMRAAM) if it was funded. They could be safely discounted for a contingency fit, and in any event, others were responsible for those programmes.

On 2 August 1990, Saddam Hussein dictated the agenda by invading Kuwait, setting in train a blur of activity in the MoD. The officers with specialist responsibility for the Tornado F3 were split between two departments. An RAF Wing Commander, OR31(Air), handled the development projects until the point when equipment was declared 'mature'. At that time it was deemed to be 'in service' and was handed over to another RAF Wing Commander on the single-service Air Force staffs known as Air Defence 1. In parallel, my own office, OR32(Air), provided specialist electronic warfare expertise, working closely with the individual platform experts. With Saddam rolling down the highway to Kuwait City, OR31(Air) announced that a meeting would be held to decide which aircraft would be deployed on operations. He was set to argue that the Tornado F3 should deploy forward into theatre given its—arguably—better radar capability and situation awareness over the Phantom. After a short discussion about the F3's lack of defensive aids and vulnerability to engagement by surface-to-air missiles, I pressed the case that it would be wrong to send an unprotected F3 and that the Phantom might be better placed as things stood. I suggested that a modification programme to fit essential upgrades to the F3 might make it a better option for the planned theatre of operations. OR31(Air) asked for details and I printed off my contingency plan. After a few muttered words of thanks, he left for the crucial meeting. For the next hour I doodled on a notepad, musing on the complexities of implementing such a plan before the meeting broke up and a harassed OR31(Air) returned. The subsequent direction was short as he returned my notes and issued his edict: 'The modified F3s deploy to Saudi Arabia in four weeks. Do it!'

My jaw dropped. At times I wished I'd just stayed in the cockpit.

No. 5 Squadron, which was already at RAF Akrotiri in Cyprus on an Armament Practice Camp, was immediately placed on readiness to deploy forward into theatre. It would take a few days to prepare for the move and the squadron would deploy initially with its existing aircraft. In the meantime, back in UK, a production line was being set up at RAF Leeming to modify forty selected airframes rapidly to a new 'Stage 1 Plus' standard. What that actually meant was yet to be finalised. The RAF website captured the momentous events in a few simple lines:

HMG announced its intention to send forces to the Gulf on 9 August 1990.

Within 48 hours of the order being given, a squadron of 12 Tornado F3 fighters was operational at Dhahran Air Base in Saudi Arabia.

Two hours after the squadron's arrival, 2 Tornados were airborne on an operational mission.

[Crown Copyright, UK MoD (1990)]

What the innocent bystander did not know was that the aircraft flying that first operational mission were woefully ill-equipped due to systemic procurement delays. To rectify that situation, the specialists in the MoD and the dedicated individuals on the Tornado F3 Operational Evaluation Unit would work twenty-four hours a day for the foreseeable future to equip the aircraft to go to war. As was so often the case, the service personnel would pick up the pieces, albeit assisted ably by some dedicated civilians.

One of the key factors in contingency planning is that you will probably need to use equipment you have on the shelf. The ideal would have been to fit the dispensers which were already being procured under the staff requirement. This was immediately discounted as it would have taken six months for the production line to be set up and, as yet, only prototypes had been tested. A stop-gap solution was needed—fortuitously, I had inherited a staff requirement to fit tactical chaff dispensers to fast jet aircraft such as the Jaguar, Harrier, and Tornado GR1. Although day-to-day management lay with the specialist electronic warfare staff in the Air Force Department, the requirement had not yet been formally handed over, which meant, technically, I still 'owned' the equipment. A quick sprint up one flight of stairs to the fourth floor and a ten-minute discussion later, I had *carte blanche* to use some of the dispensers at my disposal. The only caveat was that Jaguars and Tornado GR1s were also deploying so I was cautioned against trying to purloin any of their assets such as the BOZ chaff pod.

The Harrier GR5/GR7 was not involved and I was intimately familiar with the Phimat chaff dispenser which we had recently evaluated during the testing of the Zeus electronic warfare suite on the Harrier. It was a French-designed, lightweight, bulk chaff dispenser which was fitted onto the aircraft on a pylon. It had the advantage of being a low drag pod, although *any* additional drag on an F3 was unwelcome. It was 3.6 metres in length, 18 cm in diameter, and weighed 73.5 kg when empty and 105 kg when full of chaff. It was made up of a main centre section which held the dispense motors and the chaff payload, a nose cone which held the electronics, and a mantle and diffuser which dispersed the chaff into the airflow. There were thirty-six packets of chaff in each of the six tubes within the main body, giving 216 packs in total. It was operated by a small controller in the cockpit and dispensed chaff according to a pre-programmed sequence when the button was pressed. My first task was to get a couple of chaff pods and cockpit controllers up to RAF Coningsby to do a test fit on the F3. The Operational Evaluation Unit was already busy so the engineering staff on the Operational Conversion Unit was tasked to undertake the initial work. Within hours, two pods had been allocated from the bay at RAF Wittering and were *en route* to Coningsby. The senior engineering officer's task was simple. Mount the Phimat pods onto a Tornado F3 pylon and get a firing signal from the cockpit to the pod.

In parallel, I needed a flare dispenser. I knew that the Phantom force had plenty of AN/ALE40 systems and, given that the F3 had been selected in preference to my old aircraft, they could be available for use. I therefore had a flare countermeasures system immediately available in significant numbers.

We had to ensure that better alternatives were not available despite the tight timescales so my colleague who was responsible for the formal staff requirement began pressing his contacts. Could the Americans give us AN/ALE 47 dispensers which could carry the larger flares used by the F-15? These were the dispensers which the Saudis had procured to fit to their Tornado F3s so would be particularly suitable. The immediate answer was that every single spare dispenser was earmarked for use on an aircraft which would deploy to the Gulf. Our cosy thoughts, nurtured in 1982, that the US would provide equipment off the shelf if we ever went to war, were shattered. The Americans needed their kit for themselves. With that setback, efforts switched to whether the Vinten flare dispensers could be produced and fitted rapidly. Unsurprisingly, although the company was extremely supportive, the lead times were still many months rather than the many days to which we were working. Despite this, Vinten were keen not to lose the contract and stepped up the development effort to try to bring deliveries forward.

If the F3 was to have a flare dispenser with which to go to war, AN/ALE40 it would have to be. The dispenser was designed with a base plate and a bolt-on canister which carried the payloads. Depending on the requirement, this could carry either chaff or flares. On the Phantom, the dispensers were fitted to each side of the inboard missile pylon. In order to achieve the correct trajectory for the flare when ejected from a Phantom pylon, a 45-degree adaptor plug was fitted between the base plate and the canister. This meant that the flare was fired downwards and below the aircraft. A similar fit would not have been appropriate for the F3 as there was insufficient space on the missile pylons and other options had already been agreed for mounting dispensers on the engine bay doors. The AN/ALE40 dispenser could be configured to take a 1-by-1-inch flare to protect smaller engines such as those fitted to helicopters. In the version fitted to the F3, a magazine to take 2-by-1-inch flares could be loaded, although this would mean fewer flares could be carried.

The payload was a magnesium-based pyrotechnic flare, known an MTV flare, which when fired, ignited in the airflow in milliseconds and burned brightly to emulate the infra-red signature of the engines and the hot metal of the aircraft it was protecting. As it slowly separated from the host, it was designed to drag a missile seeker head away from its target. Sequences were developed by the operational trials unit to give the flare the best chance of seducing the threat missile seeker heads, which were expected to be prevalent in theatre. The flare payload, known as the MJU7 (in its NATO guise) or PW218 (in its UK version), had been tested on the Phantom which had a larger and hotter engine than the F3 and had been proven to be effective against the typical missiles which might threaten the Tornado F3 in Iraq. It also worked well on the Harrier, albeit in a different configuration. Saddam fielded older generation infra-red guided missiles. In the air-to-air arena, these were mostly AA-2 Atoll, AA-8 Aphid, and some older French missiles which were not equipped with infra-red counter-countermeasures. Luckily, successive years of arms embargos had ensured that these missiles, particularly the French ones, had not been upgraded. One of the most significant threats, and widely proliferated, was the SA-7 Grail man-portable missile. The 2-by-1-inch flare which was carried by the AN/ALE40 was perfectly adequate against this threat, providing the pilot pulled the engines out of afterburner in a 'chill' manoeuvre. No conventional flare at the time, including the larger American flares, could protect a Tornado F3 in afterburner, so pilots and navigators learned defensive tactics which reduced the infra-red signature of the aircraft when entering an engagement. Criticism that the flare was too small to protect the Tornado F3 or that the modification was ill-conceived was unfounded. Fitting a different dispenser was not an option; it was AN/ALE40 or nothing.

A flare dispenser installation had already been designed for the Tornado F3 and I had seen a test aircraft at BAE Systems Warton where the modifications were being evaluated using dummy equipment. A section was cut out of the lower engine bay doors at each side of the lower rear fuselage and a mounting plate was fitted to the doors. The base plate of the countermeasures dispenser was bolted onto that plate standing proud of the lower fuselage. The first task was to determine whether the AN/ALE 40 could be fitted instead of the Vinten dispenser without further changes. As the doors were already being modified for the Saudi F3s which would be fitted with AN/ALE 47, I was confident we could find a solution, but it would need to be quick. The first challenge seemed straight forward. I had dispensers, I had a design for the engine doors, and I could find as many flares as I needed from war stocks. However, there would still be challenges. Only a few sets of modified engine bay doors had been produced and the plans were to deploy forty aircraft. Immediately, BAE Systems placed their welders on twenty-four-hour manning. Doors were stripped from the F3s being prepared on the production line at Leeming and were sent immediately to Warton for modification. Time was tight but the company responded magnificently. The 'To Do List' was taking shape as the first set of modified engine doors was dispatched from Warton to the OEU at Coningsby. These were closely followed by a number of Phantom AN/ALE 40 chaff/flare dispensers from the logistics depot at RAF Stafford. The first pieces of the jigsaw were in place.

An active jammer proved problematic. The Skyshadow pod fitted to the Tornado GR1 was considered, as was the American AN/ALQ 131 pod, but Skyshadow was quickly discounted as the GR1 force needed every available pod to support its own commitments. Efforts concentrated on the American jammer and requests went out to our allies to borrow a pod to see if it could be hung on the inboard pylon. Its impact on airframe performance and how it would affect the radar and RHWR would need to be carefully assessed.

My first task after receiving the news that I was now responsible for implementing a £37 million modification programme was, in true staff officer fashion, to call a meeting. Staff officers who control current Urgent Operational Requirements nowadays will be familiar with a complex, well-oiled process which reviews and agrees urgent requests for modifications, identifies contingency funds, and delivers these urgent programmes. Nowadays this is called an Urgent Operational Requirement and it is funded from Treasury contingency funds. There was no such system in place in 1990. The last operation which had needed such procedures was Operation Corporate in 1982, the operation to recover the Falkland Islands. Everyone involved in that process had long since moved on and, as newcomers, we had no model to copy. A select group of key players was called to an emergency meeting in the MoD stressing the urgency, even though I could give no details over an insecure phone line. It required an act of faith from the attendees. I also called my colleague in the MoD Procurement Executive who funded the routine EW modifications as I knew that we would need contingency funding quite early in the process. How to do that would be his problem, but he rose to the challenge. At that point I climbed aboard a train and headed north for RAF Coningsby to take a look at progress on the chaff dispenser mount. It was Wednesday afternoon and still only Day 1.

When I arrived three hours later, a team was already working away on the Phimat dispenser which had arrived from RAF Wittering. The senior engineering officer on the OCU, fuelled by adrenaline, had been hard at work on the fit. The pylon on the Phimat did not mate to the pylon on the F3, but after scratching around, he had found that a particular bomb rack, and if memory serves me correctly it was a bomb rack from a Jaguar, would mate to both the chaff pod and the tank pylon. By inserting this between the two he was able to physically hang the pod under the wing. With an appropriate electrical adaptor he was able to hook up the pod to the electrical system of the Tornado. The physical mating was already achieved and the pod was hanging below an OCU Tornado F3, but the missile monitoring system (MMS) was confused. It was not expecting to see a Phimat pod as no one had ever programmed it to expect one. Software experts on the ADV Software Management Team at Coningsby were already working to make the pod talk to the MMS, with help from the contractor who had designed the system. It was not a show stopper as the pod could be operated independently with a simple electronic interface if necessary. The major problem was that there was no wire which ran from the pod to the cockpit to send a firing signal from the cockpit controller to the chaff dispenser. The senior engineer had experts poring over the technical manuals to identify a suitable piece of 'electronic string' to make a connection. Eventually he found a redundant wire, which had been installed during build to operate a redundant function, and it was co-opted for the job.

With the first progress made it was decided that a test bed aircraft would be modified on the Operational Evaluation Unit (OEU). The OEU engineers were joined by engineers from BAE Systems and a task force was formed. A controller was fitted onto the JTIDS data link panel blanking plate in the rear cockpit, allowing the navigator to program the dispenser and eject chaff in continuous pulsed or burst modes using a dispense button on the panel. A further panel to control the AN/ALE 40 was fitted alongside in the rear cockpit. The Phimat dispenser was fitted to the inboard pylon and the engine bay doors were removed in anticipation of the arrival of the modified doors. The operational settings to be used in the air would be determined in a trial which was planned for later in the next week.

As I left the OEU late that night, a van pulled up carrying the modified engine bay doors for the flare dispensers. A separate cell of technicians began to document the work and produce a 'special trials fit', and by using these instructions, engineering staff on the production line at RAF Leeming would be able to copy the fit on each of the forty nominated Tornados. The plan was coming together.

I returned to MoD the following morning to chair the initial meeting which proved to be one of the most positive meetings I ever attended as a staff officer. Traditionally, MoD meetings were turgid affairs. The company representatives would spout the company line, explaining the technical problems and why the project was behind time and over budget. The MoD (PE) project manager would express his displeasure and insist that the company produce more evidence before the next meeting. The operational sponsor would add his disquiet at the impact of the lack of progress on the front line. A date would be set for the next gathering three months hence when the same story would be repeated. The cycle was soul destroying, or so it seemed at the time. On this occasion, the mould was broken. The meeting was attended by a contractor from each of the key companies who I needed to contribute to the modification programme. A senior representative from BAE Systems had been sent to represent the company and, as the design authority, their cooperation was fundamental. He took me aside in advance and explained that all normal policy was set aside and that they would do whatever it took to get the vital equipment onto the jets as quickly as possible. There 'was a war on' and normal commercial process was, temporarily, suspended; they would work closely with the other contractors to make it happen. I was staggered and heartened simultaneously. He made the same speech to the assembled group and the company stuck to its word. I outlined my contingency plan with precise goals and timescales which, even to me, sounded impossible to meet. It was met with nods of agreement, scribbled notes, and positive reactions all round before the meeting broke up and everyone left to tackle the problems.

One of the contractors approached me afterwards. He explained that he was going away to put his factory on twenty-four-hour manning, but could I just give him a covering note. The note on a loose sheet of paper read: 'Dear Chaps, cut along and produce the stuff required, Love, The MoD.' Well, it was something along those lines. With that, the modification programme stepped up a pace. It was a graphic example of true British determination in adversity and those

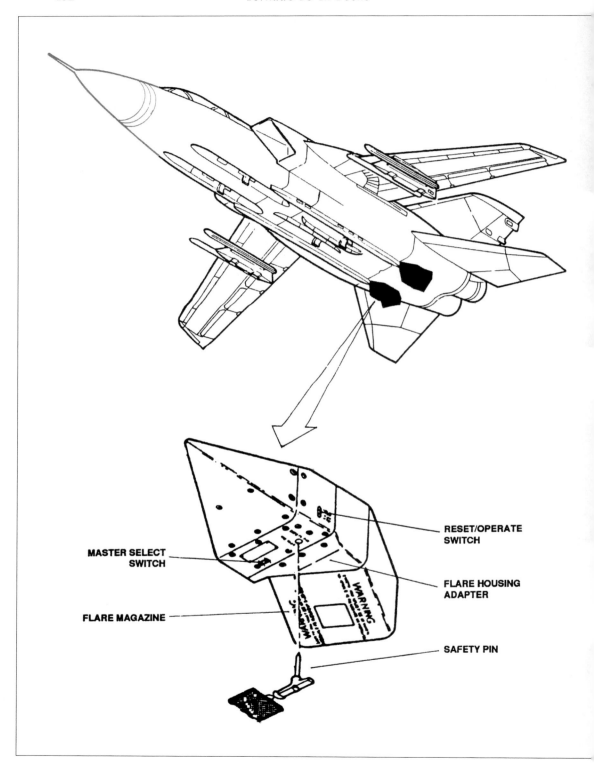

The Operation Granby AN/ALE40 dispensers fit. (*UK MoD Crown Copyright, 1990*)

The original Operation Granby fit AN/ALE40 flare dispensers. (*Mark Wilson*)

A Phimat chaff dispenser.

A Tornado F3 Stage 1 Plus aircraft of the Tornado F3 Operational Evaluation Unit.

A Phimat chaff dispenser fitted to the missile pylon. (*Mark Wilson*)

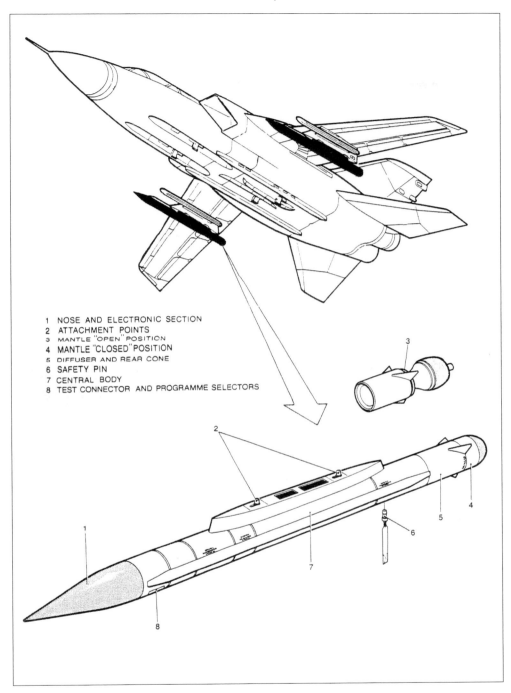

1 NOSE AND ELECTRONIC SECTION
2 ATTACHMENT POINTS
3 MANTLE "OPEN" POSITION
4 MANTLE "CLOSED" POSITION
5 DIFFUSER AND REAR CONE
6 SAFETY PIN
7 CENTRAL BODY
8 TEST CONNECTOR AND PROGRAMME SELECTORS

The Operation Granby Phimat chaff dispenser fit on the inboard pylons. (*UK MoD Crown Copyright, 1990*)

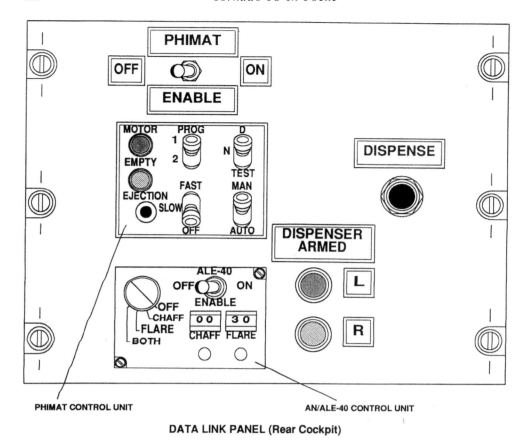

PHIMAT CONTROL UNIT　　　　　　　　**AN/ALE-40 CONTROL UNIT**

DATA LINK PANEL (Rear Cockpit)

The Operation Granby Phimat chaff dispenser control panel. (*UK MoD Crown Copyright, 1990*)

involved could feel immensely proud. They would never be recognised with a medal, but they undoubtedly contributed to the war effort.

One of the more controversial modifications, and much misunderstood at the time, was the radar signature reduction measures. Given that over twenty years have passed, that the Tornado F3 is now in a museum, and that the technology is no longer secret, I can finally explain what a journalist was able to announce at the time. Had I done so then, I would have been in breach of the Official Secrets Act and would have likely gone to jail.

As we have since seen with the F-117 and most recently the F-35 Joint Strike Fighter, reducing the radar signature is a fundamental element of design; a programme such as that for the Tornado F3 would be unnecessary today. Radar can be reflected from flat plates but the most effective way to bounce radar back is a corner reflector. Where metal comes together, a right angle is formed and this is a very efficient reflector; the F3 was covered in such shapes. By far the greatest contribution to the overall radar signature of the aircraft was that from the face of the engine. Radar waves enter the intake, bounce off the spinning fan blades and are reflected back towards the host radar. Close behind is the return from the big tub below the cockpit canopy which houses the crew. After these two, there are hundreds of small elements such as the gun port and the navigation lights which add small amounts to the overall signature. If treated, these contributing elements can be minimised making the aircraft appear smaller on radar, leading to a later detection. This is the concept behind a 'stealth' aircraft.

As the programme moved ahead at full pace, tasks had been delegated to individual project officers and were proceeding well under the watchful eye of the commander of the evaluation unit. I was to take the lead on the radar signature reduction programme. The principal measure was to treat the intake ducts to suppress the response from the fan blades which make up nearly 50 per cent of the radar signature. Reduce these returns and the aircraft becomes less visible to another fighter's airborne intercept radar or, more importantly, its radar-guided missiles. Studies had been completed to decide whether radar-absorbent material applied to the intakes could reduce these reflections, and the results were promising. The material used had been developed by the MoD research community many years before. To the layman it looked like rubber matting, but it was high-tech material loaded with small metallic reflectors which divert and slow the passage of radar signals. As a radar signal passes through the RAM, it is absorbed and only a fraction of the original radar signal is returned. This material is produced in large sheets and then cut to size depending on its application. For the F3, these tiles were about 2 inches square and were fitted using epoxy glue. Each intake required 500 of these small tiles which were laboriously fitted by a dedicated technician working in the cramped and confined environment of the intake. It was a truly appalling task. The gaps were then sealed to hold them firm. To survive the heat and stresses of an air intake, the RAM had to be extremely robust. Other reflectors were assessed, including the navigation lights, the gun port, the bulkhead behind the radar scanner, and the cockpit 'tub'.

The cockpit area contained a number of significant reflectors and radar waves entering the cockpit from opposing air intercept radars, particularly from above, would be returned. If the 'tub' could be protected a significant part of the radar signature would be masked. A manufacturer had proposed applying a transparent stick-on material which looked remarkably similar to 'fablon' sticky back plastic. If the material could be applied to the canopy without degrading the view from the cockpit it would eliminate a major source of radar reflection. In the few days which followed, he arrived with rolls of the material and began to apply it to a canopy. In a story which would have been worthy of a West End farce, he applied the film, attempting to persuade me that it would be acceptable on operations. The Tornado canopy was a series of complex curves and no matter how the 'fablon' was applied, wrinkles and aberrations were apparent. There was no way this treatment could be used operationally unless a spray-on application could be devised. Even then I had concerns that helmets and lifejackets might scratch the coating and degrade the view from the cockpit. A spot on a canopy can be misinterpreted as an opposing aircraft and cause unnecessary defensive reactions from the crew. Small distortions were apparent across the canopy. The value just didn't warrant the risk so the measure was quietly dropped, much to the disquiet of the contractor.

The bulkhead RAM was a much easier solution. The radar scanner was mounted on a flat bulkhead ideally angled to reflect radar. Inside, the radome was protected from the airflow so the material could be more agricultural; a large collar was fitted to the bulkhead produced from a less aerodynamic material. A number of smaller contributors were assessed, some of which led to modifications, some of which were dropped. The gun port proved impossible to treat. A polystyrene plug was cut to fit the gun port snugly. This was covered in metallised 'speed tape' which would prevent reflection. The concept was that if the gun was fired, the round would force the plug out and away from the aircraft. On each test sortie, even without firing the gun, the tape peeled back and deposited the plug down the engine. With fears of imminent damage to the engine, the measure was also quietly dropped. The infamous gun plug became the butt of a number of jokes.

The final measure, ironically, was the one which attracted attention to the modifications. Radar absorbent paint was applied to the leading edges of the wings, the pylons and the fin. Although the contribution of these aerodynamic surfaces was small, every little measure helped. To be effective, a certain depth of paint was needed and twenty coats were applied. The paint was a 'loaded solution' and looked more like underseal, which was applied in the 1970s to protect cars from rust. Its high-tech function was less apparent. Unlike the tiles, this measure was well received by the engineers and was retained long after the other modifications were removed because it acted as a protective layer against sand blasting in the desert. How often it was touched up to maintain its effectiveness was less clear, but by then, Saddam had proved to be a less than determined opponent.

An aircraft signature can be mapped out on a radial diagram and it looks like the spikes around a porcupine. Each 'spine' shows where an aircraft would be most visible to hostile radars. Once treated, a modified Tornado F3 lost its spiky appearance and the average value of its radar cross section was reduced to a fraction of its original value. This was a significant gain against the older generation pulse radars which the Iraqis operated. Against high-powered radars such as the Foxhunter, the value was less evident, but Saddam did not have many high-powered radars. His regular fighters such as the Mig-21 and the Mirage F1 were equipped with old pulse radars with much shorter detection ranges. Importantly, their radar guided air-to-air missiles with their tiny radar dishes were much less effective than our own. They would have been adversely affected by the reduced radar response. If the modification made already short ranges even shorter, crews would gain a significant tactical advantage and operational analysis backed up this view. Any radar relying on radar tracking such as air-to-air missiles or radar-guided surface-to-air missiles would have greater difficulty tracking the modified F3. The reality was that this would never make the F3 into an F-117 stealth fighter, but it was felt that the gain was significant for a low-cost enhancement.

Imagine my surprise when within days of completing the first highly sensitive trial fit, an article appeared in a leading aviation magazine. The article written by a respected aviation journalist described the modification programme in almost perfect detail. Having conducted the installation in secrecy, within hours of completing the test flights, the full details were published and became open source. The article with the dramatic title, 'Tornado uses RAM on leading edges and Phimat chaff/flare pods. RAF Reduces Radar Returns', went on to describe that RAF Tornado F3s deployed to Saudi Arabia had undergone a radar signature reduction programme including coating the forward facing surfaces with radar absorbent material (RAM). It correctly identified that the leading edges of the wings, tailplane, and fin had been treated, including the underwing stores pylons. Although it suggested that the spray-on coating of radar opaque material was to prevent radar signals penetrating to internal bulkheads, which give a strong radar return, the assertion was slightly misleading, although the conclusion that the treatment considerably reduced the frontal radar cross section was also true. The final revelation, however, was of concern. The fact that the bonding agent used to attach the tiles has been strengthened because RAM tiles fitted in the engine intakes had detached on at least two occasions was only known to a select few. That the engines ran after tile ingestion, albeit suffering minor nicks on fan blades, and were changed on landing, could only have come from someone close to the programme.

The article had us scratching heads and demonstrated the classic dilemma for an MoD staff officer. Starting a witch hunt to track the leak would have raised considerable interest and merely confirmed the truth of the story. Trying to repudiate the facts would have seemed ill-advised as the modifications had clearly been made to the aircraft and were externally visible; the fact that we were about to go to war was also no secret. In a later breach, an unclassified video appeared on my desk showing each activity in precise detail and was passed out to interested desk officers hoping to generate interest and future business. Our sensitive project had become the worst kept secret of the whole war. Worse was that compromise to the enemy might allow modifications to threat weapons to overcome the defensive measure. With the aircraft retired, the modifications are consigned to history, but I asked at the time what would be the price of the breach in Operational Security?

Efforts to fit the active jammer stalled quickly. It became apparent that to provide the power which the pod needed, heavy-duty electrical wiring would have to be provided to the inner wing pylon. To carry a fuel tank, all that was needed was a jettison signal via a simple wire, but this would be inadequate to power a hungry jamming pod. Without extensive rewiring, the plan was not feasible within the four-week timeframe. Although efforts never stopped, the immediate problems proved insurmountable until the advent of the urgent requirement for a jammer in the Balkans theatre, which produced the towed radar decoy system some years later and necessitated a much more radical solution.

By the time I returned to RAF Coningsby after the initial meeting, the new engine bay doors had been fitted to the test aircraft, the AN/ALE40 flare dispensers were bolted in place, and a Phimat pod hung from the inner pylon. A technician was already tucked inside the engine intake and was slowly gluing the radar absorbent tiles into place. The smell of epoxy was strong and I felt sorry for him as he worked through the fumes, protected by a simple respirator. The intake lining had already turned from its natural metal state into a black jigsaw.

The cockpit controls I had requisitioned were being installed in the back cockpit under the watchful eye of the operational requirements officer for the F3. He had already begun to consider a number of ergonomic improvements which had been wanted for some time. Locally manufactured 'grab handles' were about to be fitted which would allow the back seater not only to pull himself around in the cockpit to gain a better view in 'the 6 o'clock', but would also mount dispense buttons to allow the navigator to 'pop' flares while looking backwards. These simple but effective additions were an example of the innovation which flourished. Designed by experts on the Operational Evaluation Unit, they were fabricated virtually overnight in a local engineering factory and delivered to the unit. Fixed with a few bolts and wired into the dispense release circuit, they later became standard fit. The RHWR display unit was relocated to a position on the upper side of the left-hand TV tab at eye level, making it much easier to read in a tactical situation.

Alongside these first modifications, the Operational Evaluation Unit had identified a raft of improvements to the much-maligned radar, and rapid progress was made. A dizzying array of designators appeared for each variation and attracted new designations such as Stage 1A, Stage 1AA, and Stage 1A+, each with an associated missile monitoring system improvement. Every potential enhancement was loaded into the radar data processor, the effect was evaluated, and the most promising candidates were developed further. A company radar expert worked hand-in-glove with RAF personnel and Foxhunter made more progress in those few months than in the following few years combined. This was only possible through the skill, effort, and dedication of a small band of experts both from the Service and from the manufacturers.

It was not all plain sailing. The development test organisation had lived a sheltered life, taking years to evaluate modifications and produce supporting paperwork. I made a warning call to the desk officer responsible for the F3 at the test centre at Boscombe Down. I asked for switch-on clearance for the modifications and that he should begin to prepare some aircrew information leaflets, only to be informed that it was impossible! He explained that six months was needed to schedule it into the programme and that such notice was unacceptable. Clearly the prospect of war had not yet percolated down to the comfortable offices at Boscombe Down. Undeterred, some rapid exchanges from the Director of Air Defence at One Star Level secured the services of a test pilot to carry out the immediate clearance activity. The publications office was also tasked to produce aircrew information leaflets for the new equipment and development test staff became quickly interested in the activities at Coningsby. Feathers were ruffled but the progress was relentless as the operational experts

1. A No. 65 Squadron Tornado F3, ZE785, wearing the commemorative colour scheme for the squadron's 75th Anniversary celebrations. (*Geoff Lee*)

2. Tornado F3 front cockpit.

3. Tornado F3 rear cockpit, single-stick variant. The original navigator's hand controller is fitted.

4. Tornado F3 rear cockpit, twin-stick variant.

5. Tornado F2s of No. 229 OCU prepare for the Queen's Birthday Flypast.

6. Tornado F2s form up over Lincolnshire.

7. Tornado F2 ZD934 of No. 229 OCU.

8. A No. 65 Squadron Tornado F3, ZE907, wearing the display colour scheme. (*Geoff Lee*)

9. Tornado F3 ZE253 of No. 56 (Reserve) Squadron.

10. Tornado F2 ZD903 over the London suburbs.

11. Windsor Formation peels off after overflying Buckingham Palace.

12. Tornado F2 ZD935 of No. 229 OCU.

13. Tornado F3s of No. 65 (Reserve) Squadron refuel from a VC10 tanker. (*Bob Burden*)

14. A Spitfire of the Battle of Britain Memorial Flight and a Tornado F2 of No. 229 OCU fly a coordinated air display. (*UK MoD Crown Copyright, 1986, courtesy Andrew Lister-Tomlinson*)

15. Tornado F3s of No. 65 (Reserve) Squadron deploy on Operation Buhl.

16. A Tornado F3 of No. 65 (Reserve) Squadron over Saudi Arabia.

17. Tornado F3s of No. 65 (Reserve) Squadron formate on a Tristar tanker during the deployment work up.

18. Tornado F3s of No. 65 (Reserve) Squadron over the Mediterranean.

19. A Tornado F3 of No. 65 (Reserve) Squadron lines up for departure at Bahrain International airport.

20. A Mirage F1 of the Qatar Air Force intercepts the formation *en route* to Doha.

21. Tornado F3s and a Tristar tanker on the ramp at Bahrain.

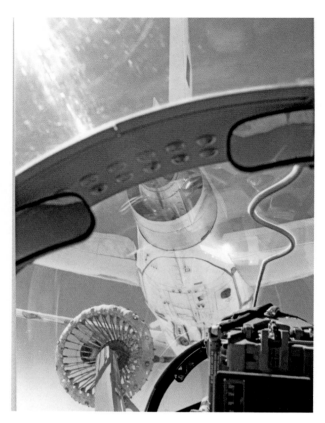

22. Refuelling from a Tristar tanker.

23. Tornado F3s finish refuelling. The aircraft in the foreground is full and fuel is venting from the fin.

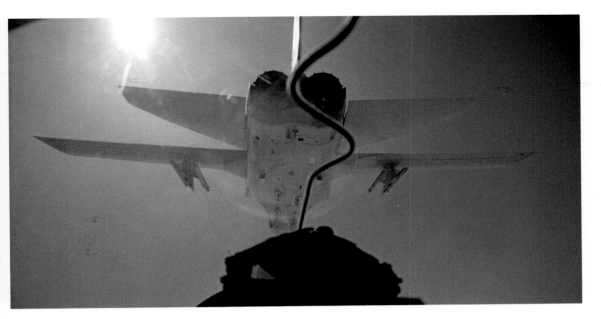

24. A Tornado F3 of No. 56 (Reserve) Squadron seen from the box position.

25. Tornado F3 ZE253 formates on an E3D Sentry, ZH105, over the North Sea.

26. Tornado F3 ZE253 of No. 56 (Reserve) Squadron.

27. Tornado F3 ZE787 of No. 56 (Reserve) Squadron at RAF Wildenrath. The airframe was 'zapped' by the resident squadron and wears the colours of No. 92 (East India) Squadron.

28. Tornado F3 ZE787 of No. 56 (Reserve) Squadron with the No. 92 (East India) Squadron chequerboard.

29. ZE758 *Charity* holding Quick Reaction Alert at RAF Mount Pleasant. The Skyflash missiles are mounted beneath the fuselage.

30. Just airborne from the main runway at RAF Mount Pleasant, the Falkland Islands.

31. In front of ZG799, Ian 'Shiney' Simmons and the author accept the final Tornado F3 single-stick variant from the BAE Systems factory at Warton.

32. The author flying over the Mediterranean.

33. Tornado F3 ZE839 of No. 56 (Reserve) Squadron wearing the display colours for the 1993 air display season.

34. The aircraft parking area at the Kauhava airbase prior to the Midnight Air Display.

35. Tornado F3 ZE839 of No. 56 (Reserve) Squadron over Finland.

36. Tornado F3 ZE832 of No. 56 (Reserve) Squadron is intercepted by a Finnish Hawk *en route* to Kauhava.

37. Tornado F3s of No. 65 (Reserve) Squadron line up for take off at RAF Coningsby.

38. Tornado F3 ZE832 of No. 56 (Reserve) Squadron carrying long-range 2,250-litre fuel tanks.

39. A Tornado F3 Stage 1 Plus variant deployed on Operation Granby. (*Mark Wilson*)

40. A Tornado F3 of the Tornado F3 Operational Evaluation Unit receives the Stage 1 Plus modifications. Phimat chaff dispensers are fitted to the inner fuel pylons.

41. A Tornado F3 Stage 1 Plus variant of the Tornado F3 Operational Evaluation Unit.

42. Tornado F3s of No. 65 (Reserve) Squadron deployed to IAF Decimommannu.

43. Tornado F3s of No. 56 (Reserve) Squadron deployed to the Belgian airbase at Florennes for the Tactical Leadership Programme.

44. Tornado F3s of No. 65 (Reserve) Squadron return to the UK via Sigonella airbase.

45. A Tornado F3 of No. 111 Squadron intercepts a Russian Tu-95 Bear *en route* to the Fairford air display. (*Steve Smyth*)

46. A Tornado F3 of No. 111 Squadron alongside a Russian Tu-95 Bear. (*Steve Smyth*)

47. A Tornado F3 of No. 111 Squadron intercepts a Russian Il-78 Midas tanker *en route* to the Fairford air display. (*Steve Smyth*)

48. The author's Tornado F3, ZE253. The aircraft sports the squadron commander's pennant under the front cockpit.

49. A Tornado F3 of No. 111 Squadron deployed to RAF Gibraltar. (*Steve Smyth*)

50. Tornado F3s of No. 65 (Reserve) Squadron deploy on Exercise Swift Sword 1.

51. A Tornado F3, ZE165, of No. 229 OCU conducts an early clearance sortie behind a Tristar tanker.

52. Tornado F3s of Nos 5 and 11 Squadrons deployed to Nellis Air Force base, Nevada. (*Giz Taylor*)

53. A Tornado F3 of No. 1435 Flight, RAF Mount Pleasant, in close formation with a C130 tanker of No. 1312 Flight.

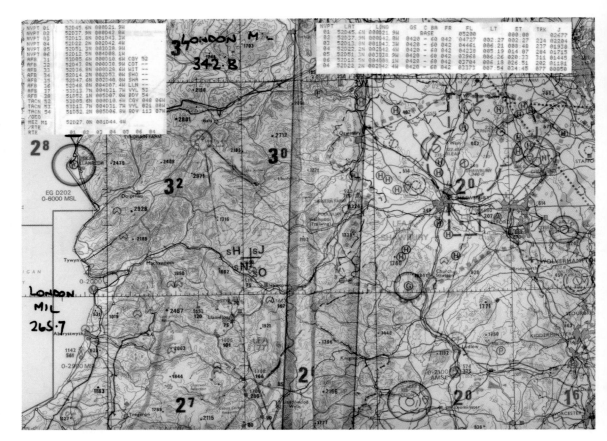

54. A low-flying chart of LFA7 Wales showing low-level operating areas and F3 navigation print outs.

55. Tornado F3 ZE253 of No. 56 (Reserve) Squadron.

56. Tornado F3 ZE256 formerly of No. 56 (Reserve) Squadron but sporting No. 11 Squadron markings and ZE343. The airframe was refurbished by Chris Wilson of Jet Art Aviation of Selby.

57. Tornado F2 ZD903 flies against the sun.

58. A Tornado F3 formates on a Tristar tanker during a work-up sortie for Exercise Swift Sword 1. (*Bob Burden*)

59. A Tornado F3 formates on a Tristar tanker during a work up sortie for Exercise Swift Sword 1.

RAF *AIR POWER*

THE
ROYAL
AIR FORCE
CALENDAR
1988

60. The cover of the 1988 RAF Calendar. The image was captured by the author from an RAF Hawk. The photographic equipment was set up by the renowned aviation photographer Richard Cooke. (*UK MoD Crown Copyright, 1988*)

61. A No. 111 Squadron Tornado F3 deploys infra-red decoys from its Vinten dispensers. (*Geoff Lee*)

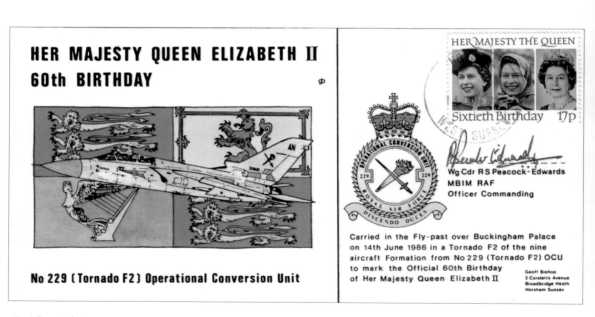

62. The 60th Anniversary First Day Cover, presented to each crew by Geoff Bishop.

The chaff and flare dispense buttons mounted on the grab bars.

The relocated RHWR display mounted at eye level.

at RAF Coningsby supported by industry continued to put in twenty-hour days.

There were a number of other enhancements which would prove essential, not least of which was the fitting of the AN/ARC 164 secure radio to allow secure and jam-resistant communications between the deployed aircraft and the controllers on the ground. In parallel, a number of missile tests were carried out. Attempts were made to integrate the more capable AIM-9M onto the F3. This missile had been bought by the Royal Navy for the Sea Harrier but was never intended to be used by the RAF. After a number of problems with the missile monitoring system, stray voltages caused some damage to the test missile. Attuned to the risks of inadvertent firings after an incident on the Phantom, it was decided that the problems were too great and the initiative was shelved. Meanwhile eight AIM-9L firings were conducted at the test range at Aberporth in Wales to evaluate a new infra-red counter-countermeasure. This gave the AIM-9L protection against infra-red decoy flares which Saddam was known to use. After a successful test, the modifications were speedily incorporated into service missile stocks providing a huge but unseen improvement in capability. The system was responding magnificently and hundreds of long-needed improvements were being incorporated at break-neck speed.

Once each of the individual modifications had been fitted, the prototype aircraft was rolled out and the efforts turned to testing. The OEU aircrew took the brunt. Hurried discussions with the operators had agreed that the AN/ALE40 system would be used exclusively as a flare dispenser, giving a respectable fifteen infra-red decoys from each dispenser. The immediate task was to determine how many flares would be programmed for each defensive manoeuvre. Using only one flare was a risk if it proved to be a dud, yet firing too many flares would waste the valuable payload. A compromise was needed. One of the constraints was that the Phantom required a 45-degree adaptor between the breech plate and the magazine to ensure that the flare separated cleanly and safely from its position on the side of the missile pylon. In theory, the flare magazine could be bolted straight onto the base plate, called the breech assembly, and the flares would fire straight behind the aircraft. In the haste of the modification programme, no one knew whether there would be a problem if the adaptor was not fitted. We decided to run the first release tests with it installed as designed for the Phantom, which meant that when the dispenser was mounted onto the engine bay doors, the flares were fired slightly outboard at an angle of 25 degrees away from the centreline. There were potential advantages but also potential disadvantages of this trajectory, and we would have to carefully assess the implications during the tests. By then, test assets had been positioned on a testing range; as the Tornado flew past, the crew dispensed potential sequences of flares. The effect on the threat missiles was measured and the effectiveness of the sequence was evaluated. In short order an operational sequence was determined and the crews were briefed.

The Phimat testing proceeded in parallel and sequences were needed which would give the potential to break the lock of threat radars which the crews would face in Iraq. Chaff was dispensed to ensure clean separation from the pod in its new position before moving on to effectiveness testing. The reduced radar cross section, achieved by installing the radar absorbent material, meant that any jamming effect from the chaff would be enhanced as there was a smaller signature to mask. To quantify the improvement, a trusted expert was dispatched to the army range at Larkhill on Salisbury Plain with a suite of measuring equipment and was able to map the new radar signature of both the F3 and the chaff. Potential sequences were employed as the Tornado was threatened by a surface-to-air missile tracking radar; the data was recorded and then given to analysts to decide how best to use the new capability operationally. Countermeasures programs were written and OEU experts incorporated them into operational tactics to disseminate to the crews. It would have been ideal to test against a Russian-built SA-2 or SA-3 surface-to-air missile which Saddam operated, but at that time the Cold War had just ended and no suitable instrumented systems were available in the UK. Even so, the results were extremely promising against the selected test system and the expert was confident. Much additional testing would be done in slower time, but the modification was promising.

Meanwhile, proof was needed of how effective the signature reduction measures had been. A sortie was flown on the instrumented Air Combat Manoeuvring Installation at RAF Coningsby. Pods carried on the F3s recorded the precise positions of each aircraft on the range and could be used to analyse the test scenarios. A modified Tornado F3 was flown in battle formation (2 miles apart) with an unmodified F3 in loose formation. Detection ranges on each aircraft were logged during a number of simple intercept runs. Each aircraft was assessed in a look up and look down profile against another Tornado F3 with its Foxhunter. I would have been overjoyed had I been able to run the test against a Mig-21 or a Mirage F1 which crews would face in theatre, but like their ground-based equivalents, such assets were not available for testing. A few years later the situation might have been radically different. Although this would not be a truly scientific assessment, it gave a broad appreciation of the effect of the modifications. The radar detection range had reduced considerably, often by up to 15 miles compared to an unmodified Tornado F3. Against the high-power Foxhunter this was impressive. Against the shorter range, less powerful Iraqi pulse air intercept radars, it would be even more significant. Against the tiny seekers in an AA-7 Apex or the AA-2c Atoll radar-guided missile which the Iraqi Air Force used, it could have been so significant that it might have prevented a front sector engagement by a hostile fighter. Sadly this fact was never well understood, even by the crews flying the F3, and the modification was criticised. It did, however, give us confidence that if the shooting war began, the F3 was better equipped against its opponents than hitherto had been the case.

Meanwhile, back on the OEU, a cell of tradesmen had painstakingly recorded the engineering changes needed to incorporate the modifications onto a front-line aircraft. The instructions would be used by the modification teams at RAF Leeming to fit the various enhancements in preparation for deployment to Saudi

Arabia. Time was extremely tight. Although it had taken only four days to fit the modifications, the senior engineer at RAF Leeming, where the production line had been set up, made it very plain that unless the documentation was with him within the next hour he would not meet his deadline for deploying the first aircraft into theatre. I was in a quandary. I had assumed we would send a courier to Leeming but that would take four hours. Did he have a secure fax? Yes. What was the number? I immediately faxed the paperwork which the engineers needed to begin to cut metal but asked him to ring back to confirm receipt. After ten minutes the phone was worryingly quiet so I called again and the phone was answered by his colleague. 'Has the STF paperwork arrived?' I asked nervously, and was told there was no sign of it. He would call me back. There followed a few brief moments when I considered the implications of sending a highly classified operational modification to the local Chinese takeaway in Ripon! With great relief, the phone rang again and it was confirmed that it had arrived safely. In the heat of the moment it had been rushed to the appropriate experts without acknowledgement. All was well; I would not be standing before a court martial and my heart rate returned to normal levels.

Once the modifications were agreed, flight clearances were needed to operate them in the air. There was insufficient time to secure a full manufacturer's clearance so the desk officer in the Air Defence office in the MoD generated clearances known as 'Service Deviations'. Although the responsibility for airworthiness ultimately fell to the Assistant Chief of the Air Staff for a modification which was not manufacturer approved, a Service Deviation had to be signed off. This meant that the normal airworthiness responsibilities were shifted away from the manufacturer to the service approving officer for each individual modification. This also meant that a rigorous assessment had to be undertaken to collect evidence that the modification was safe to operate. In the case of jamming equipment and avionics, this was generally straight forward, but when hanging stores or releasing weapons, perhaps less clear cut. The desk officer would collect the evidence and present a case to the appropriate senior officer, inviting him to assume the risk. As would be expected, senior officers took this responsibility extremely seriously and often took some convincing. The process could take weeks, but with a war looming, time was critical. Without his agreement the modified F3 simply would not get airborne and there were a few nervous hours before the paperwork was cleared and the clearances were forthcoming.

No plan survives first contact with the enemy. The F3 could operate without external fuel tanks and achieve a respectable radius of action, typically one hour forty-five minutes on a low-level intercept mission. The penalty of flying with the large 2,250-litre tanks had been debated many times and in order to carry two fuel tanks, the additional weight required more power and effectively cost the contents of one fuel tank. In other words, to carry two fuel tanks you received the benefit of one extra tank of fuel if operating at height. As the deployment progressed, basing options were agreed. It was assumed that the F3s would operate close to the border with the other tactical air assets. It transpired that the

Tornado F3 would be based many miles in the rear area at Prince Sultan Air Base, or PSAB, in Saudi Arabia. To reach the main operating areas in Iraq it would have to transit long distances and, to do that, it would have to carry the 2,250-litre fuel tanks. In order to mount the Phimat dispenser and provide it with power, it had been fitted under the inner wing pylon where the fuel tank normally hung. Given the operational decision, the Phimat would have to be relocated onto one of the stub pylons which normally carried an AIM-9L Sidewinder missile. To do so would mean that only three Sidewinders could be carried, but having self-defence chaff might be even more important than the final missile. The missile monitoring system software had not been designed to take a chaff dispenser on the stub so a further software rewrite was initiated to re-host the new store. Flexibility was, indeed, proving to be the key to air power.

Between the 'go' decision on the morning on Wednesday to a fully modified Tornado F3 being rolled out on the ramp at RAF Coningsby was a staggeringly short five days. The Tornado F3 was ready to go to war.

The operational build-up coincided with my return to flying and I had been promised a posting to No. 5 (AC) Squadron and had high hopes that I would be able to test the modifications for real. In a cruel twist of fate, the Flight Commander Training on the Operational Conversion Unit had decided to retire from the RAF and, as the only F3-qualified navigator able to re-qualify quickly, I lost my opportunity to deploy on operations. My posting was switched back to the Operational Conversion Unit to train new crews, so it was with some frustration that I handed off my remaining responsibilities, dusted off my aircrew manual and refocused my efforts to return to the cockpit. By the time I arrived back at RAF Coningsby after my brief lead-in courses, an OEU crew had already re-evaluated the chaff programs from the stub-mounted dispenser and the evaluation effort was moving on.

Both Nos 5 (AC) and 29 (F) Squadrons played an important part in the Gulf conflict. No. 5 (AC) Squadron was deployed to the Gulf for three months in August 1990, flying air defence missions from Dhahran, while No. 29 (F) Squadron operated from Saudi Arabia for three months from December 1990, flying over 500 missions. Much to my relief, after a few teething problems, modified aircraft performed well. But for a scribbled plan on a computer in the MoD, the Phantom might have had one final operational fling. I felt just a little pang of regret and guilt at denying my old mount the opportunity. Tornado F3 might never have deployed at all and its future could have been markedly different. Excluded from the operation, ammunition would have been given to the detractors, funding would certainly have been cut and the later programmes to fit AMRAAM and ASRAAM would, without doubt, have been terminated.

Back at Coningsby the atmosphere was tense as modified aircraft had been committed and had arrived in theatre. The squadrons were being reinforced and we had been warned to convert as many crews to the F3 in as short a timeframe as possible. A new syllabus had been agreed which converted experienced aircrew onto the jet in a shortened time. Chillingly, we expected the Iraqis to fight and we

A Tornado F3 Stage 1 Plus aircraft deployed on Operation Granby. (*Mark Wilson*)

expected losses. In the event, there were no losses and the F3 was often relegated to less glamorous duties defending the rear areas against an attack that never came. The inability to fit an active jammer meant that commanders were reluctant to employ it in an offensive counter air role over Iraqi territory. Had our efforts to fit AN/ALQ 131 come to fruition or the towed radar decoy been available earlier, the situation might have been different. There were indeed incidents when F3s pushed forward and one crew came close to engaging a hostile contact, but incidents were few.

On 24 August 1990, after three years on the ground, I flew my familiarisation sortie in a Tornado F3 prior to starting my re-familiarisation course. There were no luxuries such as lead-in training in the Hawk. I was given a truncated groundschool phase lasting only a week, and just eight weeks after leaving my desk in the MoD, I was flying instructional sorties with new students. I had no chance to catch breath for the next four years.

There was an amusing sequel some months later. I was by now the Flight Commander responsible for training matters on the Operational Conversion Unit. As the newly modified aircraft had been accepted into service, a handful of the 40,000 tiles fitted in the intakes of the forty aircraft had become detached and had been swallowed by the RB199 engines. During early evaluations we had carried out ingestion testing and the size of the tiles had been determined based on what the RB199 could 'digest'. Even so, the engineers in theatre decided to change engines as a precaution and carry out a check on the remaining tiles to make sure they were all securely attached. While this was going on, the unmodified jets manned by No. 5 (AC) Squadron crews from RAF Coningsby were delayed in theatre and the crews had an extra two weeks enforced holiday in sandy places. Only when the new jets were checked and cleared were the aircrew able to return to the UK in the unmodified aircraft. Including the Cyprus detachment, it had been a long spell away from home, leading to frustration among the aircrew at the delay. At cease work I was enjoying a pint of beer in the Officers' Mess Bar, feeling just a tad guilty at my inability to influence events further, when one of the No. 5 Squadron navigators arrived. His opening remark was, 'Which idiot put all those tiles in the intakes.' I explained that that would be me and enjoyed the next thirty minutes listening to his energetic rhetoric based largely on conjecture rather than fact. As we parted, he a little better educated and me with a slightly tender chest from the finger poking, we shook hands. My parting remark was, 'I'm your new Flight Commander'. He had just received a posting to the OCU as an instructor and within days he would be working for me. I have still been unable to convince him of the value of the modification even after the passage of time, although we remain friends.

If I was to summarise those hectic few weeks, a much-maligned procurement system had been bumped into action and stop-gap defensive aids had been installed onto the Tornado F3, along with vital ergonomic improvements. The aircraft would now appear as a less attractive target on an enemy radar screen and its own radar was significantly enhanced. Within two weeks those modifications had been tested and validated and operational tactics written and briefed to the crews who would deploy. A modification programme had been documented and the first aircraft were being modified on a production line. The new equipment was cleared to fly and, within four weeks, those same aircraft deployed to Saudi Arabia to operate alongside coalition partners to remove Saddam Hussein from Kuwait. When pressed, the system had delivered.

In an ironic twist, in my later guise as Air Defence 2, I would be responsible for the formal qualification of the contingency modifications into fully endorsed modifications to the Tornado F3. The quick fixes would have to be approved and integrated into the weapon system by the aircraft manufacturer and my contingency plan would return to haunt me.

8

The Operational Conversion Unit

Formed as No. 229 OCU, the Tornado F3 Operational Conversion Unit adopted a shadow numberplate, No. 65 Squadron, to allow it to take on a NATO commitment in 1986. The squadron colours of No. 65 Squadron were laid up and it assumed the mantle of No. 56 Squadron, a famous Battle of Britain fighter squadron, in 1993. In keeping with tradition the switch to the training role meant, the less glamorous title of No. 56 (Reserve) Squadron was adopted, losing the (Fighter) designation.

The role of an OCU is to deliver new crews to the squadrons trained to 'limited combat ready' status. Inevitably, due to scheduling problems, the final events to confer full operational status are left to the squadrons and completed during a combat ready work-up. On the unit, a typical flying programme would begin with twelve sorties on the first morning wave followed by ten on a midday wave and a much smaller final wave in the mid-afternoon. The reduced numbers later in the day reflected the fact that aircraft had a predictable tendency to break. Most rectification would be carried out overnight, although if the snag was simple and could be fixed with a box change, an aircraft which was declared unserviceable on the first wave might be ready to fly again on the third wave. If night flying was planned, either the whole programme would slip and begin later in the day or a long gap would be programmed before a final wave was flown in the dark. In midsummer, this final wave could be as late as 10 p.m. to ensure it was completely dark for the night training. Within a typical flying programme individual courses would be allocated slots so each of the major phases could appear on a given day as successive courses would be at different stages of training.

Ground training preceded flying events beginning with a phase brief and interspersed with academic subjects. To prepare for the airborne sortie, students rehearsed the missions in the air intercept trainer and the simulator. A typical training sortie on the OCU was somewhat different to squadron flying in that it followed a carefully scripted profile. A comprehensive syllabus guide contained detailed profiles for each flying event explaining exactly how the target aircraft would behave and showing techniques to be employed. This allowed students to practice different techniques against different categories of target. There was a clear explanation of what the student crew would need to demonstrate in order to be awarded a coveted 'duty carried out' or DCO.

A thirty-minute briefing would be conducted before each flight, normally delivered by the instructor crew, although the instructor pilot would usually fly with the student navigator and vice versa. This allowed more flexibility should, for example, a video recorder fail to capture the intercepts as a sortie could be deemed successful by the instructor on the strength of a verbal debrief. Occasionally, the student crew would be nominated to brief and lead the sortie flying together as a crew and would be expected to cover each aspect of the sortie, demonstrating their understanding of the aim. These events were known as crew solo missions.

After donning the bulky flying clothing and safety equipment, crews walked to their nominated aircraft, stopping briefly at operations for a final out-brief. A normal start sequence took typically fifteen minutes before the pair of F3s taxied to the in-use runway for take off. For some exercises, particularly during the air combat phase or the advanced radar phase, three-ship or even four-ship formations were scheduled with the additional F3s acting as targets or aggressors. By flying specific profiles and tactics, the additional F3s would simulate targets as varied as Soviet Bears or Iraqi Migs. On the way to the play area, crews would complete ancillary exercises using every available moment of airborne time for training. These ranged from medium-level visual identification profiles to sighter exercises and low-level visual evasion work-up serials. For the latter, the instructor pilot would begin a series of manoeuvres in the low flying area at 250 feet above the ground, turning at up to 4G simulating a loaded fighter bomber. The student pilot would attempt to manoeuvre his aircraft into a missile and a guns tracking position while the instructor held the 'tow'. The manoeuvring would continue for some time before reversing roles for the benefit of the student navigator. This showed the navigator the additional challenges of operating the radar overland behind a target. With the advent of the air-to-air combat modes, and in the absence of a threat against the F3, this exercise became much more front-seat centric than in the Phantom.

In the play area the intercepts would vary depending on the particular stage of training. Profiles could be as diverse as a basic medium-level intercept sortie, to a one-versus-one air-combat exercise, an intercept against a supersonic target, or a two-versus-two advanced-radar intercepts against two Hawks in the Welsh or Cumbrian low flying areas.

Once the intercepts were complete, the aircraft would recover to base to land. The type of approach would depend on the weather. In good conditions the preferred recovery was a visual run in and break in which the pair approached initials in battle formation before making a high-G break into the circuit, lowering the undercarriage to land. In more marginal weather, the duty officer flying might well declare radar approaches mandatory, in which case pilots would fly a ground-controlled approach or an ILS (instrument landing system) approach to land. Each type of approach had to be practiced during the course so, even on a good day, OCU aircraft would be seen pounding the radar pattern often with pilot flying instructors in the back seats, much to the chagrin of the navigator instructors.

As the aircraft were turned around by the groundcrew ready for the subsequent wave, the crews signed in and, after a mandatory cup of coffee or tea, would debrief the sortie in some detail to extract the training lessons. The instructor pilot would analyse how well, or how badly, the sortie had been conducted, followed by the staff navigator who would debrief the recordings of the intercepts from both aircraft, dissecting each intercept and discussing how it might have been flown better, picking out strengths and weaknesses. It was rare to demonstrate a perfect intercept and that included staff navigators as well as students, and errors in both cockpits would be used as learning tools. The main points were then recorded in a comprehensive write-up before recording the coveted 'DCO' on the progress board, allowing the students to move on to the next event. Occasionally, a 'DNCO', the 'N' denoting duty not carried out, would result in the scheduling of a remedial exercise to reinforce the points. Costing tens of thousands of pounds per hour, remedial flying was strictly rationed and progress was relentless. For that reason, remedial work could often be a prelude to suspension if the lessons were not learned quickly. The pressure was enormous and the more contentious debriefs would, inevitably, spill over into the Officers' Mess Bar at the end of the flying day.

With the new track-while-scan and situation displays, the way in which intercepts were flown in the Tornado F3 was revolutionised. An intercept is broken down into phases. Firstly the target is detected and the target parameters are analysed before an intercept is set up. The type of intercept—frontal attack, stern approach, or visual identification—depends on the target and, in the real world, the instructions from the intercept controller. The intercept may lead to a long-range missile shot but it can continue into the visual arena; this is known as 'the merge'. At any time after 'the merge', crews begin to plan a 'bug out' or disengagement and that decision point is absolutely crucial. To remain engaged for any length of time in an F3 was to risk being out manoeuvred by a more agile opponent. With a well-flown disengagement, you would survive to fight another day; the Tornado F3 was well-equipped to disengage at high speed with the wings fully swept.

With track-while-scan or TWS, an additional phase known as 'sorting' was added to the intercept once a target was detected. The ability of the TWS to differentiate targets within a formation meant that each attacking fighter could be allocated specific targets within the formation. If both fighters engaged the same target, missiles would be wasted, so scripted radio calls ensured that separate targets were selected. Techniques were significantly different to those employed on a Phantom or a Lightning squadron. The scan patterns were much more complex, searched a larger volume of airspace, and were designed to take advantage of the improved situation awareness. To further enhance detection, different sectors were allocated within the formation; for example, the leader searching low and the wingman searching high. The navigator with first radar contact became the tactical leader for that intercept and controlled the sort plan. Once the targets had been entered into TWS, the navigator analysed the formation, identified the parameters (heading, height, and speed), and decided on a profile appropriate to the target classification; for example, to engage if the target was declared hostile or to identify if the target's identity was unknown. A 'side-side' sort meant that each F3 took its natural opponent on its own side, bracketing the target formation. A 'lead-trail' sort was used when a target formation had depth—namely elements in trail formation. In this case, both F3s approached from the same side with the tactical leader targeting the lead 'bogey' and the wingman talking the trailer. A sort could be modified if the attacking formation was split in height, becoming a 'low-high' sort. The details are less important than the principle that each fighter should target a different 'bogey' and sort plans often varied between squadrons and over the service life of the F3. Once 'sorted', each F3 would manoeuvre for an intercept on its nominated target, often becoming widely spaced from its wingman in order to set up the most effective missile shot.

Where the missile was fired depended on missile type. An AMRAAM is 'fire and forget', although in long-range mode it takes information from the host radar at mid-course before going 'active'. For Skyflash, the radar must remain locked to the target throughout the time of flight of the missile to allow the radar to update the guidance information. With a Sidewinder or ASRAAM, the shot is taken closer to the target, but like AMRAM, these missiles are 'fire and forget' and do not rely on the host aircraft for updates. The later the shot, the more likelihood there is of entering a merge. At close range the target designator, or TD, box in the head-up display helps the pilot to acquire the bogey visually and can be critical for success. The most effective pass during a merge is to fly a minimum separation pass, passing as close to the bogey as possible, often known as a 'dust off'. An agile opponent will attempt to 'lead turn' to gain angles before the merge. This means that he already has an advantage, having used displacement to turn towards his opponent prior to the pass. A less agile opponent will try to keep the separation to an absolute minimum to give the bogey pilot a harder problem after the pass. As the players pass, often at supersonic speeds, the reaction of the opponent dictates tactics. Against an Su-27 Flanker, an F3 crew would not turn as this would invite a quick kill. A savvy crew would sweep the wings and fly through at high speed, attempting to avoid a stern missile shot as the agile opponent turned quickly in behind. In the time it takes an opponent to turn and threaten, ideally the F3 would have made its escape before the opponent could fire a shot. Against a less agile opponent, perhaps a heavily loaded bomber, the crew may decide to enter a turning fight. As the fight developed, the crew would constantly reassess whether disengagement might be more appropriate than staying to fight. A heavily loaded yet agile opponent, such as an F-16, might still have extremely good performance. Constant assessment was vital as an ill-timed 'bug out' would merely offer an easy stern aspect missile shot. A further well-executed minimum separation pass would

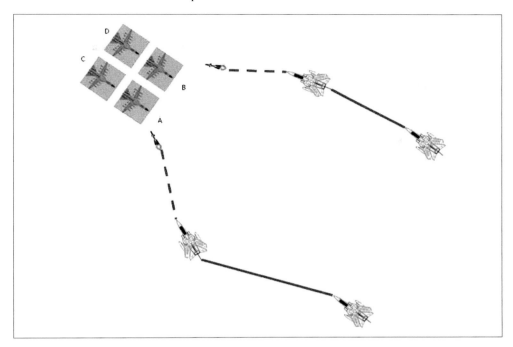

A 'side-side' sort.

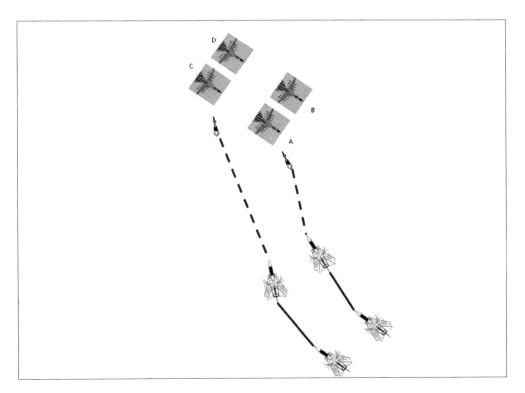

A 'lead-trail' sort.

probably put the F3 outside missile parameters and offer the chance to disengage. Air combat was a game of cat and mouse.

Defining and keeping these tactical plans relevant was a key feature of the OCU syllabus. Teaching had to reflect operational practice, but there might not be a consensus across the squadrons and different wings adopted different tactics. Even so, the Operational Conversion Unit syllabus of the 1990s had not changed much since it had been drafted by the Course Design Team in the early 1980s. In the meantime, the weapon system had matured enormously and the cockpit ergonomics were quite different. Squadron procedures had matured significantly and the OCU was in danger of being left behind. It was clear that a syllabus rewrite was needed to refresh the training syllabus and to reflect the arrival of the latest Stage 1 standard weapon system.

After a review, the squadrons were canvassed to determine what changes were needed. New radar set handling techniques taught the navigators how best to use the new navigator's hand controller and radar 'switchery'. In the front, the new stick top and air combat modes revolutionised cockpit routines. The training material for each flying event was rewritten and validated using carefully selected 'guinea pigs' before the instructors were briefed and standardised. Using a car analogy, although the bodywork was the same, the old V4 engine had been replaced by a V8 and while, outwardly, the package was the same, behind the scenes much had changed. Most people outside the F3 force, including the armchair experts, had no inkling of the step change, and yet bigger changes were in train.

The concept of graduating a student as only 'limited combat ready' was reviewed. It was a source of frustration that many operational techniques had to be delegated to the squadrons due to a limit on training hours and a lack of assets. If training could be completed on the OCU, the burden on the squadrons would be eased. Some things such as electronic countermeasures training were a step too far as the system software was immature and much work was still being done by the Operational Evaluation Unit to fix the bugs. Sufficient No. 360 Squadron Canberra sorties simply weren't available to ensure that six student crews could be graduated on a specific date with the appropriate skills. As a compromise, a ground-based academic phase was added to introduce the techniques, but the flying element to train this core skill remained with the squadrons. Air-to-air refuelling was introduced and, for the first time, students began to experience tanking as part of the OCU package. Weapons events were also impossible as a training missile firing for each crew would have been prohibitively expensive. Setting up an air-to-air gunnery phase would also have been similarly impossible given the poor UK weather and the extent of the qualification requirements. Despite best intentions, much training would still be done on the front line.

Some changes reintroduced old favourites. A new profile had been introduced for intercepting a high-flying target. It had been designed during a Weapons Instructor Course and involved a 'double 90' attack profile, flown at Mach 1.3 in which the fighter completed a series of elegant lunges before, hopefully, rolling out behind the target which was flying at 50,000 feet plus. Although the profile worked, it required split-second timing to execute the two turns or embarrassment followed. An old profile inherited from Phantom days—and therein may be the reason for the changes—was the easiest profile in the world. A very slack stern attack displaced from the target heading by 15 miles and allowed a supersonic fighter to roll out 5 miles behind the target and convert the speed into height to complete a visual identification profile. Anyone could do it! It was dusted off and reintroduced, making that particular event less of a confrontation.

No sooner had the syllabus been validated when a number of former exchange aircrew and weapons instructors began to look at fundamental changes to how intercepts were done in the F3. Intercepts had traditionally been set up using track crossing angle, or the angle between the fighter's heading and that of its opponent. By determining lateral displacement, an intercept profile could be calculated. The Americans used 'aspect', or the way a bogey presented to the fighter, as the way to determine the intercept geometry. Aspect gave an idea of the bogey's intent. A high-aspect bogey was pointing at the fighter and might be targeting you, whereas a low aspect bogey was nose-off and probably no threat. Although our 'cousins' were hugely capable, there was often a danger that Brits would adopt their way of doing things without good reason. Aspect, however, had much merit and was worthy of debate, yet with a major syllabus rewrite just completed and the prospect of further changes being required when Stage 2 was introduced, there was little appetite for an immediate revision. Lack of change is insidious. Experts can become unchallengeable to the point of dogma. Change on change is equally bad. Experience can be diluted to the point where the blind are leading the blind. The OCU had to deliver a rigid standardised syllabus to ensure that students were measured against a known yardstick. Instructors had to 'toe a Party Line' as without such discipline, millions of pounds of taxpayers' money could be wasted. Aspect was eventually adopted a few years later as part of another major update, and drove thinking on the new AMRAAM tactics. It proved to be a good change at the right time.

Unlike the squadrons, there were precious few detachments for the instructors on the OCU so it was a welcome break from the relentless training routine to be scheduled for a rare overseas detachment. I joined a small group from 'C Flight' who ran the weapons instructor courses, for a detachment to the Air Combat Manoeuvring Installation (ACMI) at Decimomannu in Sardinia. The staff aircrew on the weapons flight ran two weapons instructor courses per year during which specially selected aircrew from the squadrons were trained for four months to become weapons instructors. Every year applications were received from the squadrons and the OCU executives sat down with Group Headquarters staff and selected the best candidates. It was an accolade to be selected and the competition was fierce, but it was not unusual for candidates to have to apply two or three times before being selected. During the course the students learned how the Tornado F3 weapon system and all its components worked at a level of detail far beyond that required of normal squadron aircrew. They were also schooled in the skills of instruction, both on the ground and in the air, and how to brief and debrief sorties. One of the keynote phases was the detachment to the Italian base at 'Deci' to conduct dissimilar air combat training with other NATO nations. The opponents on this occasion were to be F-16s of the Royal Netherlands Air Force and the students needed 'victims' on which to practice. Instructor aircrew were invited along to act as pseudo students.

The ACMI was an instrumentation system which tracked the position of any aircraft carrying the ACMI pod; the first system in Europe was installed at Decimomannu. A tracking and instrumentation sub system, called the TIS, was equipped with distance measuring equipment giving the range of the aircraft from interrogator sub stations. The TIS comprised a master station and up to seven interrogator stations mounted on buoys anchored to the sea bed; by triangulating, a precise position in space could be calculated. Data transmitted from pods on the aircraft was sent via each station back to a control cabin on the ground and recorded for debriefing purposes. Up to twenty aircraft could be tracked simultaneously, allowing quite complex air combat scenarios to be recorded and played back for debriefing purposes. The pod that collected the data was a modified Sidewinder missile body and was carried on one of the missile pylons. The pod transmitted positional data, flight parameters, and weapon system information to a control system which displayed the data in real time in the control room, showing the position of all the participating aircraft in three dimensions. Cockpit views could be displayed on screens to analyse tactics, missile shots, or gun shots. As missiles were launched, the system recorded the parameters and computed whether the shot was valid. If validated, a small coffin would appear around the victim and the range training officer in the cabin would call a 'kill removal', taking that aircraft out of the fight. The crew which had been 'killed' could regenerate and re-enter the fight after a short delay. At any time, the RTO could see the position of each participating aircraft and could act as a safety coordinator or, on rare occasions, as an air combat instructor. Unfortunately, OCU instructors bore no resemblance to Kelly McGillis from the movie *Top Gun*, although anyone who has watched the movie will recognise the ACMI cabin from the debrief scene.

The sortie was to be a two-versus-two air-combat mission against the F-16s, and I was flying with another seasoned OCU instructor. I would relearn some old lessons as well as enjoying some rare continuation training. We had found the F-16s on radar and after 'sorting' to our respective target, we had manoeuvred for a Skyflash missile shot. With the missile in the air we had been threatened by an F-16 who had locked his radar onto us; having seen the indications on the RHWR screen in the front cockpit, my pilot decided to abort the attack. This was known as a 'pump' manoeuvre, more aptly described as 'running away bravely', in which a maximum 'G' turn was followed by a descending break to reverse the track and disengage. Either crew member could call the manoeuvre but it was often the pilot who recognised the threat as the navigator would be engrossed in ensuring the Skyflash missile timed out. On this occasion my pilot pulled the maximum 7G allowed for that particular configuration during which my head fell forward helped by my 5 lb flying helmet, which now weighed 35 lbs.

I knew from experience that once this happened, I should leave my head where it was and wait until the G relaxed before recovering my dignity and an upright posture. In the Phantom this phenomenon was known as 'listening to the radar' as that would be where your head rested. For me, it was the first time I had been caught out for many years and, in an F3 with its better sitting position, it was less likely. Foolishly, I tried to regain my normal sitting position despite my head having been pulled down under the sustained 'G'. There was little prospect of counteracting the weight of my helmet using out of practice neck muscles and inevitably a neck strain resulted. A reminder that old lessons are wise lessons was of little consolation. This was sortie number one and a further four sorties during the short detachment would be a painful reminder of my error as my neck slowly recovered. Checking my 6 o'clock became remarkably harder for a few days.

QWI student debriefs were legendary. In order to prove their emerging skills, the students would debrief the sortie at some length and, once complete, the staff would debrief the debrief, finishing up by dissecting the briefing slides. A typical training debrief, even on the OCU where new students were being schooled, would last thirty minutes at most. QWI student debriefs had been known to last four hours and go into excruciating detail to extract the last drop of learning from an unwilling subject. This particular phase had culminated in a four-versus-four air combat sortie which is a demanding scenario in its own right and taxes even experienced aircrew. Against the F-16s flying effective defensive tactics, it was hard to achieve a successful Skyflash shot as the F-16 pilots had thwarted every attempt to achieve a kill against them. At that time the European F-16s were armed with older generation stern-aspect Sidewinder missiles and AMRAAM had not yet arrived. In the highly charged environment of the ACMI, any hint of a lock from Foxhunter would result in a defensive reaction from the F-16 as it broke through 90 degrees onto the beam. If the defensive manoeuvre was well flown, it would defeat the Skyflash but suck the F3 much closer towards its more agile opponent. It was a brave F3 crew who pressed in under these circumstances. If the Skyflash was defeated, the F-16 would recommit, turning hard back towards the F3 and, with its superior performance in the visual arena, it could quickly achieve a kill against the less agile F3. A 'pump' if executed by the F3 crew in sufficient time would allow the crew to abort the attack and remain outside weapons parameters. In a real engagement that would probably be the end of the fight as no sane crew would recommit against an aircraft with the performance of an F-16 or an Su-27. During a disengagement, the F-16 pilot would lock his radar to the departing F3 trying to goad the departing crew hoping for a turn back. Meanwhile the F3 crew would know the rough position of the opponent from the intercept controller and at some stage fuel would dictate the outcome. If the F3 crew held the bizarre notion that trading shots might be a good plan, the F3 would have to turn at maximum 'G' and using one of the head-up display combat modes, reacquire the F-16 and launch a head-on weapon before being acquired by the opponent. With similar missile capabilities, at best, shots would be traded and both would be 'killed'. At the worst, the F-16 would get the first shot away before executing a breakaway, often deploying infra-red flares to defeat a possible 'revenge' Sidewinder shot. It was a dangerous 'tit for tat' and bad odds.

On this occasion, we had already been threatened by the F-16 and aborted the attack, returning east at well over Mach 1, and were approaching the range boundary. We would have 'dropped a boom' on Sardinia without action as the coastline was fast approaching. As we reached the boundary the rules of engagement dictated that we would be excluded from the fight. We could carry on east at subsonic speed and return to base with spare fuel—a less than satisfying option—or recommit to the fight knowing our chances of success against the F-16 were marginal. Being a dumb but aggressive fighter crew, we chose the latter knowing that we would at least provide a debriefing point for the QWI students as it was by far the worst plan. We broke hard to the north, washing off the speed, and as we passed through north we became subsonic just inside the range boundary. We skirted the edge of the range, timing our moment to recommit, trying desperately to see the F-16 which was advertising his presence with a spoke on our radar warning receiver in our 9 o'clock. Holding a tactical speed we finally saw our opponent and my pilot selected a combat mode turning hard back towards. Miraculously, the radar locked up and we fired a missile at the F-16, waiting all the time for the call of 'Fox 2' from our opponent, signifying his return Sidewinder shot. It never came. Our missile timed out and we heard the satisfying call from the range training officer announcing that the F-16 was dead. Why he failed to engage us would come out during the debrief, but it was highly unusual to succeed in such an exchange. As the engagement was terminated, we were now certainly out of fuel and it was time to return to 'Deci' for tea and medals!

In the debrief cabin some hours later, the recording approached the point at which we had disengaged. Our speed had picked up rapidly to Mach 1.5—one and a half times the speed of sound—to ensure we stayed ahead of the F-16 and outside of his missile envelope. At the eastern boundary of the range the north/south line known as the supersonic line was clearly marked, and to ensure that sonic booms did not affect the islands, all participants had to be subsonic as they passed the line. For an instructor, compliance with the rules was a major debriefing point and we were to become a tool in the box of learning. As the student instructor dissected another engagement, he seemed to gloss over a major error by the other student crew. Being understanding, we didn't attract attention to the omission as we were sure our colleagues on 'C Flight' would have spotted it and would raise it later in the debrief of the debrief. It was then, however, that attention focussed on us and we were admonished for 'busting' the supersonic line during our turn back. We explained that we had been carefully monitoring the speed in the cockpit and that by the time we hit the line, not only were we subsonic but we were heading north away from the islands. Our inquisitor was having none of it and, seemingly backed up by the ACMI data and much to my chagrin, laboured the point. Being 'old and bold' we should have let the point drop, realising that we were merely pawns in the game of learning. Much heated discussion and a few bruised egos later, we eventually moved on, but I promised never to be involved in the drama of student QWI missions again. Even the attractions of a Sardinia trip, a bottle of 'Deci Red' wine and an authentic pizza, were no compensation for the 'head banging' of a QWI Course debrief.

Far more satisfying was leading a detachment of four Tornado F3s to support the Tactical Leadership Programme at Florennes in Belgium. Acting as 'Red Air' for TLP offered high-quality staff continuation training for instructor crews, which kept our own skills current. The course had finished the applied phase and was moving into composite air operations missions, utilising all the ground attack, reconnaissance, suppression of enemy air defences, and air-to-air fighter capabilities at its disposal. The types on the course ranged from ground attack Tornados through F-16s to Mirage 2000s. The defensive fighters were provided by USAF F-15s, NATO F-16s, and German F-4Fs.

At the arrival briefing I give a brief introduction to the F3, its capabilities and weapons, and as a parting shot, explained that we were from the Operational Conversion Unit and would be happy to support in any way, including being constrained if it helped increase the training value. Immediately afterwards, a pilot from my own detachment remonstrated, suggesting that we were here to 'kick ass'. I had been an instructor for too long and my younger colleague was absolutely right. It was indeed time to show what the F3 could do as it would be an ideal opportunity to dispel some of the myths which still haunted the aircraft.

For the first sortie we were to escort the twelve-ship bomber package which was tasked against targets in Germany and would be attacked by the eight defensive fighters *en route*. During the mission we would be threatened by surface-to-air missiles on the ground, however, as escorting fighters, our main role was to tie up the defensive fighters to prevent the bombers being engaged. To do this we planned to position two F3s ahead of the first bombers to sweep through the area and engage the combat air patrols. A further pair would be embedded within the formation to strip out when engaged and to fend off any fighters which broke through the sweep. For a first event it proved challenging, but the F3 was well equipped for the role as our air-to-air weapons were more easily employed in that scenario, being less constrained by restrictive rules of engagement. One of the usual challenges was to decide who was 'hostile'. Operating ahead of a package, simulating operating in hostile territory made that determination much easier. Our excellent navigation suite allowed us to be where we were needed at all times. If separated from our charges, a rendezvous at nominated points around the route would be straight forward. Although we were flying without external fuel tanks, we had enough fuel to complete the route with fuel to spare. The first mission went well and morale among the detachment crept upwards. Even Foxhunter was behaving.

The next day the weather was poor in Belgium and Germany and low flying was impossible. Ironically, having flown from the UK to Belgium, we were soon heading back across the English Channel to fly a sortie over the southern North Sea with the package tasked against shipping targets in the Channel where the weather was better. Operating with a pair of Hawks, who were also acting as 'Red

Air' aggressors, we flew a mixed fighter force against the escorted package before landing at RAF Wattisham for a turnround. On the return sortie to Florennes, we repeated the exercise with eight defensive fighters attacking the twelve bombers over the sea off Essex. Up to now the scenarios had been evenly matched and each side had experienced simulated losses.

It was during the final sortie when we were to prove just how far the Tornado F3 with its Stage 1 radar modifications had come since its introduction to service. Again tasked as 'Red Air' we were to repeat the same profile, attacking the escorted package, but this time overland at low level in German airspace. We elected to use unconventional tactics and to operate as loosely coordinated singletons. We risked being picked off by the escorts but the loose coordination gave us freedom of manoeuvre. The lack of a wingman meant that our agile opponents such as the F-15s and F-16s would probably pick us off if it became a one-versus-one engagement. Set against that was the flexibility of being able to harry the package as it worked through our fighter area of responsibility. The box was small enough that we could call for help should we be attacked by the escort; in effect, we would give mutual support by presence. We agreed procedures to ensure that we were unlikely to launch missiles against each other as such antics could be extremely embarrassing at the debrief, even when acting as 'Red Air'. The combat air patrol was positioned at the end of the area looking towards the point from which we knew the package would arrive, as their route had been constrained to ensure interaction. At the appointed time the package entered the area and we made our first engagement working together as a pair. In the absence of a defensive reaction, Skyflash shots prior to the merge brought kills against some of the ground attack aircraft. In trying to meet a time on target some crews were failing to comply with Rule 1: 'Survive to fight'. By staying 'on track, on time' an old lesson would be relearned.

In the midst of the engagement, the Hawk pilots operating on a visual combat air patrol in the centre of the area were also engaging the package. Occasionally they would cross our track as they returned to their patrol position. The radio chat increased to ensure that we would not engage each other in error. A call of 'heads up' would have each crew checking the radar warner to ensure that we were not targeting each other—a so-called 'blue on blue'—although in this instance it would have been a 'red on red'. With the potential risks, the Hawk pilots would have liked a radar warner in their own cockpit.

As 'World War 3' developed, the escort fighters engaged, forcing us to withdraw 'down threat' to our original combat air patrol paralleling the line of advance. As we fell across the other participants we nibbled away at the package, and with twenty aircraft penetrating the fighter box it was a 'target rich environment'. Reaching the edge of the operating box we recommitted, taking further shots at the formation and their escorts staying at high speed and at low level. Combat aircraft were 'wheeling and dealing' at extremely low altitudes in scenes reminiscent of the *Battle of Britain* movie, and the radio channel was alive with calls of missile shots.

Out of missiles and out of fuel, after a relatively short time on task, we returned to Florennes at low level. To the best of our knowledge we had survived without being engaged, although one F-4F had come very close and a shot seemed to be a strong possibility. At the debrief, our eight shots against both bomber and fighter targets, including a hapless F-16, were analysed. In a tense exchange, the air-to-air kills were discussed and the tally leaned heavily in our favour. I could sense an air of disbelief from sceptical F-15 drivers, but we were able to validate most of the shots, although in the heat of the engagements and with good defensive reactions, some of the shots had been defeated. As we returned to RAF Coningsby, we had raised the profile of the Tornado F3 among a previously sceptical NATO community, and felt vindicated.

A deployment to Germany provided another 'First' for the Tornado F3. My former squadron, No. 92 (East India) Squadron was due to disband and the Phantom would be retired from its role defending the NATO Central Region from RAF Wildenrath. As part of the celebrations, an exercise was held on the Friday, after which the participants landed at Wildenrath and the squadron hosted a disbandment party. A Hunter was specially painted in a commemorative blue colour scheme, celebrating the Blue Diamonds aerobatic team, and a No. 92 Squadron Phantom was also decked out in a matching blue scheme. We parked our Tornado F3s in a spare revetment on 'Delta' Dispersal and joined the festivities, albeit with a tinge of regret at the disbandment of a fine squadron. Most of my fellow Tornado aircrew had served on the squadron.

On Monday morning, when it came time to returning home to RAF Coningsby, we signed out the aircraft and walked across to the dispersal. My aircraft, ZE787 *Alpha Victor*, which had only just arrived on No. 229 OCU and sported a pristine air defence grey colour scheme absent of squadron markings, had acquired a new livery. Red and yellow chequers and a 'Hissing Sid', the No. 92 Squadron mascot, had been carefully applied by the squadron groundcrew during the weekend. To the best of my knowledge, this was the only time a Tornado F3 appeared in the colours of No. 92 Squadron. I was hugely proud of my old squadron but my current squadron were slightly miffed that a hasty paint job was needed to adopt its true No. 229 OCU guise. Nevertheless, unofficially, the Tornado F3 served briefly on an RAF Germany squadron.

Despite the fact that the OCU had the most experienced aircrew in the Tornado force, it did not stop us from experiencing our fair share of incidents. The first involved an experienced staff crew. The front seater was a former Lightning pilot and the back seater a second-tour Tornado F3 navigator. As they recovered from the sortie, a bizarre chain of events ensued. There are two controls on the leg guards at the upper front side of a Martin Baker Mark 10 ejection seat. On the left side is the emergency oxygen control handle which is painted yellow and black. When pulled, a small emergency oxygen supply mounted on the seat is released into the oxygen masks allowing the crew to descend to a safe height. On the right is the manual separation handle which is also painted yellow and black and is used in the event that the ejection seat fails to fire. Manual separation is not for the faint hearted. Pulling this handle sets in progress a sequence of events: the straps holding the occupant into the seat are released and the drogue parachute and personal parachute are pulled into the airflow, literally dragging the occupant from the cockpit. The quote in the aircrew manual was, 'This procedure is dangerous and offers little chance of survival'. Who am I to argue and, if I had ever had to consider such an egress, I would have hoped to jettison the canopy first.

The crew had completed the sortie and were recovering to RAF Coningsby when a problem occurred. After they experienced fumes in the cockpit they ran through the emergency drills, deciding that emergency oxygen was needed. The pilot pulled the handle on his ejection seat to initiate the flow. At this stage there was a loud bang and the manual separation sequence on the front ejection seat operated, shattering the canopy. Although it became extremely noisy in the cockpit and they must have been thoroughly disorientated, the aircraft was controllable and, after completing a slow speed handling check, they decided to recover to base. At some stage, although disconnected from his seat, the pilot realised that he was still attached by the strap of his kneeboard which had, inadvertently, been threaded through the manual separation handle. Bearing in mind that the whole aim of a manual separation was to pull the occupant bodily from the jet, it was remarkable that he was still in the cockpit. They made a relatively predictable recovery over the Lincolnshire countryside and the approach seemed as if it would be normal until the pilot throttled back to final approach speed. The reduction in airflow allowed the drogue shoot to billow pulling the main chute into the airflow. With the extra pull the pilot was sucked upwards and lost his grip on the controls, still held to the seat by the flimsy strap of his kneeboard. The aircraft was trimmed out but flying itself. Very fortunately, the aircraft was a two-stick trainer variant with dual controls in the rear cockpit and, as he saw the pilot's predicament, the navigator took control. In an amazing feat of airmanship, he landed safely and deployed the thrust reverse, slowing the aircraft to a halt with the pilot still onboard. Had the crew been forced to eject, the pilot's chances of survival were zero. Although the kneeboard strap would have failed under the stresses of 18G ejection, the chute which was already deployed might have been shredded in the high speed blast. It was a harrowing incident that earned the navigator a commendation. In my view it deserved a medal of the highest order for skill and bravery. Such incidents rarely surface in the public view as they do not result in the loss of an aircraft. For me, they continued to prove how easy it was to make a simple mistake, the implications of which had massive knock on consequences and could lead to the loss of an expensive airframe. Thankfully, on this occasion the aircraft landed safely.

In another similar incident, with the Boss on leave, making me Acting Squadron Commander, another instructor crew was returning from a sortie when they suffered a failure of the landing flaps. This should not have been a major problem as pilots practised flapless approaches on every dual ride with a QFI. Without flaps the approach speed is much higher and, depending on the configuration, it can be as high as 192 knots. It was prudent to dump fuel to lower the landing speed. The crew elected to engage the approach end cable but the limit was 165 knots. To prevent the aircraft exceeding the limit the crew would need to lose up to 30 knots before engagement. The approach was normal and the aircraft engaged the cable before coming to a halt. It was towed back to the hanger for inspection but stress damage was found around the rear bulkhead where it joins with the centre section. This is where the two parts were mated during build and was colloquially known as 'The International Dateline'. The engineers began to scratch their heads, trying to decide the implications of a high-speed engagement. The aircraft was immediately grounded while the airframe specialists from BAE Systems inspected the problem and designed a fix. It was on the ground for some months pending repair, which cheered my Boss up no end when he returned from leave. The crew was proven to have engaged the cable at about the maximum speed of 165 knots—well, maybe a few knots extra—which, given the damage, caused much head scratching and a reconsideration of the prudent limit.

To forget to lower the undercarriage and land wheels up is probably the greatest sin an aviator can commit. It can cause expense and can damage both the aircraft and the pilot's (and navigator's) reputations. Much research has gone into understanding why it can be forgotten and to implement procedures to minimise the likelihood of it occurring. In the F3, gear indicators were fitted in the rear cockpit of a trainer variant, but surprisingly, not in the rear cockpit of a single-stick aircraft. The first wheels-up landing occurred with an OCU aircraft in the early 1990s, although on that occasion, far from forgetfulness, the crew were well aware that they had a major failure throughout the incident.

Problems with the Tornado undercarriage on take off were quite common. A complex built-in-test system was notoriously unreliable and often aircraft had to recover prematurely after erroneous captions suggested the gear had not retracted correctly. Problems on landing were much less common, although the same built-in-test could cause similar issues when the undercarriage was lowered. As the crew began their recovery, a landing gear problem illuminated a red 'UC' caption on the telelight panel. If the caption stayed on after selecting the gear down, the pilot would attempt a further up/down selection, hoping to clear the problem. If that failed, the handle was left down and the emergency lowering system was operated using an entirely different system. For both systems to fail was uncharted territory for the crew. Having attempted to rectify the failure using the main and the emergency lowering systems the crew worked through the emergency drills to identify the configuration of the aircraft. They decided whether to jettison external stores, what effect the runway conditions would have and if the area adjacent to the runway was safe, given a crosswind. If any of these aspects appeared unfavourable, the crew had the option to eject at a safe altitude. With the F3s flat underside, which lends itself well to landing wheels-up, they decided that this might be preferable to an ejection. Asymmetric gear configurations would have been more problematic and had one main wheel been up but the other down they would, undoubtedly, have decided to eject. The crew flew past the tower for an external inspection and confirmed the position of the undercarriage and elected to land. A wheels-up approach is flown using mid-flap, which puts the aircraft in a very flat attitude, albeit adding about 10 knots to the threshold speed. If the aircraft is settled onto the ground gently, damage should be minimised apart from a few skin panels which might need replacing. All this had been decided by aircrew on a test squadron discussing the hypothetical situation. This crew was about to try it for real. In the event, the aircraft settled gently onto the runway and stopped in a very short distance with little damage to the airframe. Within a short time the airframe was repaired and flying again after a number of panels were replaced. It was proven that a foreign object, known as FOD, had lodged in the undercarriage selector mechanism preventing the main gear selector from operating correctly. In a secondary failure, a leak from the emergency lowering system had prevented it from operating and coming to the rescue. Despite the double failure, the crew proved the value of emergency training and minimised the damage to a very expensive airframe, earning accolades for their performance.

A colleague who served on the OCU with me described his own incident on an online forum and provided a good insight into the thinking that goes on behind the facade:

> The only potential problem is a crosswind that takes you off the runway after the rudder loses control effectiveness. The wing tip is not far from the ground and it might dig in and flip the aircraft if you're on the grass. In my case, we agreed that the Nav would command eject us out if the aircraft started to go near the edge of the runway. What we didn't realise was that operating the crash bar to kill the engines and operate the fire extinguishers also cut off the intercom. Caused a moments excitement as we turned a little and I didn't want to be fired out with full rudder on and one thigh off the seat. Stopped OK in the end not too far from the centre-line.

Calm words after what must have been an adrenaline-fuelled experience.

One of the more pleasant duties was to host aviation photographers for the occasional photographic event. The OCU was a good place to host such events as we often flew a third aircraft in a formation, acting as a target. This jet could carry a photographer without needing to dedicate a sortie to the task and could call on two photogenic subjects.

Geoff Lee is a legend in the aviation photography world and he and his company, Planescene, has produced some of the finest images of aircraft ever produced. A sortie was planned to capture some airborne shots of a No. 56 Squadron Tornado F3 carrying a drill missile load. The sortie was to be part of a three-ship formation and was scheduled to take off in the early afternoon on a winter's day. Inevitably, a photography event was lower priority than other training sorties and as aircraft began to fall over with various unserviceabilities, we began to fear that we would lose the sortie. Those who have lived and worked on squadrons will be familiar with this feature of life. You brief the sortie and after checking with the Duty Authoriser on the Operations Desk you retire to the crewroom, waiting for the promised jet to materialise. This was one such day and the 1230 take off slipped to 1330, and then to 1430. Geoff was visibly concerned as his schedule would not allow him to repeat the sortie for many months. Having loaded drill missiles onto an F3 which was to be the subject for the pictures, I was equally keen to see the sortie go ahead. His biggest concern was that on a winter's day, light levels were rapidly dropping to the point where the quality would be affected. With only minutes to spare to the cut-off time, the promised jet was pre-flighted and the crews walked for the sortie. Geoff produced the usual raft of impressive pictures, including a shot of an armed aircraft in the vertical, but his best was saved for last. As the sun set, he snapped a photograph which is still my all time favourite shot of the Tornado F3. Framed against a setting sun, he caught the F3 in full reheat in the most dramatic pose with perfect light conditions. The photograph eventually illustrated the introduction to the outstanding book *Tornado F3 – 25 Years of Air Defence*, published by Squadron Prints, and would grace any book cover.

On another occasion we were visited by another respected aviation photographer. A Hawk had been specially modified to carry a rearward facing camera pod which captures amazing photographs of aircraft in dramatic poses, uncluttered by cockpit canopy rails. On the day of the flight the photographer was suffering from a heavy cold which will ground even a seasoned aviator. Colds cause congestion in the ear canals and with the pressure changes experienced in a fighter, it is very easy to rupture an ear drum when less than fully fit. With a few hours to go he decided that he was not fit to fly and I was substituted to take his place in the rear seat of the Hawk. He briefed me on how the pod had been set up and where the lens was focussed. A simple trigger arrangement had been installed in the rear cockpit which allowed me to operate the shutter of the camera mounted in the pod. We would operate with a pair of our F3s over the sea before moving into Low Flying Area 11 in Yorkshire, taking more shots at various altitudes and with different backgrounds. The photographer explained the images he wanted to capture and we briefed the detail of formation positions and how we would choreograph the individual serials. On the way to the area the F3s flew various formation positions on the Hawk. Once in the area, the Hawk pilot flew an orbit and, once again, the F3s tucked in behind, looking particularly photogenic with me clicking away with the shutter. When I returned I thought I might have caught that elusive shot of an F3 framed in the halo of the sun. A long debate ensued as it was explained that the best pictures relied on the strength of the image and that background was irrelevant, so feeling somewhat deflated I went back to work. Some months later copies of the 1988 Royal Air Force Calendar arrived and on the cover was the picture that had captured my imagination. Feeling quite the heretic, I admit to feeling a degree of vindication.

One of the highlights of my tour was the opportunity to host the Formula 1 World Champion Damon Hill for the day. Damon was offered a flight in a Tornado F3 and came along to the squadron with his wife and son who is now also a racing driver. At that time, he had yet to win his first Grand Prix. Such trips followed a fairly strict format given the stresses of flying a fast jet and the high-profile nature of flying a celebrity. Even so, we had no doubts about this particular 'back-seater's' ability to withstand the 'G' forces. Although passengers are not expected to operate much of the equipment, in the F3 some essential avionics such as the IFF (identification friend or foe) box are only found in the back cockpit and a passenger has to be able to set the codes as well as stowing the ejection seat pins and operating a few other key controls. Additionally, there are quite a few do's and don'ts. The function of any switch painted yellow and black needs to be carefully briefed. Pressing a jettison button could cause a good deal of embarrassment and cut the trip short, and turning the radar on at an inopportune moment could cause injury. The functions have to be carefully explained and rule number one was to listen to the pilot and do exactly as he said during the flight.

After the cockpit and safety briefings were complete I took Damon along to the air intercept trainer and ran through each of the more important cockpit switches, what they did and when to operate them. He nodded at the appropriate moments and ran through the sequences without much prompting. Returning to the squadron, we began the laborious process to fit his flying kit; although the items are not tailored, they have to be adjusted to fit comfortably. A badly fitted 'G' suit or a tight helmet can turn a sortie into an absolute misery. Equally, a helmet which is too loose could be ripped off during the force of an ejection causing injury and leaving the ejectee unprotected during a parachute descent. The safety equipment technician on the squadron routinely adjusted each pilot and navigator's equipment to ensure it continued to fit properly.

Briefings over, the Boss, who was to fly the sortie, signed out the jet while I took Damon out to the aircraft. I ran through the ejection seat checks as normal and fired up the main computer and inertial navigation system. On this occasion, rather than climbing in myself, I would be handing the cockpit over to our newest recruit. I strapped him into his ejection seat, fitting the various connections and straps, leaving just the seat pan firing handle pin to remove. After pointing to the most important switches which he had to turn on, and receiving a final thumbs up, I climbed down the ladder leaving him to settle in. The jet spooled up and, within minutes, he was on his way in the company of another Tornado F3. The sortie went exactly as planned and within the hour they were back on the chocks. As I climbed up the ladder he dropped his mask and I was met with a huge grin. Unlike some 'first trippers', he had clearly enjoyed the experience. I'd guess the stresses of supersonic flight are not too dissimilar to those in an F1 car.

As we wrapped up, there was a final presentation. Damon's own No. 56 Squadron name badge adorned his flying suit, which the squadron had prepared in advance. At the time, the Mk 3 flying helmets were being scrapped and replaced by a newer version; they would have ended up in a skip or painted a gaudy red to be used for sea survival drills. The safety equipment fitters had rescued a written-off shell and had painted it in Damon's racing colours of blue with the white hashes. It was a beautiful job and someone had spent a lot of time and effort to prepare it. The presentation clearly made a big impression and we often wondered if his flying helmet had ever found space among his many helmets and trophies he collected over the years.

As a racing driver, Damon would have fitted into the squadron easily as he shared the same love of high technology as the aircrew. He popped into the bar for a quick pint following his flight and enthused about the experience, commenting on the complexity of the flying kit and the cockpit environment. He was thoroughly under-impressed by the acceleration as the jet rolled down the runway and felt he had a good chance of beating us from 0 to 100 mph, although we never had the chance to find out. Races for *Top Gear* came much later! He did, however, concede that we had him firmly beaten from 400 to 600 knots. He also chatted easily about his Williams F1 car, its strengths and weaknesses and the techniques needed to drive it. He had a rapt audience. The lasting impression was that he was a thoroughly nice bloke with a wonderfully supportive family. A few weeks later I received a thank you card signed by the great man himself. A few kind remarks concluded with an admission that as soon as the cockpit canopy had closed he forgot everything I'd told him at the briefing. I remembered my own first trip in a Phantom so many years before when I too had suffered from 'brain-dump-itis' as soon as the wheels were in the well.

In a nice sequel, my son Tim attended a Formula 1 testing session at the racing circuit at Catalunya and had the opportunity to chat to Damon who was by then a commentator with Sky TV. Even after all those years and having enjoyed the dazzling success of his F1 career, Damon still remembered his flight in the Tornado F3.

Another highlight of my career came during my time serving as an instructor. There was a small window of opportunity which gave navigators the chance to fly a demonstration sortie in the front cockpit. Most navigators had previously trained as pilots although few retained currency. As part of the role, it was vital to understand the pressures on a new pilot and to understand what he was doing in the front seat and why. The senior officer responsible for the Tornado F3 fleet at Headquarters No. 11 Group was an experienced qualified flying instructor and the former commander of the Phantom OCU. The Boss of the F3 OCU at the time was also a qualified flying instructor or QFI and was well-versed in his ability to fly the aircraft effectively from the rear seat. Given the exceptional ease with which the services could be operated from the back, the flying instructors were confident in their ability to cope with any situation with little help from the front cockpit. He made a case to allow instructor navigators to complete a series of reverse role simulator exercises, leading to a single demonstration flight in the front cockpit. This experience had the potential to be a vital part of the navigator instructor staff work-up.

As the deputy commander of the unit, I volunteered without much arm-twisting at all to conduct one of the early flights. A couple of similar events had already been flown but without structure and I was keen that this event should become a regular feature. Apart from the obvious, it would be a huge incentive to attract instructor navigators to the OCU where the downside was that navigators

The author familiarises the Formula One star with the Tornado F3 cockpit. (*UK MoD Crown Copyright, 1986*)

Damon Hill experiences high-speed flight in a Tornado F3. (*Geoff Lee*)

received fewer flying hours than their squadron peers. Along with an extremely experienced QFI, we drafted the content of the simulator phase to ensure that navigator candidates would experience each of the major emergencies that they could potentially be asked to handle for real. In addition, pilots had to be word-perfect on 'Bold-Face Drills', which were the immediate actions needed to tackle emergencies. Pilots were expected to complete these drills while the navigator pulled out the flight reference cards and then talked through the drills and the implications in slower time. Although each crew member was expected to know the drills by heart, as they progressed through the conversion course, it was easy to become a little more blasé as the navigator's role was to follow the flip cards accurately, not to guess. For a navigator occupying the front seat, his bold-face actions would need to be as instant and accurate as a pilot's. Five simulator sorties were detailed and the nominated navigator instructors were carefully schooled over a single week. Once the work-up was complete, the sortie was scheduled based on the Exercise C2, the pilot's first familiarisation sortie with a flying instructor. It would include general handling over the North Sea, a supersonic run in 67 wing (the wings fully swept), before descending to low level for some low flying over the sea and overland.

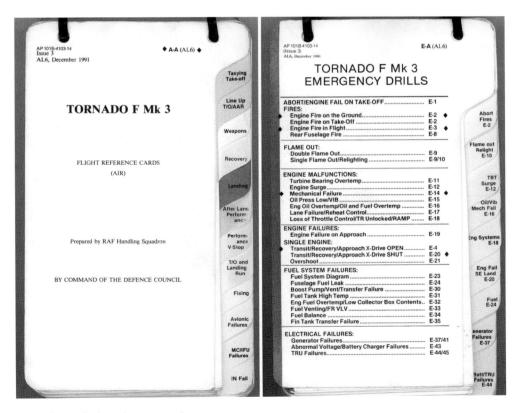

Tornado F3 flight reference cards.

On the day, the weather dawned fair and Tornado F3 ZE205, 'AM', (AT016) was allocated by the duty authoriser. Although I had qualified as a pilot in 1972, and unlike RAF pilots at that time I actually held a pilot's licence, the aircraft I was to fly was a quantum difference from the small, light piston on which I had trained. The briefing was uneventful as we had already flown the profile in the simulator and we knew exactly what was involved. As captain, my QFI, Ian 'Shiney' Simmons, who also flew the Spitfire on the Battle of Britain Memorial Flight, signed for the aircraft in the line hut in the usual way. The walk to the aircraft was surreal as I watched him climb into my usual cockpit and carry out the checks I normally completed. Meanwhile I walked around the aircraft and completed the external checks to ensure all the relevant bits were attached as expected. Climbing into the front I strapped into the ejection seat, bemused by the unfamiliar view from the cockpit. I spent more time going through the pre-flight checks than even a brand new student on his first flight would have taken. I was paranoid to make sure that I would not make any mistakes. We ran through drills, such as a CSAS (fly-by-wire system) built-in-test, to watch the in-cockpit indications for real. Eventually, there was no putting it off and after confirming that all was well in the back, I called Coningsby Tower for taxi clearance. I had listened to this same routine hundreds, if not thousands, of times from the back of a Phantom and also from a Tornado F3. Pulling the wings back to 45 for taxi made our girth that much narrower.

For once it was down to me to release the brakes and push up those throttles to get us moving forward. A dab on the brakes to confirm they were working and the jet eased off the chocks. The OCU operated from the aircraft servicing platform, or ASP, so as I moved forward I was aiming towards the grass in front of the squadron. Now that would be impressive if my first act was to pop an F3 onto the grass! Engaging the nose wheel steering, I eased the rudder bars to the right and we turned the corner to pass in front of the other F3s on the line. Off the ASP, onto the parallel taxiway and we taxied towards the in-use runway while completing the challenge and response pre take-off checks. This part was a routine I had gone through thousands of times, although now it was in reverse.

Calling for take off was a truly adrenaline-provoking experience, despite my thousands of hours of fast jet flight time. Clearance given, I eased the jet around the corner across the 'piano keys' and lined up. There were always a few vital engine checks to complete before rolling, and I ran through those before releasing the brakes and pushing the engines forward to military power. A final check of the engine instruments and into reheat, and the jet began to accelerate. It felt light and responsive and as I eased the stick back, feeling the nose wheel rise off the ground, it leapt into the air like a thoroughbred. This part was a well-rehearsed routine, and despite the thrill of being airborne I brought the gear up, the flaps up, and at 350 knots pulled the engines out of reheat. It was at this moment that capacity began to tell as I made the airborne call and announced my intention to switch to the departure frequency. The QFI switched frequency for me as I had done myself so many times in the past, and I was now expected to make the departure call on the radio. My available capacity was exceeded as I checked around that all was as expected in the cockpit and eased the jet around the corner onto an easterly departure heading, while climbing swiftly through 3,000 feet. I now knew how young pilots felt on their first solo. In an immediate act of contrition, I had to ask my trusty and trusting back seater to make the radio call. I could waggle my arms and legs or I could talk on the radio. At that moment I could not do both. With the call made and capacity returning I now had the chance to relax and look around my new, slightly unfamiliar, environment. The telelight panel was reassuringly blank, the engines were behaving impeccably and the gauges all showed readings which were entirely normal. I was beginning to enjoy myself. Fuel was not an issue for what was planned to be a sortie of just over an hour, so I was persuaded to reengage the reheat and make a rapid climb to 15,000 feet where the first exercise was planned. By now under radar control of an air traffic control unit and over the North Sea, we began to explore the basic flight envelope. Turns in 25 wing with the wings fully forward with and without the manoeuvre devices was followed by similar exercises in 45 wing to demonstrate the differences. Basic stalling showed the characteristics at slow speeds when the aircraft might be vulnerable to loss of control. Without experiencing it, feeling how the aircraft responded could not have been communicated by my QFI even if he had chatted for a week. This section of the sortie finished with a few basic aerobatic manoeuvres such as a loop and a (very shabby) barrel roll. Any illusions of ever becoming an aerobatic pilot evaporated. At this stage we called for clearance to accelerate to high speed. In the Tornado this involved a complex series of climbs and descents to reach optimum speeds and heights, bringing the wings gradually back to their fully swept position. As the aircraft accelerated transonic, it became a totally different aircraft. As the speed reached Mach 1.3 we climbed to the nominated height in the mid-thirties before beginning a gently loaded turn, which took in a large section of the North Sea. Although the aircraft felt responsive supersonic, its turning diameter, unless significant 'G' was applied, was huge. By now, and well towards the Scottish border, our turn took us back southerly and we pushed the speed up to about Mach 1.5, which was plenty fast enough for a first effort. My QFI was chatting happily in the back and was obviously used to the whole process. With Norfolk rapidly approaching we cancelled burner and the speed began to slowly drop off. We watched the needles shudder briefly as we returned to subsonic flight. The thought that I had just dropped a sonic boom passed briefly through my mind. Use of airbrakes could be problematic at high speeds so I let the speed slowly trickle back. When I thought of the heroes who had explored this very flight regime before me, my own first experience was somewhat less dramatic. The F3 was completely benign and handled impressively. The regulations only permit supersonic flight outside 30 miles from the coast and, normally, pointing away. With the cost of Norfolk painting on the scope—and I may even have uttered praise for how my pilot was handling the radar—it was time to explore the effects of the huge slab airbrakes on the upper rear fuselage as we decelerated to cruising speed and dropped down to the lower airspace again. The plan was to descend to low level over the sea, completing a few turns in the descent before navigating back to a visual entry point using the navigation displays. At that moment the air traffic controller called a contact and a Jaguar from the base at Coltishall crossed my nose a little over a mile away, also in a rapid descent to low level. My QFI called me to turn right to follow and began to demonstrate his own prowess in handling the radar in the back. I selected Sidewinder and fumbled with a number of supposedly familiar controls, but in the heat of the moment could not decide which switch would allow the drill Sidewinder missile head to lock to the target. So while I was firmly in 'the saddle' only a mile behind my target, my lack of skills prevented me from making that final step of locking the training missile onto its prey. A critical demonstration eluded me. As the Jaguar made its escape, I was able to reflect on how different it was to be staring through the HUD at a target rather than watching the event on a grainy video after the flight.

As we approached the coastline I looked ahead for our low-level entry point at Anderby Creek on the Lincolnshire coast. We were to enter at the coast and fly through the local low flying area past Alford towards Coningsby. My transit was to have been at 250 feet which is the normal operating height at low level and the F3 is extremely stable at that height. Despite constant entreaties from the back cockpit, as soon as I settled at the lower height I would immediately pop back up to 500 feet where life seemed so much easier. It was some time before I persuaded myself that 250 feet really was a comfortable height at which to fly. Eventually, we hit 'initials' and pulled up to 1,000 feet and broke into the circuit before cleaning up and turning downwind for a ground-controlled approach or GCA. The aim of this exercise was to demonstrate the utility of the head-up display in setting an approach angle and following the 2.5-degree approach all the way down to touchdown. Some timely and well-directed advice from the rear allowed me to make an approach from which we could have landed. The final event was to be a number of normal circuits so, after overshooting from the GCA, we turned downwind again carrying out the checks before lowering the gear for a touch and go. The wind on that particular day was a fairly healthy 18 knots across, which made the finals turn quite challenging. After exploring the dead side of finals I overshot into what was to be my final landing. After a less than perfect effort with the circuit ever tightening because of the crosswind, I vowed never to make disparaging remarks about the quality of a pilot's circuit ever again. My vow lasted just a few brief sorties! Touching down I had pre-armed the lift dumps and thrust reversers so as soon as the weight was on the wheels I pushed up the throttles and the 'buckets' popped out into the airflow, slowing the jet down below 90 knots at which time the re-ingest audio sounded and I pulled the throttles back to idle, stepping on the brakes to slow to taxi speed. The taxi back to the ASP and the shutdown passed in a blur before I was unstrapping and climbing out of the front cockpit for the one and only time.

As personalities changed and risk aversion grew, the programme was stopped. The leadership decided that, although the sortie was valuable, the risk if an emergency developed when a navigator was in the front cockpit was too high.

While a commander must always manage risk, an invaluable training opportunity for instructor navigators was lost. I can still say that even after all these years, that one sortie taught me more about helping a pilot through those early conversion sorties than any other sortie I flew in the back seat. It had been the most exhilarating one hour twenty-five minutes of my professional career.

One of my less stellar moments was when I was tasked to lead a pair of Tornado F3s to conduct a flypast at the Sunset Ceremony for our own Battle of Britain Cocktail Party at RAF Coningsby. The cocktail party is an annual event at every RAF Station and celebrates the heroes of the Battle of Britain and their contribution to our history. After a formal reception, guests are invited to assemble in front of the Officers' Mess at the appropriate hour. In a moving ceremony the bugler plays the last post as the RAF Ensign is lowered at sunset to the haunting strains of 'Lights Out'. Our two Tornado F3s were to overfly the flagstaff as the ensign was lowered, so timing was critical. As we crossed the dais we would turn outwards through 45 degrees, rotate into the vertical in full reheat and climb away from the spectators into the gathering dusk.

We launched well in advance and set heading for the datum which was near a small Lincolnshire village some miles from base. Fortuitously, the mast I had chosen as my datum sat on a small hill giving vertical extent, making it easier to see. Even so, leaving the initial point as the darkness descended, the features of the run-in would become less distinct. By planning the track carefully I would pass over the flagstaff on the correct heading at exactly 1900 hours flying away from the dais in full view of the guests. As we approached the holding pattern, in full daylight the mast was obvious and we established our timing racetrack. With minutes to go and the light fading we set off from the initial point. I would have to adjust my timing which was, by now, a few seconds adrift. I looked down for my first check feature. When the expected landmark did not appear I began to feel a slight nervousness. There it was, and we were behind time so a call of 'Speed up to 450 knots' brought a swift selection of reheat and we accelerated rapidly. Staring at the ground I looked for my next check feature but what should appear but the one that I had been anticipating. I was actually ahead of time. With the call of 'Speed back 250 knots' I could feel the waves of frustration emanating from the front cockpit. Apologies were redundant but the debrief in the bar would be merciless if we arrived early. The airbrakes popped out and the retardation was immediate as we slowed down now, not surprisingly, ahead of time. Had I done nothing my timing would have been almost perfect. In the meantime, my wingman, who had watched the burners ignite, had matched our acceleration and was closing in on the right to drop into line abreast formation as briefed. As our speed came rattling off he was spat out, unceremoniously, and wallowed on our right wing as he tried to match our reduced speed. There followed a very uncomfortable few minutes as I stared at my stopwatch, willing the 'time to go' to match the estimated time overhead the dais. I could do no more. Thankfully, as we flew overhead the flagstaff the timing was almost perfect, but it had been far from a smooth arrival. As we conducted a rather gentle outward turn, the pilots needed no prompting to engage full reheat as, without it, a climb out would have been extremely uncomfortable. I heard from those who witnessed the flypast from the ground that it was one of the most impressive ever as the jets were almost silent before arrival, having been throttled back for some time. The crescendo which followed broke the sombre mood of the bugler's refrain, although the zoom climb into the upper air had to be curtailed given our limited energy, and the rather unceremonious roll off the top came quite early.

I retired to the Officers' Mess bar to accept my fate and, sure enough, the banter was fierce. On reflection it would have been hard to make my wingman's job harder on that particular night, but there was never an excuse for a wingman not to be in position despite my 'assistance'. That's life on a fighter squadron.

I received constant ribbing from my peers for some time, but a while later my good friend was to let me off the hook. A four-ship of F3s from No. 29 (F) Squadron was tasked to provide the flypast for the annual formal parade for the Air Officer Commanding No. 11 Group. The formation held perfect timing but for some reason flew directly over Tattershall Castle rather than the parade dais, which was over 2 miles away from the airfield. It became known as the 'Beyond Visual Range Flypast' in a nod to the radar tactics the aircraft employed. I quizzed my friend but even after many years he was still a little sensitive about the incident and his threatened demotion to flying officer!

Delivery flights had been a constant feature of life on the squadron since the early days of the Tornado F2. I was to play a small, albeit unglamorous, role in the history of the Tornado F3 as I collected the last single-stick variant of the Tornado F3 delivered to the Royal Air Force. On 20 November 1993 I climbed into ZG799 at the flight ops facility at BAE Systems, Warton, and we departed without fanfare. During the one-hour-fifteen-minute sortie we visited venues that had been associated with the F3 over the years. After an overshoot at RAF Leeming and flypasts at RAF Boulmer, RAF Staxton Wold, and RAF Coningsby, we landed and delivered the jet to the engineers for acceptance checks. The accolade for the final delivery flight went to the Air Officer Commanding No. 11 Group, who flew ZH599, the last trainer variant of the Tornado F3 with OC No. 56 (R) Squadron in the back seat. They received somewhat more pomp and ceremony for the occasion.

I flew my final sortie on No. 56 (R) Squadron on 23 September 1993. After a short operational work-up I found myself bound for the Falkland Islands to take up my appointment as Officer Commanding No. 1435 Flight, responsible for air defence of the Falkland Islands.

There was a sad sequel to my departure when my old squadron lost its first Tornado F3, ZE789, resulting in the tragic death of the navigator. Having had a superb safety record, the loss underlined the risks of fast jet flying yet again. On 10 March 1995, a crew had finished a practice interception mission against an electronic warfare training aircraft and were returning to base at medium level. As they passed Spurn Point they heard a thump from the rear of the aircraft and it began to roll, pitch, and yaw violently. They were faced with a baffling array of failures and quickly diagnosed that the left engine had failed catastrophically. Almost immediately, the F3 became uncontrollable and, after warning his navigator, the pilot ejected. The pilot landed safely after a short parachute descent and was picked up by a search and rescue helicopter. The navigator was picked up by a second helicopter but was found to have suffered fatal injuries during the ejection. In a summary worryingly similar to the famous sequence in the movie *Top Gun*, the Board of Inquiry said that, although it could not be concluded with certainty, the navigator had probably been struck by the canopy. He was a talented aviator who died in the service of his country and will never be forgotten. The aircraft crashed in open water but within sight of the coastline. Given the serious nature of the accident, it was decided to recover the airframe—particularly the engines—for investigation. After some incredible efforts by the recovery crew, the wreckage was raised and it proved possible to determine the cause. Thermal stress in the high-pressure nozzle guide vanes had caused an uncontained failure, severing hydraulic systems and wiring which controlled the flight control system. The failure literally ripped apart the engine bay, causing a major fire fuelled by hydraulic fluid which burned through the mechanical back-up flight control rods and crippled the aircraft. From the moment the relatively small component had failed, the accident was unavoidable. It was a tragic loss of a talented aviator in an unpredictable accident.

9

Air Displays

The airshow debut for the Tornado F2 followed shortly after its introduction to service. The Boss, Rick Peacock-Edwards, and his navigator, Andy Lister-Tomlinson, designed a sequence in concert with the Spitfire from the Battle of Britain Memorial Flight flown by Paul Day. Paul was at that time the most experienced Spitfire pilot in the world and became a Tornado F3 pilot and OCU instructor himself. The coordinated opposition manoeuvres and passes in close trail formation were an instant success with the crowds. What was remarkable was that the work-up began less than six weeks after the crew had converted to the Tornado F2 at Warton. The first display before the crowds at RAF Valley in Wales in August 1985 drew universal praise.

Providing an aircraft for the display commitment was a significant undertaking for a squadron. Display crews flew normal training sorties during the week and spent weekends at airshows, returning on Sunday afternoon or Monday morning to begin a new working week. It could be a punishing schedule, albeit hugely rewarding.

Different aircraft were selected from across the squadron fleet as display flying incurred significant fatigue penalties; indeed, a display can rack up a month's fatigue use in just a couple of weekends due to the high 'G' forces during the display sequence. Unless managed, the commitment would reduce the operational life of the aircraft rapidly. If an airframe is specially selected and painted in a unique colour scheme, it takes a beating. Enthusiasts are keen to see the commemorative colours but regular appearances can have an impact on its operational capability. High fatigue sorties such as air combat manoeuvring may have to be limited and the airshow aircraft might be relegated to flying only low intensity sorties such as basic air intercept profiles.

The selection process starts many months before the first air display of the year with the nomination of a display crew. A number of volunteer candidates are selected from the squadron and develop their own sequence to be presented to the Boss for consideration. A short fly-off in-house leads to selection to fly the display

The Spitfire/Tornado F2 synchronised pair. (*UK MoD Crown Copyright, 1986*)

for the season. Once nominated, the winning crew begin to develop the detail and three sequences are designed. The 'Full Display' is flown when the weather is good and the airspace is clear. This involves the full demonstration of the aircraft's capabilities and includes all the traditional aerobatic manoeuvres. Loops, derry turns, aileron rolls and barrel rolls are interspersed with 'dirty passes' where the undercarriage is lowered and airbrakes are extended. A 'Rolling Display' is a halfway house and can be flown when the cloudbase or visibility is such that the full sequence is impossible. It involves many of the main aerobatic manoeuvres but is limited in height and is, to a certain extent, a compromise. Rather than full loops, flatter rolling manoeuvres are flown, allowing the pilot to remain below a cloudbase and in sight of the crowd and the ground. The final sequence is known as a 'Flat Display' and is constrained by a low cloudbase. A flat sequence includes tight turns and fast and slow passes give the crowd a spectacle despite the limitations of the weather.

One of the skills of a good display pilot when designing a sequence is to include manoeuvres which display that particular airframe to its maximum advantage. Although the Tornado F3 was not the most agile of aircraft, it was a hit at airshows as virtually the whole display was flown in full reheat, leaving the crowd's ears ringing for many minutes after the event. Without external fuel tanks and flown well, the aircraft might not match an F-16 in turning ability, but it would certainly stay inside the airfield boundary. It also had a few advantages which other aircraft lacked. Different configurations could be shown to full advantage during the sequence and there was nothing more dramatic than the final high-speed pass in 67 wing just below 'The Mach' before rotating into the vertical for a zoom departure into the blue sky.

Few people ever have the privilege to experience the thrill of flying a display. The skills demonstrated at an airshow lie firmly in the front cockpit and there is only a limited amount a navigator can add once the wheels are in the well and the display is underway. Nevertheless, putting on that show starts well before the display itself and, on a two-seat squadron, much of the administrative burden falls to the back seater, ranging from detachment planning through to coordination with display managers. Once into the sequence, 100 per cent of the pilot's concentration was on the real world outside the cockpit. Navigators could remind the pilot of the next manoeuvre in the sequence, although such details were normally imprinted indelibly in the pilot's brain by then. Another invaluable role for the navigator in the F3 was that he could confirm the position of services such as gear, flaps, and airbrakes, ensuring that the aircraft configuration was appropriate to the manoeuvre. Most importantly, he could monitor that final vital commodity: fuel. Once airborne, the pilot flew the carefully scripted routine to precise limits. Each manoeuvre runs in sequence and at every check point during the display, certain heights and speeds, known as 'gates', must be met to ensure that the manoeuvre can be completed safely. If a high-speed pass is flown along the crowd line pulling up into a loop, the pilot must hit a specific height at the top of the loop to ensure he has sufficient performance to fly the next pass at his minimum safe height. Failure to achieve this has tragic consequences, and a Phantom crew was lost at RAF Abingdon in 1988 in such circumstances. After completing a looping manoeuvre, the aircraft struck the ground during a sequence and tragically the crew were lost.

For safety reasons, a 'crowd line' is clearly delineated for every air display and during manoeuvring a height limit of 500 feet is applied for additional safety, although the F3 was cleared to fly down to 100 feet for some flypasts. Each manoeuvre has to remain 'airside' of the crowd line, except under exceptional circumstances, as a consequence of past accidents. Even so, given that the jet would pass within 250 metres of the crowd during the display, impressive results could still be guaranteed. Pilots do not work to these limits immediately. As a display is developed, practices begin as high as 5,000 feet above ground level and each element is repeatedly practiced until it becomes routine. Only then is it stepped down in height in carefully controlled stages. Eventually, the crew become comfortable at their lowest display heights. Once the work-up was completed, the final test was to display in front of the group commander, normally the Air Officer Commanding No. 11 Group for a Tornado F3 display crew. At this stage, there are no excuses and a flawless display is the way to receive the coveted 'Public Display Authority'. From then on the crew can display in front of an enthusiastic crowd.

Undoubtedly, the unsung heroes are the display groundcrew. While the aircrew commute to and from the displays in a Tornado, the groundcrew spend hours in transit between the home base and the display destinations in a minibus.

The hours are long and the ignominy for failing to have a serviceable jet for the display is immense. The engineering personnel did an amazing job on the road with limited resources.

No. 56 (R) Squadron provided the display crew for many years, and at various times Headquarters No. 11 Group was persuaded to allow the squadron to paint an airframe in a special colour scheme. An adventurous effort during Fred Grundy's first display season was known as 'The Raspberry Ripple'. The scheme, applied to ZE907, commemorated the colours of No. 65 Squadron with its red spine and the red and white chevrons prominently slashing the fin. The all-red tail of ZE839, 'AR', followed during the 1993 season sporting No. 56 Squadron's Phoenix symbol enclosed in a white disk.

Commemorative schemes became less prominent as operations became more prevalent. By 2005 painting was a thing of the past and politics dictated that fatigue use was even more of an issue as the life of the airframe was stretched out. A more subdued red flash on the fin was approved for the OCU display aircraft, which by then was based at RAF Leuchars. The aircraft sat alongside the normal squadron markings resplendent with its 'Firebirds' logo. To spread the load among other squadron airframes, decals rather than paintwork were applied to these display aircraft, allowing flexibility in the programming. Nevertheless, No. 56 (R) Squadron produced a glorious piece of artwork on ZE735 for the 90th anniversary of the squadron the following year. The red spine blended seamlessly into the traditional flames below a huge stylised Phoenix which filled virtually the whole fin.

Tornado F3 ZE839 of No. 56 (Reserve) Squadron over Finland.

My own short exposure to display flying occurred during Exercise Radlett, which was the demonstration tour around the Gulf States. During the detachment, BAE Systems hoped to display the Tornado F3 to selected officials at each of the nominated venues and a crew was needed. The visit to Kuwait had been cancelled at an early stage leaving just Bahrain, Doha, and Abu Dhabi on the schedule. I was a willing volunteer to join the display pilot from the previous season to deliver the displays which would take place at each venue. The main display season had ended a few months before and the display currency had lapsed. We had not worked up as a crew, so before leaving for the Middle East we flew a practice sequence to refamiliarise my pilot with his routine. We then sat down to study each venue and work out if any obstacles might affect the sequence. My pilot had flown a complete season with his regular navigator so was entirely familiar with his routines. Even so, it was decided not to try to use all three displays—flat, rolling, and full. The rolling display was selected as a good compromise as it contained most of the aerobatic manoeuvres short of looping and fully inverted passes, yet remained relatively close to the crowd line. With the excellent weather in the region, it was unlikely that a flat display would be needed.

Looking at the fuel gauge as we taxied for our first display at Bahrain, I was conscious that it might be more appropriate to announce that it was time to land rather than to roll down the runway for take off. I recall sitting at the holding point in total silence after completing the pre take-off checks. The concentration in the front cockpit was intense and infectious. Cleared to roll, as the gear retracted, the sequence started with a minimum radius turn, almost before the jet was clean, manoeuvring inside the airfield boundary at the surprisingly slow speed of 250 knots. Coming back to crowd centre, it led into a sequence of derry turns, high G turns, and a dirty pass with gear, flaps, and probe extended, before concluding with a high-speed pass in 67 wing, rotating into a vertical departure. From start to finish was a scant five minutes. I talked him through each sequence giving those vital check heights, speeds, and reminders to retract the services at the appropriate moments. Despite constant reference to the details on my kneeboard, it was impossible not to glance down at the airport terminals just below the aircraft, wondering what the departing passengers must be thinking about the crazy Tornado in full afterburner which was delaying their boarding. As we dropped the jet onto the wide runway and the pilot engaged the lift dumps and selected maximum thrust reverse, the jet rocked to a halt at crowd centre. It was all quite surreal and, at any other time, an unauthorised display at an international airport would have earned us both a court martial. The most telling feature at the end of a display is the sudden release of adrenaline. The cockpit discussions would be familiar to anyone who has listened to a Formula One driver who has just won a race and celebrates with his team over the radio. Truly memorable, despite my limited contribution.

Back to reality at home. With the relentless drive to graduate new crews, there was little chance on an OCU to enjoy the more pleasant aspects of life on a squadron. My second tour of duty on the Tornado F3 OCU was a stark contrast to the first. Detachments were few and far between and the old adage of 'all work and no play' came to mind on more than one occasion. It was a huge treat when the opportunity for a rare visit to Finland emerged. Occasionally, rank had its privileges and the Boss and I, by then the Executive Officer, or XO, were first in line for a seat to the show. We had been invited to provide a static aircraft for the Midnight Airshow at the Finnish air base at Kauhava. As the show was planned to close at midnight, we checked in for duty at the squadron later in the day, having completed all the flight planning in advance. The two jets were prepared and I filed a flight plan. The route took us over Denmark and Sweden before crossing the Baltic into southern Finland. A quick hop up the coast of the Gulf of Bothnia and we would arrive at the base, which sat just outside the town of the same name. As we headed north a pair of Hawks from the training unit pulled alongside and escorted us the final miles to our destination, landing in brilliant sunshine to join a Jaguar and a Nimrod which had also been invited to the show. The end of the Cold War was still recent so sharing the parking ramp with a flight of Mig-21 Fishbeds, which the Finns operated at that time, was still a novelty. It emphasised our location in close proximity to the Russian border, only 200 miles to the east. At that moment we were as close to the city of St Petersburg as we were to the Swedish capital Stockholm. After arrival, we sought out the display coordinator to find out where he wanted our F3s to be parked. We were welcomed enthusiastically and thanked for taking part in the airshow. Being such esteemed visitors, the coordinator intended that we should fly the last display to close the show. Far from being a static exhibit we were to be the star of the flying display! I watched the Boss's face drop as he realised the implications of disappointing the hosts by failing to perform. Where the misunderstanding had arisen was unclear, but we were unmistakably expected to be active participants. Luckily, the Boss had just flown a display sequence for a Station Open Day at RAF Coningsby and the routine had been approved by the Station Commander. I had acted as display navigator for the Gulf tour and 'knew the ropes'. If we adapted the sequence we could save face and still satisfy the locals. We grabbed a ream of paper and retired to a quiet spot and began to map out a potential sequence based on the Boss's recent display. A safe minimum height was selected, although the surrounding countryside was familiar and looked remarkably flat, like Lincolnshire. Armed with the briefing notes, the Boss disappeared to find a phone to explain the problem and seek approval from the Station Commander at Coningsby. Some minutes later, after hurried discussions with the Air Officer Commanding No. 11 Group, we had approval to carry out a 'performance demonstration'. Fortuitously, the aircraft we had selected for the trip was ZE839 'AR', which was painted in the commemorative scheme with an all-red fin. The fact that it sported the huge 2,250-litre fuel tanks under the wings would further limit the sequence, but a performance demonstration was better than a refusal.

In the event, the demonstration was flawless and we dropped into a familiar routine as we worked through the sequence. It probably looked relatively tame from the ground, lacking any true aerobatic manoeuvres—rather a series of tight turns and a dirty pass. We hit each element perfectly before closing the show with a high subsonic pass along the crowd line, pulling into the vertical in 58 wing, again limited by the fuel tanks. Somehow, landing after midnight in broad sunlight still seemed very odd. As the crowd drifted towards the exits we received a number of raucous congratulations in Finnish, which seemed to suggest that the demonstration had been well received. The first beer that night, or rather the following morning, slipped down very nicely.

Another associated commitment which fell to the OCU was to provide the spare and static aircraft at each airshow at which the display aircraft was due to perform. I took the static display Tornado F3 into the Royal International Air Tattoo at Fairford in 1993, and it was to prove to be memorable for many reasons. The Russians were extremely active at the airshow after the fall of the Berlin Wall, and a large contingent was present at RIAT. A pair of brightly painted Mig-29 Fulcrums was providing a spirited display, which included high-G sequences in close formation. Some minutes into the display the pair split to carry out opposition passes before attempting to rejoin. The wingman arced the turn to rejoin into close formation but misjudged the manoeuvre and struck the leader, slicing the nose off the lead Mig just behind the cockpit. The pair collided overhead the area where aircraft waiting to take part in the display were parked, generating a dramatic fireball as the leaking aviation fuel ignited. The nose of the lead Mig bent back at a crazy angle as the airframe disintegrated and pieces of broken airframe rained down, narrowly missing the Battle of Britain Memorial Flight Lancaster which was parked below. Both pilots ejected safely, but the leader's ejection can only have been traumatic as the nose separated from the tail section and became completely unstable, tumbling in the airflow. One airframe crashed just beyond the parked aircraft and exploded in flames. The other Mig entered a flat spin and crashed outside the fence. The pilots hung in their chutes for scant seconds before coming to earth. A video sequence captured at the show showed one of the pilots, still clutching his bonedome, lighting up a cigarette. Reportedly, the leader was less than diplomatic about the fate of his wingman. In a clip circulating on the internet, a commentator explained the words spoken in Russian. The offending pilot was surprised about a neck collar being put onto his partner. He said:

'Hey, everything is normal?'

'Normal'

'What is this thing on your neck?'

'Don't worry, they are going to put one on you too, ha ha!'

All aviators have a sense of humour, even in the darkest moments.

More drama was yet to come as the emergency services responded to the crash alarm. The RAF fire truck, in its haste to reach the crash site, punched a hole through the perimeter fence before screeching to a halt and applying foam to the burning wreckage. Happily there was little damage and no injuries.

The following day, a navigator colleague who had been lucky enough to serve on exchange duties flying the F-14 Tomcat at Oceana Naval Air Station in Virginia was keen to show us the Tomcat cockpit. We sought out the static F-14 which had flown in from a US Navy aircraft carrier but the crew was nowhere to be seen. My friend, sporting his 1,000-hours Tomcat badge, asked the American guard who was stationed inside the wire if we could take a look. Without a moment's hesitation the request was refused despite my colleague's protestations that he had flown the jet. Sitting alongside was the Tu-142 Bear which was attending RIAT for the first time; a tangible example of the end of the Cold War. I had spent many years on alert ready to intercept Bears and it was a surreal sight to see the huge aircraft on British soil. Our sister squadron, No. 111 Squadron, had intercepted the Bear on its way into Fairford, for once a gesture of friendship, and it now sat alongside the IL-78 Midas tanker which had accompanied it. On the ground, as in the air, it was an unwieldy beast with its four huge engines and eight contra-rotating propellers. It sported the Russian flag proudly on the nose and the huge red star on the fin left no doubt that this was the same type that had been our target during the Cold War. It seemed beyond the realms of possibility that we could blag our way onboard, but when a likely looking officer in Russian uniform wandered our way we pointed to our flying suit patches with the red triangle and Tornado F3 printed across the bottom and then pointed, hopefully, at the Bear. Amazingly, he nodded enthusiastically, lifted the rope, and we were on our way onboard. It seemed surreal as we climbed the wooden steps which had been propped up into the nosewheel bay. I had spent years sitting in the QRA shed unsuccessfully waiting to intercept a Bear from my bases at Wattisham and Wildenrath. My first real encounter would be to sit in the cockpit!

Inside, the huge aircraft was reminiscent of the Vulcan in which I had sat as a young flying officer, although much more spacious. The taste in colour of the Russian designers left much to be desired and, in contrast to the stark black of a British aircraft, it was painted in a strange duck egg blue, or was it green? In the aft cabin was the massive radar display screen which the Russian navigator must have used on many occasions to designate his targets. Although this was a maritime version, his bomber colleagues would have used a similar radar set to target our air defence radar sites in the Scottish Islands. I would have liked to delve deeper but with no power and a guide who spoke no English, sign language was the best I could achieve. After a tour of the Bear we were received, equally enthusiastically, onboard the Midas air-to-air refuelling tanker. I heard afterwards that one of the escorting Tornado F3 pilots had pulled alongside the Midas as they flew down the North Sea. Using the universal symbol he had extended the refuelling probe which is the request to take on fuel. His gesture elicited little response from the Russian tanker captain, which is perhaps fortuitous. I suspect the Tornado crew may have had some difficulty explaining that he had just completed the operational testing for clearing the Tornado F3 to tank from an Illyushin IL-78 Midas. The events were a bizarre juxtaposition of the norm, being firmly rejected by our closest ally, the United States, and welcomed aboard with enthusiasm by our former foes.

Although not an air display, one largely unknown event worthy of mention was a guided tour offered by the air traffic controllers at RAF Manston, known as 'The

A Russian Bear at the Royal International Air Tattoo in 1992.

The author in the cockpit of the IL-78 Midas tanker.

White Cliffs Tour'. RAF units rely on visiting aircraft to fly practice approaches to keep air traffic controllers current. If crews were willing to fly a precision approach radar talkdown for controller training, the favour would be returned with a 'White Cliffs Tour'. Leaving Manston Zone after the practice approach and flying past Reculver Bay, Margate, Broadstairs, Pegwell Bay, the Cinque Ports, and the White Cliffs of Dover, they would be offered a running commentary on the history of the memorable features. In a unique example of mutual 'back scratching', the unit generated fast jet traffic for essential training while the crew had a brief respite from the hectic events of a typical training mission. It qualified as one of the most select guided tours in history and I was lucky enough to experience it myself on one occasion. Flying with a good friend *en route* to Biggin Hill to deliver an F3 which was taking part in the static display, we dropped in to Manston. My pilot just happened to fly the Spitfire with the Battle of Britain Memorial Flight and showed me how to thread through the London Zone at low level, through a little-known gap in the controlled airspace. Spitfire pilots still led a charmed life. Slightly chastened by his outstanding navigational skills, we shot an approach at Manston before being given the tour. After a spectacular ten minutes at low level, we pulled up for an approach into the congested airspace around Biggin Hill before landing. It was a truly memorable experience seeing the legendary cliffs up close from the confines of a Tornado cockpit, and it evoked thoughts of 'The Few' as we saluted our illustrious predecessors. I could not help but wonder how many flyers, both British and German, had viewed that iconic landmark from such a perspective back in those dark days.

It would be remiss of me to finish the section on airshows without making a mention of another tragic loss to the F3 force. Flight Lieutenant Paul Brown, known as 'PB', was the display navigator for 1993 and 1994. He tragically passed away at a very early age after a short illness. He was a hugely talented instructor and a genuinely nice bloke who left a large gap with his passing. Although another talented aviator finished the display season that year, 'PB' left big boots to fill. I hope he is able to recount his display stories at that great Officers' Mess Bar in the sky; he is sorely missed.

10

The Tornado F3 on Operations

The respite from operations following the First Gulf War was short lived. With tensions rising in the Balkans, a 'No Fly Zone' was established over Bosnia. A United Nations resolution was passed which prohibited military flights in Bosnian airspace, but after flagrant breaches, a further resolution prohibited all flights. In order to enforce the resolution, NATO fighters were tasked to police the airspace beginning in April 1993. The operation was named 'Deny Flight' and Tornado F3s were deployed to the Italian Air Force base at Gioia del Colle to support the NATO operation. I had flown through Gioia on a number of occasions as a staging post between RAF Wildenrath in Germany and RAF Akrotiri in Cyprus. The base immediately experienced an influx of combat aircraft as the operation intensified, and a dispersal was set aside for the Tornado F3s with the crews operating from a small operations complex alongside. Shelters were rigged up to protect the aircraft from the extremes of the weather but, unlike other operational areas, the problem was the heat from the sun rather than rain.

At that time and once again 'flying a desk', as the fleet manager for the rear seat aspects of the Tornado F3, one of my responsibilities was to visit Gioia and discuss the crews' needs. The F3, with its comprehensive avionics and tactical air picture, was well equipped to act in the enforcement role. By then the jet was flying with a 'Stage 1 Plus' radar standard which gave a credible radar performance, although operating overland, particularly in the hilly terrain in Bosnia, added significant challenges. By 1993 it had been modified to take the Vinten flare dispensers and the BOL chaff system but did not yet have an active radar jammer. This was to become a crucial limitation within months.

Many of the functions which were routine in the UK were not necessarily the same on operations. A simple example was that the crews might have to refuel one day from a VC10 but the next day from a French KC135 tanker. To be able to do this, the Assistant Chief of the Air Staff, who was the Airworthiness Authority for the aircraft, had to approve flight clearances. Many UK agencies, particularly in the support area, had become accustomed to scheduling modifications and clearance activity in slow time with programmes lasting many years. For operations this was totally unacceptable and the system was given yet another wake-up call. RAF detachment commanders should not have had the need to explain to their NATO bosses why the Tornado F3 could not take part in an operation just because a clearance to operate a piece of equipment was not in place, but this was happening. As a cog in that very wheel I was stunned to hear of the problems. If the crews needed a clearance it should be produced in days if it was a simple fix or, at worst, in weeks if the modification was more complex. I returned after seeing the operation at first hand, both frustrated that I wasn't flying but fired up with enthusiasm to try to correct the problems. I spent the next few months writing service deviations to allow various new pieces of equipment to be flown and issued appropriate clearances to allow the crews to operate as tasked. Despite my willingness, I quickly hit a 'speed bump'.

The US KC135 was by far the most numerous tanker on the operation. To refuel aircraft fitted with probe and drogue refuelling systems, a short 6-foot

The Vinten flare dispenser and control panel.

hose could be fitted to the 'boom'. The basket which was fitted to a KC135 was much smaller than the RAF equivalent, and when 'prodded' over-enthusiastically with a refuelling probe, it often showed its displeasure. It had a tendency to kick aggressively and become slightly agitated. Once in contact, all was still not easy. On an RAF tanker the hose was pushed inwards towards the hydraulic drogue unit and the pilot allowed the hose to reel in and out with the minor changes in speed between the receiver and tanker. Once plugged into the KC135 basket, an 'S' kink was set into the hose and only then would the refuelling valves open allowing fuel to flow. Throughout the refuelling the receiver pilot had to fly an accurate formation position on the boom which was much more demanding than the RAF procedure. Any drift away from the correct position could seem quite dramatic as the short hose stretched alarmingly. Although much more demanding, RAF crews took the challenge in their stride and use of the KC135 was cleared by day.

Back in the Ministry of Defence, I heard rumours that an F3 had been tasked onto a KC135 at night but, on checking, found that we had never issued a formal clearance for night operations on this particular aircraft. The operational crew could be forgiven for the lapse. They had been vectored onto their tanker, probably on recovery after an operational mission. Receiving their precious fuel was more relevant than a clearance and they would have tanked from the same aircraft by day many times before. This was, after all, live operational flying. It transpired that formal clearance flights had never been completed at night. A hasty instruction was issued, asking them not to use the KC135 at night until we could issue the appropriate paperwork. I began assembling the case but only a single recorded sortie by a Boscombe Down test pilot some years before was on record, and his comments on the standard of lighting for night tanking were disparaging. He had criticised to the point where he considered it to be a flight safety risk. I agonised over the dilemma. A test pilot with possibly few hours on the Tornado F3 and perhaps with limited currency on type had made a categorical statement. It simply could not be ignored and a service deviation could not be granted without further evaluation. I canvassed opinion on the Operational Evaluation Unit and the pilots were quite bullish in their view that there were no real problems, even though the lighting was less than perfect. I did not delve further into how they knew! My One Star Commander who would sign off a service deviation would not accept a case without new evidence and it was some time before the night trial could be repeated at Boscombe Down and a more positive assessment given. In theatre, the squadron was able to tank only from the VC10 at night, limiting operational flexibility. On this occasion it was impossible to bypass the regulations until the lighting was re-evaluated. Some criticised the bureaucracy but the officer who was being asked to underwrite the risk was understandably cautious and it was some months before dispensation could be given, much to the frustration of the crews on operations.

While Croatia enjoys a long coastline along the Adriatic Sea, Bosnia, sitting just inland, is land-locked. The 'No Fly Zone' covered the area overland yet NATO assumed control of much of the airspace over the Adriatic as well. This rear area over the sea was known as 'Mainstreet' and was where the various support aircraft such as air-to-air refuellers and airborne early warning aircraft were positioned. A typical mission would see the F3s launching from Gioia, transiting to a tanker for refuelling so that they entered the operational area topped to full. The area over Bosnia was divided into four sub-areas and each formation would be allocated to a sector, and if further limited in height, a number of tactical formations could operate in the area simultaneously. The Air Tasking Order, or ATO, would determine the mission. After entering their allocated block via an entry point, the F3 navigators would search for potential targets which might be breaching the 'No-Fly Zone'. The mission was under the control of an E3 airborne early warning aircraft with instant access to the operational commander on the ground via secure radios. As they found potential targets, instructions to identify, shadow, or perhaps intervene, would be given. Once they had completed their allotted mission, the F3 crews would leave Bosnian airspace, returning down the transit corridor and back onto 'Mainstreet' in the Adriatic. Occasionally, post-mission tanking was scheduled, but given the close proximity of Gioia to the coast, the crews were mostly able to return the short distance without needing additional fuel.

The operational control of the F3 force was exercised by HQ Allied Forces Southern Europe from its headquarters in Naples with a subordinate Combined Air Operations Centre established at the Italian Air Force base at Vicenza in Northern Italy. The operations room was typical of a NATO facility. Huge digital displays covered the front wall and provided the key decision makers with tactical information on the air movements within the area of responsibility. The key tactical decision maker was the Senior Operations Officer, or SOO, a position I was to hold at a later date. For advice, I could call upon experts, including air-to-air refuelling and electronic warfare specialists and a mission director who worked closely with the E3 AWACS control aircraft. Italian controllers acted as a link to the civilian air traffic agencies to coordinate military and civilian movements. Another team monitored the Link 16 data link, ensuring that the recognised air picture was always accurate and available. Additionally, liaison officers for each aircraft type and a ground liaison officer who interfaced with army units were available on call. In the back room, the planners worked endlessly producing the daily plans. There were cells providing intelligence support and others operating the Predator unmanned air vehicle. The surveillance feed from the Predator, which was almost permanently airborne, was fed to a small monitor on my left-hand side. When a mission was underway I would watch it unfold in glorious monochrome on the TV screen. The feed was known as 'Predator Porn' and it was compulsive viewing. Frequently I would watch trucks being tracked around the Balkan countryside without knowing who the target was or why. Such specific operational details were quite rightly closely controlled and protected by a 'need to know'. All I needed to know was where the Predator was flying and how long it would be on task. I could then ensure that it did not affect my other fixed wing assets as it returned to its landing site, complying with its electronic commands.

As SOO, I was responsible for the detailed execution of the Air Tasking Order (ATO). The document issued daily directed each mission with its task for the day. During the height of Operation Deny Flight and the subsequent Operation Deliberate Force, air defence forces including the F3s had provided quick reaction alert forces in addition to the planned policing sorties. The SOO could call on these assets when breaches of the 'No Fly Zone' occurred, scrambling fighters to intercept offenders. A Battle Staff Director who was a NATO colonel or equivalent was responsible to the One Star CAOC Director for any decisions taken by the Battle Staff and often showed a close interest in my actions, being a little more detached from the hubbub of the operations room floor.

During the early stages of the operation there were many breaches of the resolution by fixed wing aircraft. Some estimates suggested there were as many as thirty per month, but it became clear that once NATO fighters began to patrol, these infractions reduced to a handful. The first serious incident came when Serbian Soko Jastreb fighter bombers attacked targets in Bosnia and were engaged by US F-16s, leading to four of the six Serbian jets being shot down. This was the first major engagement during the operation and it demonstrated to the leadership in Serbia that NATO was serious. There were few fixed wing violations in the years which followed. Subsequent pictures released in the media showed that Serbian fighter jets had been hidden in underground hangars to protect them from air attack and were rarely used.

Helicopters remained a problem, complicated by the fact that the Serbian leadership was well versed in deception techniques having trained in the Former Soviet Union. Helicopters were camouflaged to appear to be undertaking legitimate missions and unverified reports even suggested the application of Red Cross markings to airframes engaged in combat duties. Rules of Engagement were highly sensitive and rarely discussed openly. Suffice to say that there was little appetite to shoot down unarmed helicopters as the Serbian media was tightly controlled and much would have been made had a helicopter engaged on 'humanitarian tasks' been shot down. It could have been a public relations own goal by NATO despite flagrant breaches. For that reason, crews were normally tasked to intercept the helicopter to force it to land or, preferably, escort it clear of the area. Serbian pilots would often comply but once on the ground they would be hard to see. With limited fuel reserves over Bosnia and some distance from home, it would not be long before a fighter crew was forced to return to base. The intercepted helicopter pilot would then carry on with the mission once the fighter had left. On the positive side, this meant that reactive tactical support in any effective way was impossible and the helicopters were less useful. Undoubtedly, any helicopter seen to be engaging in hostile operations would have been dealt with firmly.

The F3 still suffered from an undeservedly poor reputation, but it achieved successes against the demanding helicopter targets. By 1993 Foxhunter was giving a useful capability and in some aspects was superior to the much vaunted US air-to-air radars. With heavy processing, the US fighters were often less able to see very slow targets. The F3 was extremely capable in certain areas given its excellent situation awareness with the tactical plan display. With a two man crew and the 'triplets' overlay, an F3 crew could track helicopters in track-while-scan quite well. A colleague told of first-hand experience during one particular operation when the Serbs had been able to maintain the flow of supplies into an operational area in Bosnia despite allied blockades. The allied commanders were mystified as to how. Once the F3s capabilities were explained, a pair of aircraft was tasked to search the area for potential breaches of the 'No Fly Zone' in order to enforce the restrictions. It transpired that Serbian helicopters had been moving stores at night using heavy lift helicopters and landing at a sports stadium in one of the major towns. At that point the stores were transferred to lorries for onward shipment to the Serbian troops. After close attention from the F3 crews over an intense period, the helicopter flights were suspended and the logistics chain disrupted.

Despite only limited media reporting back home, this was still very much a 'shooting war'; deployed crews trained in combat survival procedures, and combat search and rescue, or CSAR, became a topic close to their hearts. Equipped with the combat survival vests which had first been issued during the Gulf War, it was heartening to know that in the event of an ejection into hostile territory, attempts to rescue the downed aircrew would be made immediately. Firing the aircrew pistol became an essential skill which aircrew were keen to practice.

One of the key operational drivers later in the aircraft's life was its performance, or lack of, in the upper air, and this came under close scrutiny during Operation Deny Flight. In order to take part in NATO operations, the F3 was often tasked to operate at higher levels along with American fighters which enjoyed better performance. At those heights, the threat from medium level surface-to-air missiles was significant. After the loss of an F-16 in Serbian airspace to an SA-6 missile, the US sector controllers decided that all aircraft operating in the Balkans airspace should be equipped with self-protection jammers in order to have a reasonable chance of survival. At that time, the Tornado F3 was not equipped with an appropriate radar jamming system and was threatened with exclusion from Operation Deny Flight. An urgent operational requirement was instigated to fit a towed radar decoy system to the Tornado F3. The only pods that were cleared for carriage were the BOZ chaff pods and the Skyshadow jamming pods and a programme to clear a newly designed jamming pod would have taken many months, if not years. A solution was needed quickly so a BOZ chaff and flare pod was adapted by installing complex electronics. Fuel was critical for the out of area operation and external tanks were essential, so it was deemed unacceptable to replace the fuel tanks with the jamming pod. It was decided to fit Tornado GR1 outboard pylons to the F3 to enable it to carry both fuel tanks and the new jammer. The inboard pylons would continue to carry fuel tanks and the new outboard pylons would take jamming equipment, replicating the fit of the bomber version. Because the CSAS fly-by-wire system would have been adversely affected by carrying an asymmetric load, the jamming pod could not be carried alone. A Phimat chaff dispenser, which had first been used during the Gulf War, was fitted to the opposite outboard pylon, rebalancing the flight loads. Although its role was, in reality, to act as a complex 'balancing weight', it was a very capable defensive aids pod and able to provide a useful additional chaff payload which complemented the capability of the new jammer. The down side was that the F3 was now carrying not only two 1,500-litre external fuel tanks to give longer endurance, but also a jamming pod and a Phimat dispenser. This meant that it struggled to operate effectively above 25,000 feet as the engines were not designed to fight at such high levels carrying such weight. As other fighters such as the F-15 were routinely tasked in the high 20s to lower 30s, the F3s lack of performance was magnified. There were still many roles such as the anti-helicopter operations which the F3 was able to undertake, but rather than adapt to its capabilities, some planners used this fact as another stick with which to beat the Tornado F3. It did, however, cause embarrassment to the crews in theatre who felt like the poor relations. Back in the UK, this deficiency re-energised the arguments that the Tornado F3 should be re-engined with EJ200 engines being developed for Typhoon, and an enhancement measure was drafted for submission during the annual spending round. That the measure was not adopted is history.

One of the more satisfying milestones was achieved when a Tornado F3 of No. 111 (F) Squadron, crewed by my friend Shaun Vickers and his pilot, passed 5,000 flying hours for the aircraft, reassuringly when conducting live operations.

Operation Deny Flight ended officially on 21 December 1995 but I was to have a unique sequel during my later tour of duty in Vicenza. During this period, operations over Bosnia were 'normalising' in NATO parlance as the airspace was slowly returned to civilian control. Kosovo was still an intense area of air activity and tactical missions were tasked into the airspace throughout the daylight hours and into the late evening. Other than the surveillance assets, including the Predator, once the fighters landed at about 2300 the airspace was quiet. The night shift ran from 1800 to 0600 and could be quite tedious; once the next day's Air Tasking Order was prepared for the oncoming shift, the challenge was to stay awake during the 'wee small hours'. By then, the Mission Director and Sky News were my only companions as the other specialists were allowed a semblance of a normal life. Strong Italian coffee became a close cohort.

Milosevic had been ousted from power some months before when, in a coup which became known as the October 5th Revolution, his thirteen-year reign ended. By December 2000, he had been marginalised by the new leader Vojislav Kostunica and was under twenty-four-hour surveillance by his own police force in the capital Belgrade. Unbeknown to me, he had decided to make good his escape. Quick Reaction Alert had been stood down some months earlier as Serbia continued to abide by the post-conflict conditions. My only assets were fighters on a very relaxed readiness state so options to intervene in the early hours were extremely limited. It had been a quiet night shift but around midnight, Sky News, which was running on the monitor in the Ops Room, ran an item of breaking news from Belgrade. Milosevic had been seen leaving his residence and his whereabouts were unknown. Within minutes, I was to become an unreported part of the breaking news as I watched with interest a track originating in the Serbian capital. There was a strong likelihood that the news and the track were directly related. A quick call to my Operations Boss confirmed that we would not intervene, although in truth, we had few real options short of bringing one of the northern bases to readiness. Even that would have taken too much time. Now confirmed as a Serbian helicopter, the track departed Belgrade, heading south and slowly made its way towards the Serbian border and on into Montenegro, which was still friendly to Serbia. It disappeared from the screen in the area of Podgorica, close to the Adriatic coast. There was a military base close by which was home to a surface-to- air missile battery and it seemed to be the helicopter's final destination. A few years earlier I might have scrambled fighters, although in the hilly terrain and at night, it would have been a challenging intercept. As history now attests, Milosevic escaped that night and avoided being taken into custody, only finally being arrested having returned to Belgrade on 1 April 2001. He was, by then, a man wanted for war crimes with few friends. The helicopter flight south undoubtedly extended his liberty by many more months.

The First Gulf War left a defiant Saddam Hussein in power in Iraq and during the early years of the new millennium, enforcement of a 'No Fly Zone' was to be a feature of Tornado F3 operations. Unlike the wars, Operation 'Resinate', otherwise known by NATO as 'Northern Watch' and 'Southern Watch', was not widely reported in the media and remained just below the radar for most of the British public. The aircrew were less sanguine because, for them, it was just as dangerous as some of the operational missions during the conflict. The operation was split into two areas and designated by the RAF as Operation Resinate North and Operation Resinate South, mirroring the NATO division. In the north, Jaguar and Tornado GR4 bombers based at Incirlik in Turkey flew interdiction missions into Iraqi airspace on a daily basis. When NATO forces defending the 'No Fly Zone' were attacked by Iraqi air defence forces, the bombers delivered appropriate responses in self-defence.

The Tornado F3s were deployed in support of Operation Resinate South from a base at Al Kharj near Riyadh, well south of the Iraqi border in central Saudi Arabia. The formal title for the base was Prince Sultan's Airbase, shortened to PSAB, but more fondly known as 'Al's Garage'. In February 1999, six Tornado F3s replaced six Tornado GR4s and assumed air defence duties supported by VC10 tankers working from Bahrain. Although the airframes remained in theatre, each air defence squadron was tasked to provide crews for an extended period of time, typically four months, and manned the jets in rotation. They shared ramp space with EA6B Prowler electronic warfare aircraft and Mirage 2000 fighters of the French Air Force. As had been the practice in the Balkans, the UN passed a series of resolutions preventing the Iraqi Air Force from flying over Iraqi airspace and NATO air forces enforced the resolutions by policing the 'No Fly Zone' over the whole country. For the F3 crews, their operational airspace in the south of Iraq was delineated by the 33rd North parallel of latitude.

Again, the Tornado F3 proved well equipped to support the air policing role. By then, the Joint Tactical Information and Distribution System, or JTIDS, had been introduced, giving F3 crews superb situation awareness. The F3 crews had as much information as more capable surveillance platforms and perhaps more than American fighters as the information was fully integrated into the tactical displays. This allowed crews to prosecute interceptions which fighters with less situation awareness would have found impossible. With the radar homing and warning receiver, BOL and Phimat chaff dispensers, Vinten flare dispensers, and the towed radar decoy system, the aircraft was well defended if attacked by surface-to-air missiles. As always, its limitation was performance in the upper air, but there was a new concern—an increasingly obsolescent missile fit.

The Iraqi Air Force had not recovered from its blunder when it deployed its aircraft to Iran during the earlier Gulf War. Iran had welcomed the assets and put some of them into service, leaving a motley collection of aircraft remaining in Iraq. Some were still capable such as the Soviet-supplied Mig-25 Foxbats and French-supplied Mirage F1s, and they often flew to provoke the NATO crews. A former colleague described one incident:

> Back in Oct/Nov 99 I locked up an Iraqi Mig declared 'hostile' on JTIDS just inside the no-fly zone about 5 miles from the Skyflash Launch Success Zone (LSZ). Late Arm was made live and the next action was to ditch the tanks when the Mig turned around and went back over the line—my LSZ and excitement shrinking with it! Did the F3 do its job that day? You bet and the RIVET JOINT and E3 High Value Assets they were trying so very hard to shoot down were never threatened. Saddam even rewarded one of his Mig drivers a pair of Silver Pistols for getting close to some HVAs on a previous sortie; so the stakes were high during Op Southern Watch.

Back in UK, the politicians were taking a much greater interest in operations and the F3 attracted close scrutiny in the Thirteenth Report of the House of Commons Defence Select Committee after a delegation had visited the base a year earlier. It gave an interesting insight the mindset of politicians.

Appropriateness and serviceability of equipment
TORNADO F3 AIRCRAFT

During our visit to RAF personnel based at Prince Sultan Air Base in Saudi Arabia, we were told about some of the performance problems demonstrated by their Tornado F3 aircraft in undertaking no-fly zone missions. The high temperatures in the Gulf have a significant effect on the performance of the aircraft, preventing them from being able to fly high enough to reach an ideal altitude, in contrast to the US Air Force's F-15s, which regularly fly at 40,000 feet. The Secretary of State told us that all fast jets experience performance problems in hot climates unless they are specifically adapted to operate in that environment and that all F3s deployed on Operation Bolton had been provided with additional cooling equipment to counter this. The F3 was originally intended for air defence of the UK, operating primarily over the North Sea.

There were also serviceability problems with the F3. The usual pattern in practice was for four aircraft to takeoff on a mission; the two performing best on the day would continue on the mission; one would remain in the vicinity of the tanker aircraft in case it was needed; and the one performing least well would return to base. The dangerous nature of the missions means that minor problems with equipment cannot be tolerated in the way they might be on training exercises. The Director of Air Operations told us that all aircraft on operational detachments were given priority in receiving spares and that serviceability of aircraft in all of our operational attachments is more than adequate to meet the task that we have been set by the commander in the field.

In response to a parliamentary question about the serviceability of Tornado aircraft, the MoD said that 'operational serviceability of front-line aircraft fluctuates each day according to the maintenance that is required' and as an illustration provided a 'snapshot' of aircraft available on a particular day. On 26 January this year, 79 of the 86 front-line F3s were classified as serviceable. This includes those which require 'first line servicing', undertaken by the deployed squadron itself, where faults can be rectified in a few hours.

Ministers have accepted the limitations of the Tornado F3 for some time. We all recognise that the RAF's F3 Tornado has a limited further life. It is not an agile aircraft. It was designed to deal with the Cold War threat of Soviet long-range bomber attack on the United Kingdom. The missile upgrade currently being implemented will, of course, make it a much more effective system, but that can be no more than a relatively short-term solution. The MoD is undertaking a £140 million upgrade programme for the Tornado F3, announced in late 1997 and known as the Capability Sustainment Programme (CSP) which is intended to provide the RAF with an aircraft which meets its current requirements until Eurofighter becomes available. The Director of Air Operations told us that the CSP will give the F3 the capability to fire advance short range and medium range air-to-air missiles (ASRAAM and AMRAAM) and will improve the navigation equipment and radar performance. It also includes fitting the Tornados with a Successor Identification Friend or Foe (SIFF) system to allow pilots to identify aircraft flying near them more effectively by electronic means rather than relying on identification by eye. Unmodified aircraft will be kept in service until 2007 and the CSP F3s until 2010. The Director of Air Operations told us that Eurofighter would be an 'ideal aeroplane' to carry out the missions currently undertaken in the no-fly zones by the Tornado F3, that it would be similar to the US Air Force F-15 and that it would not suffer from temperature problems.

We understand the frustrations of our air-crew in undertaking difficult missions with aircraft which are not ideal for the task, particularly when they are operating alongside their US colleagues who have demonstrably superior equipment. The

Secretary of State pointed out the difference in the budgets available to him and to his US counterpart. Although we have made clear on a number of occasions our view that the UK defence budget should be increased, we accept that the realities of living within any level of budget mean that expensive equipment cannot always be replaced as quickly as would be ideal. However, we expect the MoD to provide all RAF air-crew undertaking dangerous missions in the no-fly zones with upgraded F3 aircraft as soon as possible and to ensure that the highest levels of serviceability are maintained on all aircraft participating in the mission.

House of Commons Defence Select Committee,13th Report published 10 August 2006.

While the interest was welcome, the politicians were 'late on parade' and most of the issues were already well known and had been constantly highlighted by military staff for some years. Performance at altitude had been identified during Operation Deny Flight some thirteen years earlier and it should have come as no surprise that additional cooling was needed to allow the aircraft to cope with the high temperatures in the desert as procedures had been developed as early as 1986. The Royal Saudi Air Force had, after all, operated the F3 since the late 1980s. Highlighting inadequate spares provision for the Tornado force was welcome. Successive savings measures had depleted the already lean spares pool and, with the limited spares being diverted to operations, aircrew and maintenance personnel preparing for future operational deployments met critical shortages.

The practice of launching four aircraft to ensure two fully serviceable jets, while depressing, merely reflected operational prudence. Combat aircraft are complex machines and contingency planning ensured that fully capable fighters crossed into the operational area. If tensions and tasking increased, such luxuries would have been impossible. Nevertheless, it is easy to be cynical, yet the intervention of a Defence Committee would have been extremely useful to staff officers in MoD at that time and would have provided welcome ammunition. Had such interest been shown earlier, perhaps operationally essential modifications would have been funded sooner and might have been fielded prior to the event rather than under contingency procedures.

Returning from politics to operations, Saddam's air defences had survived the First Gulf War relatively intact. He was still able to field an integrated air defence system comprising ground-based air defence radars and surface-to-air missile batteries. In its original form, the infrastructure had looked remarkably similar to that of the former Soviet Union which had provided much of the equipment. The area radars were older generation Soviet early warning systems which cued the SAMs to illuminate their targets with their own tracking radars as NATO aircraft approached. Following doctrine, the air defence commander would allocate a track to a SAM battalion. Within the battalion, an individual fire unit would be nominated and its commander would illuminate the target with his own tracking radar before launching a radar-guided missile at the target. Unfortunately for the

Iraqis, NATO analysts quickly began to locate these fixed installations. When Iraqi forces fired on a NATO aircraft the offending SAM battery could easily be identified from its radar emissions and would quickly be destroyed. Even so, horrific video footage from cameras aboard returning aircraft showed SAMs passing extremely close to the NATO jets. It was a miracle that more NATO aircraft were not lost.

Saddam's forces began to be more imaginative but realised that if they locked their trackers to the opponent, the NATO pilots would see that as a hostile gesture and would exact retribution. The F-16 Wild Weasels equipped with HARM anti-radiation missiles would lock onto the emitted radar beam and destroy the tracking radar. Many of the fixed installations were attacked and destroyed; as a consequence, Iraqi commanders began moving their SAMs around the countryside so that they were harder to locate. Vulnerable reconnaissance platforms would then have to search for the new positions, making them vulnerable to attack. The commanders also became quite cunning with how they dispersed their SAMs setting up complex ambushes, first to lure NATO aircraft into the vicinity and then force them into predictable manoeuvres which the SAM commanders could exploit. Luckily, NATO expertise and tactics outwitted Iraqi guile, but it was a more challenging battle than was ever reported in the media.

There were many incidents, but one specifically affected the Tornado F3. It occurred during an Operation Resinate mission and, although precise details may have gone unreported, I can relate the broad facts given that both the Tornado F3 has retired and the Iraqi air defence system no longer exists. If threatened by a surface-to-air missile, crews use highly complex tactical defensive manoeuvres to evade the missile. The tactics were validated on operational test ranges and practiced during training missions. Tornado F3 crews would use their defensive aids such as chaff and radar countermeasures at carefully determined critical points. By flying the defensive manoeuvre the lock of the tracking radar was broken making it harder for the threat weapon system to reacquire the Tornado. During the Cold War when low-level tactics were the norm, the safest place to hide was 'on the deck'. At medium level where the F3 was tasked during this operation the problem was more complex. To fly the manoeuvre to the limits, a Tornado F3 pilot needed to jettison the large external fuel tanks which limit the performance, thereby making the aircraft much more responsive. Once the multi-dimensional manoeuvre had been flown and the SAM had been defeated, the crew would make their escape hugging the terrain.

On this day, an F3 crew was heading into the operational area when the radar homing and warning receiver lit up with a lock from a surface-to-air missile closely followed by the warning for missile guidance. They executed a perfect tactical defence, jettisoning the tanks and descending to low level just above the desert floor, and headed back towards the Saudi border. There was no visual contact with the missile but a nervous crew returned to base feeling that they had just dodged a bullet, with the only evidence being their fuel tanks embedded in the desert floor.

When the experts began to analyse the engagement, there was no evidence of a SAM in the local area, which was perplexing. Analysts began to look for other radars but could find nothing which could have caused a lock-on indication. Luckily the incident had been captured by the onboard recorders or the crew may have faced criticism that they had invented the whole thing. Eventually, a sharp analyst noticed that an EA6B Prowler had followed the Tornado F3 into the area and at precisely the time that the F3 had been illuminated, the Prowler crew had been carrying out checks on their jamming equipment prior to an operational mission. One of the checks might have caused the indications which the Tornado crew had seen on their sensors. Everyone had acted correctly but the reason for the RHWR alert seemed to be an example of mutual electronic interference which occurs occasionally in combat conditions. No harm was done other than planting a pair of 2,250-litre fuel tanks in the desert, but even with the best military planning and the most effective avionics, errors can still occur.

There are very few accounts of what it was like during operations at that time, but a colleague and fellow Tornado F3 navigator Neil Whitehead published this gripping account of the F3's often unsung contribution, which is worthy of repeating.

An Air Defender's Perspective During Operation TELIC

Operation (or Op) TELIC is the codename under which all British operations of the 2003 Invasion of Iraq and after were conducted. A total of 46,000 troops of all the British Services were committed to the operation at its start. At the peak of the campaign, some 26,000 British Army soldiers, 4,000 Royal Marines, 5,000 Royal Navy and Royal Fleet Auxiliary sailors and 8,100 Royal Air Force personnel were in action.

Operation Telic is one of the largest deployments of British forces since WWII. It is only approached in size by the 1991 Operation Granby deployment for the Gulf War and the 1956 Operation Musketeer Suez Crisis deployment. It was considerably larger than the 1982 Operation Corporate in the Falklands War, which saw around 30,000 personnel deployed, and the Korean War, which saw fewer than 20,000 personnel deployed. The following account is given by a member of the Tornado F3 Force who took part in this operation.

I found myself on the 'trooper' to Prince Sultan Air Base, Al Karhj, KSA in Feb 2003—I was part of the final 'reinforcement crews' going to man the Tornado F3 force for any offensive operations against Iraq. Operations had been going on for some time under the guise of the Southern No-Fly Zone, but as the political events were escalating, so was the presence of men and material in theatre. PSAB is in the middle of the Saudi Kingdom and had seen quite a prolific build up of American forces there for several years—it was also the main Combined Air Operations Centre for the theatre. All of this meant that the recreational facilities there were to a very high standard—we were also a long way from the Iraqi border and with very little media presence due to the Saudi insistence of us flying from a 'secret base'.

Seeing as the final reinforcements were being deployed in the first place, we were fairly confident that there would be an escalation and a shift in operations. However, up until that point it would still be business as usual with the No-Fly Zone (termed Op RESINATE) patrolling and the corresponding rules of engagement. This had come into effect as a result of the first Gulf War and 'allowed' us to patrol as far north as Baghdad and ensure there were no Iraqi aircraft present. Targeting their air defence systems, ranging from surveillance radars to actual missile batteries, was also part of the enforcement. Offensive operations were already being carried out well before Op TELIC (as the British refer to Iraqi Freedom) commenced. There was also a large recce presence, both in terms of photographic platforms, but also a dearth of electronic 'vacuum cleaners'. Our job during any of these missions was to ensure control of the air to allow either recce or strike platforms to carry out their task.

The tempo of RESINATE missions also increased—initially we would only be over Iraq for a single hour a day, then 2 until soon we were building up to a 24 hour presence. As mentioned, PSAB is located some distance from the border, and prior to crossing into Iraqi airspace it was essential that every fast jet aircraft had refuelled—the majority also had to refuel after crossing back out just to get home. The number of aircraft required to keep a permanent presence soon escalated and the ramp at PSAB soon became quite full. Part of the political 'deal' the Saudi's had struck for the use of their base was that no bombers could be based on their soil—these aircraft had to come from Qatar or Kuwait, so the variety of types limited to PSAB was quite spectacular: RAF Nimrods, Sentrys, VC10s plus F3s—USAF KC10s, KC135s, AWACS, JSTARS, RC135Us, EA6Bs, F-15Cs, F-16CJs and U2s. Phew! Additionally there were regular transport aircraft bringing in all the supplies that all these aircraft plus their crews would require.

The Tornado F3 had been part of the No-Fly Zone for several years, and as such, we were used to PSAB and what it had to offer. With such a large influx of people though, it filled the available accommodation to bursting, and so temporary arrangements had to be made for those not considered essential. However, everyone was able to eat at canteens open 24 hours a day or swim or make use of the free cinema or a well equipped gym. As I said, fortunately there was a large American presence, and one which at the time we took for granted and considered 'normal'. I was soon to see that that was not quite the case!

Our Tornado 'bomber' colleagues flew from Ali-al Salem in Kuwait and also from Qatar. The ones based in Qatar had similar distances as us to fly prior to crossing the border and could also enjoy the comforts brought to the base by their American counterparts. The ones in Kuwait, however, were very close to the frontline!

After a short while, we knew when the 'Shock & Awe' that was the desired American effect would commence. There was a slick changeover between whether you had got airborne on a No-Fly Zone sortie or whether you were now off to war and had a new set of rules of engagement. On the first 'war' sortie that I was on, we unfortunately had a generator malfunction once we had crossed back to the friendly side of the border. As the Tornado is an electric jet, it is desirable to have two generators but essential to have one. Faced with a choice now of flying for over

200 miles versus diverting to a Tornado base just 40 miles away, the decision would seem simple enough. As a result we flew to the aforementioned base in Kuwait. We had been told to fly with our gas masks should we land somewhere in the middle of a 'chemical' attack, but we had made light of this. Now landing in Kuwait the first thing we were given was a chemical suit—still vacuum-packed—and told where the nearest shelter was. Hmm. Everybody also carried the gas masks on their person and carried their suits with them too. Back at PSAB, we only had to have our masks 'to hand' i.e. in the same room, and had no idea where the nearest shelter was.

Soon banter was flowing between the bomber losers and us air-defender heroes when we thought we'd go for a bite to eat, giving us our first chance to look around the base. Ali-al Salem is very much an RAF base with a very small American presence, and as such the facilities are on a much smaller scale. There are even bomb-craters around the HAS site from the 1st Gulf War. The catering, though by British field services, was to a very impressive standard. Suddenly, the air-raid siren went.

During training, they say that you have 9 seconds to get your gas mask on before you may feel the effects of any chemical agents. Let me tell you that it takes a lot less than 9 seconds to get your mask on for real! Now, where was that nearest shelter that had been pointed out? No idea—we were nowhere near it now that we had gone to lunch. Where is everyone else running to? Follow them! The shelters consisted of several concrete blocks that had then been covered with lots and lots of sand—lots and lots of sand. With everyone running and then getting their chemical suits on (at this time a full biological or chemical attack was suspected) so much sand was kicked up in the shelter that you needed a gas mask on just to see. The personnel at Ali had been subjected to a few of these attacks by the time we got there, and as such were slightly more practised than we were, so my next recollection is of an entire bunker watching as my pilot and I struggled to get into our vacuum-packed suits. After what seemed like a very long time we were suited up, just in time to hear the thumps of the outgoing Patriot battery firing on the incoming Scuds.

The all-clear soon went. That meant doing an individual sniff test. I was definitely going to be the last one in the bunker to take my mask off! Unfortunately we were close to the end and so had to be first to leave! However, I couldn't smell anything and as things got back to normal there was still time to finish our lunch!

That night we had 2 further air raids—we were becoming quite practised ourselves at putting on our suits and soon felt quite blasé about the air raids and associated Patriots. It was the next morning when the television news was reporting that an RAF aircraft had been shot down. At the time there seemed nothing untoward at Ali al Salem, but looking back, the clues were all there. It was only after we had returned to PSAB that we learned that it was a Tornado from the Kuwait base, and shot down by a Patriot to boot. What had I said about feeling blasé earlier?

Back at PSAB we felt grateful for being so far from the border, and went to get an ice cream by the poolside. Communication home was also much improved from PSAB, with several internet points plus phones allowing easy access to loved ones. Whilst in Kuwait, I had at least managed to send a message home but that may have well raised more questions than answered due to how cryptic I was trying to be.

We flew several more sorties before it was decided to reduce the number of air superiority fighters in the air—the Iraqis, despite being a formidable force, had shown their resistance to the regime by burying their aircraft instead of launching them to face certain destruction. We fired no shots in anger. As such, we were then able to leave Saudi whilst the troops were just entering Baghdad. PSAB soon closed, much to the Saudis' pleasure. The heroic air defenders in the F3 force returned home and had to face a public who knew nothing about what we had done, seeing as there were no correspondents allowed onto our base—this fact also delighted our mud-moving brethren!

My experience of conflict has a blinkered viewpoint, flying from the relative luxury that was PSAB. Certainly diverting into Kuwait allowed me a different insight into how lucky we had it. Looking back though, as there has been no operational F3 flying since, I do feel a certain amount of pride at having been involved.

Another colleague offered his own insight on a military aircrew discussion forum:

For Telic 1 [the Iraqi Operation], ASRAAM had arrived but AMRAAM wasn't fitted. While it's true the air threat never materialised, no-one expected that to be the case—particularly in light of the (rarely mentioned) Mig25 and Mig23 activity in the week before the campaign started. There's a lot of hoop spouted about what the F3s actually did in Telic, and I've often heard it said they were never in harm's way. Truth is, CAPing in Balad SE's overhead, committing against reported helos north of Baghdad or flying shotgun for the single GR4 over central Baghdad because he had no wingman never even made it into the MISREPs [mission reports] because it was seen as routine compared with what the muds were doing.

Suffice to say that F3 crews made a significant and mostly unacknowledged contribution which was rarely reported in the media.

An operational commitment which rarely made the news was the need to reinforce Gibraltar. Some might say it was to keep out the Spanish but the truth was that the southern neighbours were less than friendly at times. During the Libyan crisis in the 1980s, Phantoms reinforced the airfield, holding QRA to guard against rogue attacks. This commitment continued into the Tornado F3 era and saw detachments visit on a regular basis. With its short east/west runway with approaches over the sea, operating from the airfield had its challenges. Those who have, tell of some interesting conditions on short finals with unpredictable airflow around the Rock of Gibraltar. That the runway was bisected by a main road merely added to the spice. If nothing else, the setting made for stunning photographic opportunities, one of which is included in the colour section.

Another unsung operational task which continued throughout the more newsworthy operations was the enduring commitment to defend the Falkland Islands. My own contribution was a stint commanding No. 1435 Flight which was the Tornado F3 unit which defended the islands. What I had not realised at

A Tornado F3 of No. 111 Squadron crosses the road in Gibraltar. (*Steve Smyth*)

the time was that, due to radical downsizing of the air defence force in the UK, this was to be my final flying tour. Given the reduction in force numbers with the retirement of the Phantom squadrons, I would never realise my ambition of commanding a full squadron, but my experiences in the Falkland Islands would be just as dramatic and just as challenging.

As deputy commander of the Tornado F3 Operational Conversion Unit, I was responsible for the day-to-day running of the flying operations. The OCU was huge, being twice the size of a normal squadron. At peak strength, the OCU had twenty-six Tornados on charge with forty instructors and up to thirty student aircrew. The pace of life was hectic and the pressure to graduate courses on time was relentless. In comparison, the four Tornados of No. 1435 Flight, five crews and fifty-five groundcrew was a tiny outfit. The difference was that being 8,000 miles from home and three hours behind UK time, there was little, if any, hands-on control from Headquarters No. 11 Group, which exercised operational control of the detachment. My task was stunningly simple. I had four aircraft to defend the islands from air attack until reinforcements could be flown in. To do so I had to guarantee keeping two aircraft at a constant 'Readiness 10', 365 days a year, to guard against any potential air intruders. There were absolutely no excuses for a failure to do so. Within broad guidelines, I had total flexibility. This really was a very large and expensive 'train set', yet the task was critical but clear.

The Falklands operation was set up differently to other RAF units in the UK. Because the numbers were smaller, each aircraft type was technically a Flight. In the UK, a squadron was equipped with twelve aircraft and commanded by a wing commander. 'Down South', each flying unit had, at most, four aircraft, and was commanded by a squadron leader. No. 1435 Flight had four Tornado F3s, No. 1312 Flight had two Hercules, and to make matters completely confusing, No. 78 Squadron operated a Chinook and two Sea Kings but was still commanded by a squadron leader. The Officer Commanding Operations Wing was in overall command of the flying effort, reporting to an RAF Group Captain Station Commander who reported to the Commander British Forces Falkland Islands, or CBFFI.

The Tornado Dispersal sat at the north-eastern end of the airfield. The buildings were of modern construction as the airfield had only been built in 1985. A small operations and engineering complex was the hub of the squadron and provided offices and working space for the squadron personnel. The aircraft operated from 'Housies' which was a take on the term HAS, or hardened aircraft shelter. As the shelters were built of traditional steel rather than the concrete structures of the Cold War, they picked up the appropriate nickname. A quick look at Google Maps shows the two complexes with sixteen shelters built around a loop taxiway. The short runway dissected the two complexes. Given that the Flight operated only four Tornado F3s, the normal operations were conducted from the most easterly section of the dispersal. Quick Reaction Alert (QRA) was the whole focus of the flying activity and the QRA aircraft were operated from the 'housies' nearest the runway with the alert personnel living in the 'Q Shed' for the duration of their twenty-four-hour duty.

The shift pattern was brutal and was set within a ten-day cycle. The cycle began with a twenty-four-hour QRA duty and ended on day nine with a final twenty-four-hour QRA duty. In between, days on 'Q' were interspersed with days flying the remaining two aircraft for training purposes. In addition to the two alert crews, a further crew was nominated as Q3, which meant that they were on a more relaxed thirty-minute readiness. It did, however, mean that the bar was off-limits for that period of duty as they might be called upon to fly. The final stint on QRA finished at 7.30 a.m. on day nine, leading into two days rest and recuperation, or R&R. In practice, however, the next stint of QRA began at 7.30 p.m. on day ten so there was never a full day off.

Aircrew rotated every five weeks so that they could maintain currency in essential skills, particularly emergency drills, in the simulator back in the UK. The Boss of the Flight and the groundcrew spent a full four-month detachment in the South Atlantic. Although it was normally only possible to launch a pair of Tornados, the flying could still be varied. The other residents, the C-130s, the helicopters, and the Tristars, were always available as training targets. Welcoming all new arrivals to the islands by joining in formation alongside the Tristar was a tradition and the first sign for new arrivals that the islands were a little different to the UK. There were no low flying restrictions and ranging across East and West Falklands at low level was the norm. Offshore, there were no limitations in airspace and operations were conducted from sea level to 'the moon', or as high as a 'clean' F3 would fly! With three control and reporting centres and an air defence piquet ship, competition to control a pair of fighters was fierce. The biggest challenge was the weather; ensuring that it remained suitable to allow a recovery to the main 10,000-foot-long runway was a priority. There was a short secondary runway but, at only 5,000 feet long, the approach from the north over Pleasant Peak could be demanding given the gusty conditions that were prevalent.

A typical sortie would be for a pair to launch and carry out a 'Fiery Cross' tracking exercise to train the Rapier surface-to-air missile crews. Simulating hostile fighters, the F3s would position away from the airfield and carry out a mock airfield attack during which the Rapier crews would lock on and simulate engaging the F3s with their missiles. Afterwards, a transit to the area would precede a session of mutual day tactics intercepts. If a C-130 was available to play, it could provide a surprisingly challenging target. It was almost impossible to arrive at the merge unseen as the C-130 crew would be positioned in every available window watching for the inbound fighters. Even using two Tornados and ganging up on 'Albert', as the C-130 was known, would result in a good deal of 'turning and burning' at low level before a missile shot was possible. The helicopters were even less sporting as the favourite tactic was merely to land, making a visual detection extremely difficult. Additionally, a helicopter was such a slow target that it was a challenge to detect on radar as it had little Doppler closure. It was sometimes rejected as too slow to be an airborne target, making an intercept difficult. Without a doubt, the most stimulating target was the Argentinian signals intelligence aircraft which probed the 200-mile Falkland Islands Protection Zone occasionally. In the years immediately following the conflict, intrusions were more prevalent, but as tensions dropped, instances became rarer. Even so, I chased an Argentinian Boeing 707 a long way to the west on one occasion. That he made his run into the Zone around the time that we were approaching fuel minimums was no coincidence. I'm sure they would have been listening as we asked for clearance to close into formation. That we were hauled off as he left the Zone must have been a relief to the crew. Happily, no combat aircraft ever penetrated the Zone as that may have caused consternation at many levels from the cockpit to the highest echelons of command.

Personnel were accommodated in an accommodation block known affectionately as 'The Death Star' after the space ship in *Star Wars*. Each unit had its own area and No. 1435 Flight lived in its own corridor with a lounge known as 'The Goose' after the local birds. The main feature of 'The Goose' was obvious as you walked along the corridor. Artwork representing the squadron badges of every squadron which had provided crews for No. 1435 Flight had been painted along each wall. The insignia ranged from fine renditions of squadron patches through depictions of Phantoms and Tornados which had equipped the Flight, to some not particularly complimentary cartoons. As Squadron Boss, it was quite amusing to see how some squadron crews viewed the Operational Conversion Unit. The cartoon for No. 65 (Reserve) Squadron, which became No. 56 (Reserve) Squadron, was of a pair of aged aircrew, one of whom was being pulled along in a wheel chair. Around the sign for the lounge which showed a male Upland Goose were the flying patches of every aircrew member who had served on No. 1435 Flight. Normally pinned to the wall in pairs, pilot and navigator, the badges were a permanent reminder of time spent at the outer reaches of the former empire. Particularly poignant were the badges of those who had lost their lives in the service of their country. These badges were reaffixed upside down to mark their loss.

I described the operation at great length in *Fighters Over The Falklands,* so if the subject is of interest you will find much more detail there. After my sojourn 'Down South', I was to return to a very different challenge to my flying job, yet just as relevant to the Tornado F3. The next step was another stint in the Ministry of Defence.

11

Life as an MoD Desk Officer

Life as an MoD staff officer could be a thankless task. I first arrived in the Ministry of Defence 'Main Building' in Whitehall in 1987 fresh from the squadron and full of naïve enthusiasm that, being at the seat of power, I would be able to change things for the Tornado F3 for the better. In the event I had little to do with the aircraft until I was tasked to implement the Gulf War modifications. Those modifications certainly changed things and began to turn around the aircraft's fortunes although some argued that it was not for the better. I have always disagreed. During my second stint in the MoD I was to be directly involved with the aircraft and its fate as I became the single service sponsor for a number of the vital programmes which would revolutionise the F3 and how it operated.

There is one critical factor for a defence project, and that is money. Without funding, a project cannot progress even to feasibility studies. Knowing that there is an operational deficiency is not enough, and officials who have little idea of how an aircraft flies let alone how it ticks operationally have to be convinced of the need. Even when funded, there are reviews and decision points to exercise scrutiny, but these can detract from the aim which is to produce equipment that works and can be maintained in a timely way. There are conflicting objectives within a project. Aircrew want equipment which works, will win an engagement and, hence, the war. Engineers want something which can be tested and maintained. Project managers want a tight programme which comes in, on cost, on time. Contractors want to produce good equipment but need to make a profit. Most of these objectives are mutually exclusive. A tight contract and stringent performance goals are expensive. The rigid systematic hierarchy, which is designed to add 'checks and balances' often means that progress can be stifled by the very bureaucracy which is supposed to prevent delays and cost overruns. Frequently, a clear requirement becomes blurred during the staffing process. However, there is one truism. The Ministry of Defence has been likened to a super tanker and diverting it from its course to satisfy the needs on an individual project is impossible.

The procurement system has changed much since the Tornado F3 was conceived, but in order to understand why the aircraft developed as it did, I will start with the system in place at the time of its inception. No one person develops an aircraft, and what the pilots, the navigators, and the engineers see at the front line is the product of many people's efforts. In the case of the F3, it matured eventually because of the efforts of the operational requirements staff, the single service Air Defence staff, the procurement experts, the engineering staff, and the testing community, and with the exception of procurement, I dipped into each level of that development at some time during the F3's service.

During my first tour in operational requirements, equipment was bought under a process known as 'The Downey Cycle', which was driven by the funding process. The budget was prepared on a ten-year basis with the first two years being prepared to a high level of detail, the next three at a lesser level, and the remaining five years at a low level of detail. This process was known as the Long Term Costings or LTC Process. The proposed measures were prioritised into a number of categories with the first being 'realism measures'. These were measures which had been introduced in the previous year and had been funded under contingency arrangements to meet a high priority or an urgent operational need. It was assumed that, if they had been urgent last year, they would be funded as a matter of urgency this year, so they rose to the top of the list. Next would be the high priority measures, and finally lower priority measures. At some point down the list a line was drawn and those above were funded and those below went back into next year's bun fight. Additionally, a few projects were offered as savings measures if they were no longer required. In those days with flexibility in the budget, staffs were reluctant to offer savings unless demanded as, once gone, realistically there was no way a project would ever be re-approved in the future. Nowadays, 'spare' defence funding is a contradiction of terms and this is not a model that the staff officer of today would recognise.

The first link in the chain to producing new equipment was the Operational Requirements (OR) Officer who held a joint- or tri-service appointment in the Central Staff of the MoD. After the OR officer had raised a requirement and it had been endorsed, it was handed to the MoD Procurement Executive or MoD (PE). The MoD (PE) staff officer, frequently a civilian who had never flown an aeroplane, raised a specification often in conjunction with an expert from the defence research community such as the former Royal Aircraft Establishment at Farnborough. Once agreed, the specification was sent to industry. Interested companies bid for the programme and a successful contractor was chosen from the companies who submitted proposals. The winning bid then went forward to project definition then full development, production, and testing. As the equipment moved forward to testing, it was evaluated firstly by the development test agency for 'fitness for purpose', a military term which has crept into daily use. The next stage would be operational testing to ensure that the equipment worked in the environment in which it was envisaged to operate and that it met the needs of a typical operator. Finally, the 'mature' system was handed by OR to the single service sponsor for the rest of its service life.

Operational testing was often neglected because of time or funding pressures. In order to get a system through scrutiny, quite often cost estimates would be optimistic. Once endorsed, only limited cost increases could be approved unless the requirement went back to higher committees for re-endorsement. As money was spent through development and the funds were committed, shortcuts were identified to stay within budget. One of the early casualties was testing. Development testing was mandatory to prove specification compliance. In order to sign off a basic 'fit for purpose', the system would first be evaluated by the manufacturer before being handed on to the development test organisation , in the case of RAF aircraft, the Aircraft and Armament Experimental and Evaluation Unit (A&AEE) at Boscombe Down. Providing a MoD (PE) project officer could sign off the new system as safe, it could be passed into service. Operational testing would, invariably, be squeezed, leading to inadequate validation of true capability.

Using an electronic warfare jamming system as an example, development testing ensured that the new system would not cause the aircraft to crash or turn upside down. This was known as 'switch on' clearance, but it did not prove that it would jam the 'SA-97' or whichever threat it had been specified against, or that the operator could use it effectively in the cockpit. Tornado F3 suffered massively from this anomaly. Even the innocent bystander would realise that this was not a satisfactory state of affairs and change was needed.

The process was replaced in 1997 by 'Smart Procurement'. Under the new system all the 'stakeholders' were brought together under an Integrated Project Team which would take the project through from concept to introduction to service to disposal. Typhoon was one of the early candidates for this new approach. Under this methodology, the IPT leader was responsible for delivering a piece of equipment which not only arrived on time and on cost, but was proven to work as envisaged. The IPT Leader was the 'best man for the job' so could be a civil servant, but could equally be a serviceman or ex-serviceman. It was no longer acceptable to throw a broken system 'over the fence' and expect it to be fixed in service. The aim was to give the operators something which met the operational requirement and could be maintained on the front line. This led to some successes but also some spectacular failures.

There were six stages of a project:

1. Concept, which was followed by 'Initial Gate', when the decision was taken whether to proceed.
2. Assessment leading to 'Main Gate', when the project was funded allowing it to go to full definition and production.
3. Demonstration using prototypes to prove it worked.
4. Manufacture, when production standard systems were built.
5. In service.
6. Disposal, which also incurred costs.

A transition period was agreed during which systems already being produced would be classified as 'legacy programmes' and would not be as tightly controlled under the new regime. With twenty-year project cycles, these legacy systems remained in development for many years beyond the transition and some still do. Tornado F3 pre-dated Smart Procurement and was designated as a 'legacy programme', which meant that although a Tornado Integrated Project Team was formed, most procurement was under modified procedures and many of the new rules did not apply. For that reason, many of the issues which I will describe were as a result of old practice where the OR officer often was the only 'corporate conscience' and the procurement manager was congratulated for being 'on time, on cost' whether the aircraft worked or not. Fortuitously, during the critical years when F3 was being brought up to specification, one of the best assistant directors (AD) in the history of the Procurement Executive was responsible for the aircraft. Without his remarkable efforts, it would have remained in the dark ages. If the AD said it couldn't be done, it really couldn't be done!

One of the advantages of modern communications is that feedback which might otherwise have remained unsaid is posted anonymously online. Before modern networking, a sponsor relied on formal feedback which could be slow and might be distorted by the staffing process. It was not always easy to understand why a system was failing as military careers could be ended by negativity. The military ethos is to fix a problem but to complain endlessly in the meantime. The online Military Rumour network, PPrune, allows serving personnel who are often muzzled by a risk averse media posture, to vent opinions anonymously. I read a post from a respected colleague a few years after I retired. Many of his criticisms were for projects that I'd been responsible for over the years and we must have spoken about the issues in the bar at RAF Coningsby on many occasions, but if so, I had failed to influence his thinking. His summary of the problems which the Tornado F3 fleet had suffered was accurate yet depressing:

> I was, am, a big fan of the Lincolnshire Land Shark, and will spring to its defence on unfair criticism, but there were some barking things that went on with it for short spells of its 25 years in service; like uncontained engine let-goes, Radar mods [modifications] that took an age to fix against some of our likely adversaries, the fitment of too small a flare in GW1 (and the lengthy retrofit), the re-measurement of everyone for the single and twin-stickers that were over 6ft tall (and the subsequent grounding of those found too big that had flown in it for years), the reticence to fit AMRAAM/ASRAAM until way too late, the TRD lash-up, the early austere AMRAAM 'wishile', the JTIDS fleet-within-fleet, the Stage 1+ fleet-within-fleet, the CSP fleet-within-fleet, are all debacles I care to forget!

Another commentator said:

> I was a member of one modification team (there were two) installing outboard pylons to F3's. No structural mods were needed and the rods and swivels were

installed and rigged as per the GR fleet. We must've done about a dozen or so. The new wing kit was installed for fitting ECM gear to aircraft going to Gioia del Colle during the mid 90's. The whole gear weighed almost a half ton and was a typical OEM disaster—making the jets fly at full throttle to push through the induced drag reducing engine life and increasing airframe fatigue too. The cabs were limited to low G turns too IIRC. Can't say how long the ECM lasted (but I'm sure it wasn't long) and I assume the wing outer pylons were removed but probably not the internal swivel gear…. We then moved to supplying Italy with 10+ leased F3s and had to fit engines with less than ten hours on them as most engines got used up in the TRD farce. IMO this was a really badly thrown together act of desperation….

And yet another:

Yes and I was on the first F3 Squadron to go 'sausage side' over Bosnia with TRD. I agree it was a great bit of kit, but just disappointed to still be flying with the same lump of lead counterbalance [Phimat] over Iraq 5–8 years later (where the heat made a HUGE difference) and we now had chaff built into the LAUs to boot! I reckon that Phimat and the lump of lead took 2,000ft off of our max comfortable dry-power cruising height over the desert—with both drag and weight.

Harsh criticism indeed and it is worth looking at the circumstances which led to these complaints with the advantage of hindsight to understand why.

There is one reason why the Tornado F3 modifications were flawed and this is a recurring theme—money. The MoD procurement process is complex and can be unfathomable even to those inside the decision chain. Looking at any programme in isolation, what emerges might not be the solution which was originally intended. A requirements officer cannot say I want to buy a Tornado F3. He or she asks for an aircraft with two wings which can travel a long way and shoot down specific aircraft in nominated operational environments. It is for the procurement authority to turn that requirement into a specification and for industry to offer potential solutions. It is during the stage when a requirement is turned into a specification that problems often occur. Inevitable compromises are made often without the requirements staff being able to influence them, which means that in order to satisfy one key requirement, others are neglected. Sometimes the compromise is obvious but inevitable. Sometimes the compromise goes unchallenged. With appropriate and timely investment, the problems my former colleagues identified in their summaries might never have been issues.

In the case of 'fleets within fleets', logically, once an urgent operational requirement was agreed, realism would dictate that the capability needs to be extended across the entire working fleet of Tornado F3s. Not so. An urgent operational requirement is only funded for the duration of an operation and, by the rules, should then be removed. The irrefutable consequence is that if the aircraft subsequently goes to war the contingency equipment has to be refitted for the new conflict. The logic is that if the need is sufficiently important it will rise to the top of the annual funding round and be fitted formally under the main equipment programme. To fit the equipment in the first place and qualify it for use is expensive and involves complex return to works programmes or contractor working parties. No fleet manager wants equipment being fitted and removed on a regular basis and operating mixed fleets is a nightmare. How can you train effectively for an operational deployment if the training fleet is not fitted with the operational equipment? The reality is that the defence vote is always underfunded and over tasked so the list of 'essential requirements' to equip our aircraft to go to war is enormous and never ending. Last year's essential modification might be too expensive to fit fleet wide so short cuts are taken to support the modification rather than remove it, sometimes against the rules, to avoid nugatory modifications. The solution is often to modify airframes to take the equipment but only to buy a limited number of systems. This is known 'in the trade' as 'fitting for, not with'. The fleet manager may modify forty aircraft but buy only ten electronic warfare systems and rotate them through the fleet where needed.

To understand the system, how it is intended to work, and how it is modified for an urgent operational requirement, an examination of the chaff and flare requirement for the F3 demonstrates the problems. The Gulf War fit of the AN/ALE40 flare dispensers and Phimat chaff dispensers was never intended to be a final solution to provide these essential defensive aids. It was only intended to provide stop-gap protection during that conflict and would be replaced at the end of the operation when the new requirement was fulfilled. The staff requirement to equip the F3 with chaff and flares was already endorsed, had gone to tender, and manufacturers had been placed on contract. By the start of the war, individual pieces of equipment had already been designed and produced, and early prototypes had been delivered to BAES Warton where they were installed in an aircraft and tested by the company. A formal modification was agreed and the equipment was further tested at Boscombe Down. The in-service date was agreed and the equipment would begin to arrive on the squadrons in 1993. Unfortunately, the equipment was not available in numbers as the Gulf War began in 1990, and given the complex procurement process it was impossible to bring dates forward. With a full-scale conflict such as the Gulf War, the thought of deploying without protection was unacceptable. Essential modifications were needed so a contingency system was used which bypassed the full formal process.

The airworthiness authority for the Tornado F3 was the Assistant Chief of the Air Staff, or ACAS. He signed off a document known as the Release to Service which contained the advice on how the aircraft should be flown and what limits were placed on it when flown by military pilots. Who he took his advice from was his choice, but driven by his staff, he would be directed towards the most appropriate agency and seek consensus. As the aircraft had proceeded through manufacturer's testing, then development testing, and finally operational testing, guidance had been written and the best advice incorporated in the Release to Service by the Air Defence staff in the MoD. Sometimes the advice from the manufacturer could be further limited for service use for operational reasons.

As an example, during flight testing, BAE Systems issued a speed limit on the F3 airframe of 850 knots but this was reduced to 750 knots on advice from service test pilots. The lower limit was published in the Release preventing service pilots from operating to the higher limit, even though the manufacturer considered the aircraft capable of the higher speeds. There might be a variety of reasons for the more stringent limit, although at any time the ACAS could have amended the Release to give approval to fly to manufacturer's limits. If an operational requirement emerged which demanded the higher limit, he could be pressed to agree depending on risk factors. In parallel, any change to the build standard of the aircraft was carefully controlled by the manufacturer who issued a formal 'modification', staffed through, in the case of the F3, the NATO Multirole Combat Aircraft Development and Production Management Agency, or NAMMA, now known as the NATO Eurofighter and Tornado Management Agency, or NETMA. This complex process takes time and is expensive.

A process had always existed to install a 'Special Trial Fit', or STF, so that potential modifications could be flown and evaluated on service aircraft. If the trial fit showed promise it could be taken forward as a full design modification. For trials purposes, the fit would only be incorporated on an aircraft for a limited time and in limited numbers so the overall risk was much lower. While airworthiness for the aircraft was underwritten by the company, if a trial fit was flown, liability for that modification could be vested in the MoD sponsor for the duration of its life. To accept that liability, the ACAS issued a 'Service Deviation' allowing military crews to operate the modified standard. Later, the STF fit was replaced with a Service Engineered Modification, or SEM, which allowed a more rigorous engineering solution to be adopted. While an SEM mirrored a formal modification more closely, a much reduced level of testing was envisaged and the implications of the installation on other onboard systems might not be assessed as thoroughly. The advantage was that a 90 per cent solution was available at lower cost much earlier. The disadvantage was that eventually these urgent requirements would have to be formally qualified and may conflict with the formal programme in terms of priority. The manufacturer had a carefully designed schedule of work lasting many years, and feeding into that plan could be complicated. Wars tended to complicate the more structured life of a designer or programme manager.

In the case of active jamming for the F3, unlike the Tornado GR1 which was fitted with Skyshadow, the requirement never attracted sufficient priority until an operational imperative changed the status quo. With the risk of exclusion from Operation Deny Flight, the towed radar decoy, or TRD, was fitted under urgent operational procedures and tight timescales were set for the modifications. The operational requirements staff had agreed a concept for a podded TRD system some time before and an acquisition programme had already been mooted, albeit unfunded. With the operational pressure, contingency funds were identified, but initially only six jamming pods were procured, ostensibly to equip the six deployed aircraft. This was quickly increased to nine to give a small number of pods with which to train crews in the UK prior to deployment. The operators, as always, wanted more, but with the inevitable financial constraint, numbers were limited so another mini-fleet was born. Most significantly, the UOR was only endorsed for the duration of the operation, and to acquire a full fleet fit or design a new replacement meant taking the project into the core procurement programme.

A need to fit active jamming to the F3 had been suggested many times and a slimline, podded version known as Apollo, a development of the Harrier Zeus jammer, had been proposed by a contractor some years before. It had not progressed to the prototype stage as it was a private venture and unfunded. To go to full production would have taken years, not months, added to which clearance activity for a new untested pod to allow it to fly on the aircraft would also have taken nearly a year. With the tight timescales, a new design was simply not viable. Onboard systems mounted in the space occupied by the gun and its ammunition tanks had been proposed to meet a potential requirement from an overseas customer. By removing the Mauser cannon and the ammunition tanks, a considerable space could be freed up in the ammunition bay which would allow the black boxes needed for a jammer to be installed. Unfortunately, this still left the need to mount antennas around the airframe—a not insignificant challenge. Mounting points were identified at the base of the fin to fit a decoy dispenser, but there were major concerns whether the tow cable could survive the extreme heat generated by the reheat that would inevitably be used if a defensive reaction was needed. Additionally, long cable runs to take signals from the forward bay to the dispenser housing would have meant stripping aircraft down to install the wiring. This option was quickly discounted as, ironically, air policing is one role where a gun is extremely useful, particularly against helicopters where it may be the only effective weapon. A radical wingtip-mounted pod was assessed but the airframe would have needed major surgery and adapting to each wing configuration would have been complex. A towing mechanism which worked at 25-degree wing sweep might not be effective at 67-degree wing sweep. The Skyshadow pod fitted to the Tornado GR1 was considered but it was already in the midst of an upgrade programme to allow it to cope with the very threats which were prevalent. Modified pods were also needed to equip the GR1 force so they were not available to the F3. In fact, the GR1 crews were already facing a reduced supply of pods as they were recycled back through the manufacturer for upgrading to a new standard. Alternative systems bought off the shelf such as the American AN/ALQ 131 pod were also investigated. While the hardware could have been available, we would have relied on the US for programming which was against national policy. There was only one viable option which met both the timescales and the operational requirement—the TRD, more affectionately nicknamed 'The Turd'. The wing-mounted, podded system was self-contained, effective, and could be fitted relatively easily.

The TRD had been under development for Typhoon for many years and I had championed it during my time in the operational requirements division. As the Typhoon equipment is a development of the Tornado F3 system and is still in service, I will avoid detailed descriptions of its capability, but open source material describes the system well. In the late 1980s, the UK was the world leader in the technology, but it had to compete with other potential solutions for Typhoon and was mired in political delay. To meet the urgent operational requirement for the F3, electronic 'black boxes' were fitted into a stripped-down BOZ pod normally used on the Tornado GR1.

The TRD was an alien concept. A length of cable was reeled-out behind the aircraft at the end of which was a small transmitting aerial. Small antennas on the pod detected the electronic threat signals. The receiver analysed the electronic environment, scanned for potential threats, and classified them. Once a threat was determined, an appropriate countermeasure designed by electronic warfare specialists was transmitted. The signals emitted from the decoy made it a more attractive target than the host aircraft, and a radar-guided missile fired at the F3 was seduced and tracked to a point well away from the host aircraft. As the missile reached its intended target, it passed outside the range of its proximity fuse, passing harmlessly until self-destruction. The whole jamming system was driven by complex software programmed into computers within the pod.

The first challenge was how to mount the pod on the wing. During design, the requirement for outboard wing pylons on the F3 had been dropped to save weight and improve performance. The F3 wings were identical to those fitted to the GR1 bomber with the exception of the swivel gear installation. The logical solution was to fit the TRD to an outboard pylon. Not only would that allow external fuel tanks to be carried on the inboard pylons, it was a better site for the decoy as there was less risk of striking the taileron with the towline during hard manoeuvring, particularly at greater wing sweep angles beyond 45 degrees. This would allow operational commanders to decide on fuel state by fitting either of the external fuel tank types or, should conditions allow, operating without tanks. Many experts argued that the weight of carrying external tanks was not worth the carriage penalty, particularly when air-to-air refuelling was allocated to the mission. By providing additional pylons, commanders could decide. Originally, it was suggested that entire wings already containing the pylon fittings could be exchanged—effectively a wing change. The pivot for a Tornado wing is milled titanium which is frozen before mating; installation is not an easy procedure. The engineering experts decided that it was simpler to fit modification kits into the existing wings, effectively reverting to the Tornado GR1 standard. Unfortunately, there were only eighteen outboard pylon mounting kits available 'on the shelf' and lead times to build more were long. This is the reason the TRD-equipped 'mini fleet' was initially set at eighteen. The forty-aircraft mini fleet for Operation Granby became a smaller 'fleet within a fleet' of TRD-capable aircraft. Like the pods, if the capability was to be extended to the whole fleet, the requirement to buy more would have to join the annual long-term costing process. So eighteen aircraft it was, which set a further management challenge and led to frustration on the front line, which now had to cope with three different operating standards of F3. It became so complex that a Venn diagram was produced to allow managers to track modification states and to understand which airframes could be used for which operational task.

Selection of the pod design proved simple. A pod large enough to take the electronics and the mechanical components was needed and the BOZ countermeasures pod carried by the Tornado GR1 was the most aerodynamic solution which was already cleared for carriage on the Tornado and available in numbers. The existing chaff and flare system was removed, leaving space to install the new electronics. The receiver and techniques generator and power supply and cooling units were installed in the front section. A reel which housed the towline when stowed also contained a winding mechanism to deploy the decoy on its towline and occupied the rear of the pod. The decoy was a strange-looking device, reminiscent of a badminton shuttlecock on a string. An enormous drag cone at the back of the decoy stabilised it in flight, keeping the towline taut once deployed. A universal mounting joint on the nose allowed it to weathercock in the airflow to reduce strains. It could be deployed at virtually all speeds and heights and once the navigator hit the button, it ran out to the extent of its towline under gravity feed. Once deployed, the decoy could only be released by jettisoning the device. It could not be reeled back in.

The original concept for the decoy had been as a throw-away device. All the clever electronics were onboard the pod and the simple electronics on the end of the string should have been cheap and disposable. Volume production should have reduced unit costs to an affordable level. Unfortunately, under urgent operational procedures only a fraction of the conceived buy was made, meaning that the limited number of decoys would be virtually custom built and much more expensive. For that reason, the decoy was redesigned to include a parachute recovery system. At the end of the sortie, the decoy would be jettisoned overhead the airfield. The duty aircrew officer positioned in the control tower controlled the drop, calling the crew to jettison at the appropriate point alongside the taxiway. On a call of 'cut, cut, now' the navigator in the aircraft would press the cut button on the control panel in the rear cockpit, severing the towline. As the decoy sensed the retardation, a small drogue parachute deployed into the airflow and the decoy descended under the small parachute, cushioning the landing. The decoy was recovered and refurbished prior to being reused on a later mission. Sometimes fact could be just as strange as fiction.

A working party was set up at RAF Coningsby to install the extended mechanical rods and swivel joints which would allow the pylons carrying the pods to move as the wings were swept. As the equipment was designed for the Tornado GR1 wings, procedures already existed to calibrate the new pylons. As testing began, an unintended consequence emerged. The Computer Stability Augmentation System, or CSAS, could not cope with a severe asymmetric load. Mounting a TRD onto one outboard pylon without a matching store on the opposite pylon was not possible for reasons of aerodynamic stability. Mounting two TRDs might have been attractive, but insufficient systems had been approved for purchase so an alternative was needed. The Phimat chaff dispenser had been fitted during the

The towed radar decoy pod was carried on a newly installed outer wing pylon opposite the Phimat pod. (*Geoff Lee*)

A Tornado F3 of the F3 Operational Evaluation Unit carries the towed radar decoy pod on the left wing. (*UK MoD Crown Copyright, 1993*)

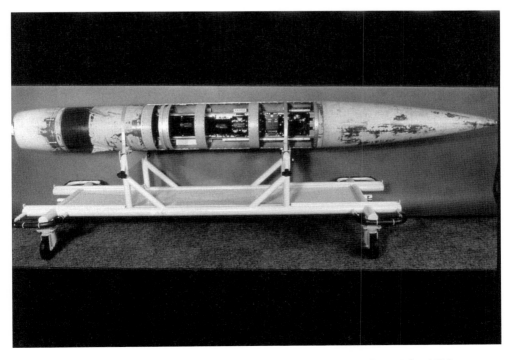

The towed radar decoy pod with panels removed. (*UK MoD Crown Copyright, 1993, courtesy of Selex ES*)

The decoy stowed in the rear of the pod. (*UK MoD Crown Copyright, 1993, courtesy of Selex ES*)

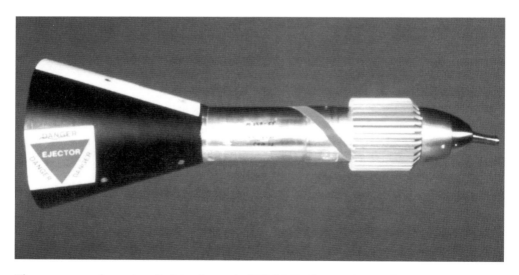

The prototype decoy installed in the pod. (*UK MoD Crown Copyright, 1993, courtesy of Selex ES*)

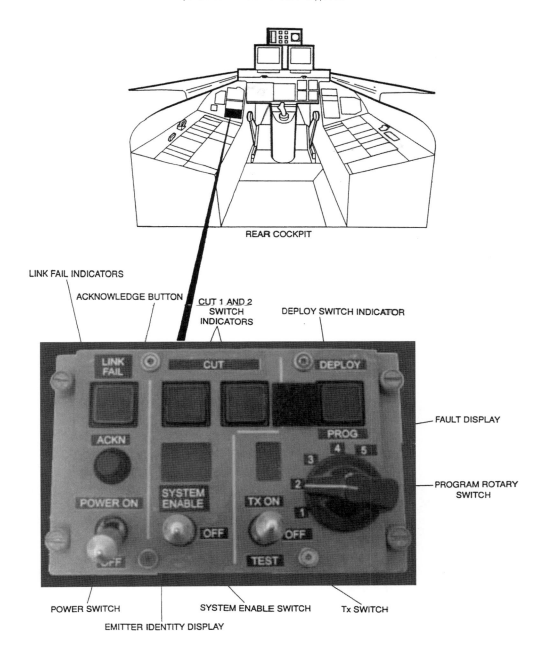

The TRD control panel. (*UK MoD Crown Copyright, 1993, courtesy of Selex ES*)

The decoy descends on its parachute after being jettisoned. (*UK MoD Crown Copyright, 1993, courtesy of Selex ES*)

The TRD recovery parachute. (*UK MoD Crown Copyright, 1993, courtesy of Selex ES*)

The decoy on the ground. (*UK MoD Crown Copyright, 1993, courtesy of Selex ES*)

Gulf War, was cleared for carriage, and pods and control panels were available. A further advantage was that chaff used in conjunction with electronic jamming from the TRD enhanced the operational protection. A combination of jamming, chaff, and manoeuvre, was highly effective against many of the threats the crews faced. Fitting two external stores added further weight to an airframe that already struggled for performance at altitude but gave a significant increase in capability. And why fly with the Phimat lead weight? In order to carry the TRD, a balance was essential so a chaff dispenser not only improved capability, but provided the necessary extra weight.

The final requirement was for a new cockpit controller. In addition to being able to turn the transmitter on and off, switches to deploy and jettison the decoy were needed in addition to a control to select the software countermeasures programs. Fitted in the rear cockpit on the left-hand lower bulkhead where the RHWR display had formerly been positioned, the new control panel was controlled by the navigator.

As clearance activity began in earnest, much work went into convincing the operational community that the concept was viable. Development testing of deployment and jettison had been completed some years before on a Jetstream hack aircraft. The decoy had also flown on the BAES Experimental Aircraft Programme (EAP) which survives and is displayed at RAF Cosford. Test pilots from Boscombe Down flew handling verification sorties with the basic fit and with decoys streamed behind an F3. At that stage, the Operational Evaluation Unit began to test the operational characteristics, to develop tactics, and to verify effectiveness of the programmed countermeasures. In a superb example of joined-up testing, the contractors, the engineering staff, the development test community, and the operational test community moved the system rapidly to a point where comprehensive guidance could be issued and training could begin.

In parallel, and often neglected in the drive for operational effectiveness, engineering procedures had to be developed to ensure that the system could be maintained in service. Spares were ordered, engineering facilities and processes were determined, and logistics chains were set up. Decoys had to be refurbished on a daily basis so rigs and equipment were procured to support the new pods. Electronic countermeasures which were to be programmed into the onboard computers had to be designed and updated and systems had to be established to deliver updates to those operational programmes. Much of this essential support was done at the newly formed Air Warfare Centre at RAF Waddington. One of the most complex tasks was to reaffix the fibre optic cable to the decoy during refurbishment. Microscopic links had to be re-established in order to ensure that the black boxes could talk to the decoy. Literally, a section of fibre optic cable the diameter of a human hair had to be re-spliced onto the decoy if it was to be reused. Watching the intricate process, I marvelled at the skills that were exercised under quite austere operational conditions. Rather than clinical technical laboratories, service technicians worked on a hastily installed rig in a rapidly deployed portakabin and achieved superb results. The complex procedures required skill and expertise of the highest order to achieve an operational capability in such short timescales. Without the skill of the service technicians and the support of industry, the aircrew would have lacked the critical protection.

Within a few months, engineering instructions, operational emergency clearances, service deviations, and aircrew guidance had been issued and the equipment was deployed to Gioia Del Colle, allowing the Tornado F3 to remain operational on Operation Deny Flight. It was a leap of faith for operational crews as they began to fly with TRD. Psychologically, crews had to be convinced of its value. They had to believe that, if the decoy was deployed, it would protect them against a surface-to-air missile targeted at their aircraft. The missile would pass within metres of their F3 as it guided towards the false electronic target, but it would not detonate—'Honest Guvnor!'

As anyone would guess, the concept of towing a small brick on a long string behind a fighter caused some consternation and only when crews were briefed on 'turd' effectiveness were those concerns allayed. Tactical flying procedures needed to be adapted. There would be no prizes for cutting your leader's towline and relieving him of his electronic 'guard' over hostile territory!

Although the concept was fundamentally sound, there proved to be practical problems. During later operational testing, decoys were lost when the towline broke during a test on an electronic warfare range. It remained 'at large' for many months until a range crew stumbled across it during preparation for another trial. This led to some strengthening of the universal joint to ensure that the decoy remained with the F3 until its 'duty' was complete. Occasionally, the parachute failed, leading to a ballistic decoy bouncing its way across the airfield after it had been jettisoned. I was assured that a 50-lb decoy bouncing towards you along the taxiway could be quite intimidating. What was certain was that in the event of a parachute failure, refurbishment was significantly more of a challenge. Undoubtedly, a throw-away device would have been much simpler to use, albeit more expensive, but with such small numbers being bought, refurbishment was mandated. Whichever option had been implemented, the cost of the TRD was a fraction of the cost of losing a Tornado and its crew to a surface-to-air missile. Indeed, the political cost of losing a crew was incalculable.

Back in the UK, one of the more frustrating consequences proved to be the need to operate the outboard pylons without a TRD fitted. Only enough pods had been approved to fit the deployed squadron plus a few to allow the next squadron to work-up. The remaining F3s modified with outboard pylons needed to operate without pods fitted. This was not a configuration ever used by the Tornado GR1 force as they always flew with BOZ and Skyshadow. A specific clearance was needed and it fell to me, as the operational sponsor, to write the clearance for my One Star Commander. In researching the existing evidence, a test pilot had flown an early Tornado prototype and had experienced minor handling effects at 600 knots. Although it was a one-off event, it was on record so could not be ignored. In the meantime, the crews on the OEU had flown the fit on a number of occasions, unaware that specific dispensation was needed. The more usual situation was a scramble to clear equipment to fly, not to clear aircraft to fly without it. To most of us it seemed like a non-issue, but it took some time to persuade the Air Officer, who had the huge responsibility of signing off the service deviation, that he really could be confident that there were no handling issues when operating this configuration. The fact that the OEU pilots had inadvertently flown the fit did not seem to impress him, understandably. In the event, additional sorties were mounted at Boscombe Down to try to replicate the handling anomaly to no avail. It proved to be a false concern and no problems were ever reported with the 'flutter' experienced on the single test flight so many years earlier.

No modification is a free ride. TRD was an extremely effective jammer and gave significant protection against anything the Serbs could shoot at a Tornado F3. Ironically, the pod also improved the fatigue life of the aircraft as the damping effect of the additional outboard weight meant that there was less stress on the wings. Indeed, Tornado GR4s were fitted with dummy BOZ pods when real Skyshadow pods were not available to benefit from this advantage. On the down side, the pylon kits were heavy and the pod added significant aerodynamic drag which made operating at typical heights a challenge. Tornado F3s often flew between 20,000 and 30,000 feet so the RB199 engines were asked to work harder as the height increased. Combat engine modes which increased power were available but at the expense of engine life. Deciding when to deploy the decoy to avoid unnecessary refurbishment was also an issue. It was preferable to leave the decoy in its housing until threatened, but there were no marks for deploying a decoy late and being shot down by a SAM. Timely deployment taxed some extremely clever tactical brains before a compromise was agreed. The tow cable and decoy could be streamed procedurally when the crew entered hostile airspace, but that meant dragging around a long cable unnecessarily behind the aircraft. Equally, it added to the workload of the technicians who would then have to refurbish the decoy and reinstall it in the pod. The secret was to know when an attack was most likely and to do that required knowledge of where the SAMs were likely to operate. Some of the Serbian SAMs were old-style fixed installations such as the SA-3 Goa, but they also operated the mobile SA-6 Gainful system. This could be moved around the countryside and used to ambush an unwary NATO crew. It did so extremely successfully when an American pilot was shot down in his F-16 over Bosnia—one of the high-profile victims during Operation Deny Flight. Much effort went into understanding how the radar homing and warning receiver reacted to a SAM lock, how much reaction time the crew would have, and how quickly it would take to deploy the decoy and begin to benefit from its electronic protection. No sooner had the experts solved this riddle when the Serbs began punting off unguided missiles. The SAM had no chance of being effective when fired in this mode, but it caused a great deal of consternation among the fighter community when missiles began whistling through formations without any warning on the radar warning receivers. The biggest risk was a chance collision with an unguided SAM, but such was the electronic chess match. With hindsight, many more pods should have been approved and more pylon kits procured to increase the smaller operational Granby fleet to the improved standard. Despite that, everyone involved in fitting this essential capability could be proud of their contribution to the operational effort. Given the funding constraints, the programme was remarkable. The system was challenged again and it delivered a world-class capability. Most importantly, the Tornado F3 was able to continue to support a NATO operation.

One of the revolutionary modifications to the F3 was the introduction of the Joint Tactical Information Distribution System, or JTIDS. As early as 1983 the UK and the USA signed a Memorandum of Understanding for British participation in the programme to improve the situation awareness of combat and support aircraft crews. The Tornado F3 was chosen as the lead platform along with the E3D Sentry, and testing of the 'Class 2' terminals which were to equip the F3 began in 1980, before the aircraft had even entered service. In January 1987 a terminal first flew in a BAE Systems development aircraft to begin to integrate the equipment into the weapon system. JTIDS was envisaged from project inception, and wiring was installed during production with provision for the control panels in the rear cockpit. The well-publicised problems with Foxhunter delayed the development but by the early 1990s it was decided that JTIDS would be introduced along with the 'Stage 2' radar upgrades. Extensive software updates and some hardware modifications were needed to allow JTIDS to work effectively, so phasing in with a major radar update was logical. A service evaluation trial followed in 1995 at Mountain Home Air Force Base in Idaho in the USA. The Tornado F3 joined the E3 AWACS, F-15, and F-14 fighters in a trial. Cooperative networks were established and fighters and airborne early warning (AEW) aircraft joined the nets, building a comprehensive air picture which was shared between the participants. The trial was a huge success, although, as would be expected with a complex system, a number of issues were identified. Correlation of externally reported tracks with those generated by the F3 radar was poor, caused by inaccuracy of the F3 inertial navigation unit. Eventually this led to the installation of a new laser ring gyro inertial system along with an upgrade to the main computer. Performance rapidly improved once these improvements came online and by the time JTIDS was introduced to service at RAF Coningsby in 1996 on Nos 5 and 29 Squadrons, the system was working well, giving a massive improvement in operational capability. The improvement was so significant that some experts likened it to the introduction of radar into fighters. A short description shows why.

The Air Defence Ground environment which included the ground-based fighter control radars, the E3 Sentry airborne early warning radars, and air defence ships had long used the Link 16 tactical data link to form a 'recognised air picture' or RAP. Battle managers could analyse threats to UK airspace and allocate fighters to destroy them. Until the advent of JTIDS, fighter crews could not see the larger air picture and relied on voice communications to build awareness. By extending the capability to fighters, crews were instantly better able to fight the local tactical battle.

Once connected to the network, a user is allocated time slots and adds their own information to the RAP. Not all users were equal. An E3 might be a 'super user' whereas an F3 would be less trusted, so by weighting, the quality of the information integrity is protected. A hostile track could be generated by a controller aboard an E3 using the long-range radar and allocated to an F3 on CAP for engagement. Once an F3 detected a target on its radar it was cross-checked against the RAP and correlated. On the plan display in the F3, a JTIDS track would be shown differently to a radar track to avoid confusion. In the final stages of an intercept, and as each F3 locked to its designated target, the tactical picture was further refined. All this could be achieved electronically using protocols designed into the operational software of the Tornado F3. Additionally, a secure radio and secure messaging function was included which meant that simple tactical messages and secure voice transmissions could be passed between friendly aircraft. Suddenly, simple data such as the weather status of your home base was always available, avoiding the need for constant chatter which could be subjected to electronic jamming. Tactical data such as the location of the tanker and its fuel offload was displayed. In addition to hostile contacts, other F3s appeared on the plan display as friendly tracks, avoiding the risk of 'blue on blue' engagements.

The JTIDS terminal fitted to the F3 was significantly more capable than the later 'MIDS' terminals fitted to Typhoon, but more user-intensive. Despite the radical improvement, the elusive colour displays which would have optimised the capability were not approved by a frugal MoD, despite the efforts of the air staff and even though the single colour displays were obsolescent and becoming increasingly difficult to support. JTIDS entered service utilising the original green displays, leaving crews to interpret sometimes confusing information. The 100 per sent solution was always elusive but, even so, this was radical stuff.

JTIDS was not the only step forward. With night tasking increasing and technological advances being made, changes were inevitable. The Tornado F3 was designed during the Cold War when night vision equipment was in its infancy and night flying relied on instruments and radar rather than the 'Mark 1 Eyeball'. A rudimentary night vision scope known as the CU-19 was fielded on Battle Flight in Germany to allow crews to identify targets visually at night. The scope measured 5 inches across the lens, 'weighed a ton', and was extremely bulky and difficult to use in the confines of the cockpit. The advent of night vision goggles, or NVGs, which were small enough to fit onto an aircrew helmet, changed night operations radically. A slider bar fitted to the front of the flying helmet behind the visor allowed the goggles to be moved into and out of the line of sight when needed. The small tubes measuring only 4 inches long looked exactly like a pair of binoculars and were powered by a small battery attached to the rear of the helmet and fixed to a Velcro patch.

The problem was how to use them safely in the air in the event of an ejection. Ideally, in a pre-meditated situation, the goggles would be removed and discarded in the cockpit before pulling the handle. For an emergency ejection where time was critical, crews had no option but to eject leaving them in place. Even for a normal ejection, the 'G' forces were huge, reaching peak levels of up to 40 G. This caused the head to be forced forward onto the chest due to the weight of the flying helmet. With goggles in place, the rotational moment forward would add to the stresses so a shear fitting was designed. The weight of the goggles would snap the fitting allowing the goggles to fall clear. To a design engineer this sounded fine. To aircrew, the thought of high-speed goggles descending unerringly towards the 'nether regions' as the seat set off up the rails was less attractive, although considerably better than a broken neck.

The advantages were enormous. Once powered, the goggles turned a dark night into day, albeit bathed in a green glow. Features which had been masked by darkness became clear and tasks which had hitherto been impossible at night became routine. Simple tasks such as tactical formation keeping became markedly easier, but using goggles was not without problems. It was perfectly viable to fly at night at low level using visual cues. Up to then, the minimum height at night had been 1,500 feet above the ground; the goal was to reduce that to 250 feet to match the daylight capability. There was a 'no-man's land' between these heights where the cues which were used to fly safely lacked perspective. The scene looked flat and lacked depth, and descending to a representative operational height was a challenge for pilots until fully trained. Sometimes the goggles were almost too effective. A set of blinking navigation lights might seem to be close but could be as far as 50 miles away. Aircraft which had been shrouded in darkness were suddenly obvious and the 'crowded sky' became a reality. Depth perception when operating in close formation was also problematic and gauging the rate of closure between two aircraft was much harder wearing goggles.

One incident was to bring the issues to the fore. After a routine intercept at night, a crew closed in to practice identification procedures using NVGs but struck the other F3, damaging the airframe. One aircraft crashed into the sea after the crew ejected, although the other was able to recover to RAF Leuchars and landed safely. Following the crash, procedures were modified and crews were reminded of the dangers of operating with night vision equipment. Operational lessons were sometimes hard won.

In order for crews to use NVGs, the cockpit lighting had to be modified for NVG compatibility. As night operations in the Balkans increased, an urgent requirement was submitted by Group Headquarters and I was dispatched to a specialist company to determine what modifications were needed to bring the F3 cockpit up to specification. NVGs are tolerant to different colours; green and red are good, but white light is not. A single unmodified warning caption could provide enough stray light to flood the goggles making them ineffective and destroy a pilot's night vision at a critical moment. The first step was, painstakingly, to identify every light in each cockpit and document it. Each light source then had to be treated to make it compatible. This could be as simple as applying a green filter to the panel, but in some cases the panel had to be redesigned. Once potential solutions had been identified, a test aircraft was modified and placed into a darkened hardened aircraft shelter at Boscombe Down for evaluation. Once proven, a specification was written and the company was contracted to modify the equipment which would then be fitted into the F3 cockpits. The modified equipment was passed to the Operational Evaluation Unit to be tested and procedures were written to introduce the new standard into service. It was unfortunate that by the time the cockpits were cleared, Operation Deny Flight, which had been the stimulus for the modification, had ended. It did mean, however, that when F3s were deployed on subsequent operations and tasked at night, there was no last minute panic to fit night vision equipment. The night capability of the F3 was radically improved at a relatively low cost, using low technology, and introduced to service quickly. The new capability seemed to be well received by squadron aircrew who began to train with it on a regular basis.

One of the more bizarre programmes to affect the F3 was 'The Airwork Saga'. Fatigue modifications known as the '25 FI' programme were carried out at the RAF Maintenance Unit at RAF St Athan. This programme had been introduced early in the service life to extend the fatigue life of the airframe and was typical of similar programmes on aircraft such as the Phantom. Although service engineers carried out some of the work, Airwork, a respected company in the aviation world, was sub-contracted to carry out work on the intake ducts. In order to gain access to the structural components, fasteners which fixed panels in the intakes were removed using an industrial-grade power tool. Whether an approved procedure was bypassed or whether the modification was flawed would only become apparent later as the legal process kicked in. What was undeniable was that the damage caused to the structure of the centre fuselage of the airframe rendered those which had been worked upon unusable. In the immediate aftermath, damage was identified in sixteen Tornado F3s which were immediately grounded, leaving a significant gap in the front-line strength of the RAF. The programme was halted, further reducing availability of airframes to the front line as the consequences were assessed. As the media speculation began, it surfaced that the damage had been spotted by an RAF technician rather than by a formal inspection process.

My colleague in the Air Defence Department, who was the airworthiness desk officer for the airframe, immediately began to formulate recovery plans but it was apparent that any solution could be wildly expensive. As they grappled with the implications, one of the most radical solutions in recent aviation management history was proposed. The Tornado F2s which had been scheduled to be upgraded to F2A standard would be used as donor airframes to provide centre sections for the damaged F3s. The donors and the damaged airframes would be disassembled and a centre section from a Tornado F2 would be fitted to a damaged F3. In effect, the MoD was sanctioning a 'cut and shunt', which had a local garage done such a thing with a car, might have made headlines. In the event it did, but for different reasons.

The reality, as always, was somewhat different to the hype. The aircraft was built in three sections and transported to the factory at Warton for final assembly. The Tornado F2 centre sections were compatible with the Tornado F3, and detailed plans already existed to join the sections during production. It was a simple task to adapt the plans and the manufacturer was contracted for the remedial work. In 1995, the trial installation was completed for the first donor swap and it was test flown successfully.

There was to be a nervous moment when one of the first reassembled aircraft was lost in an accident on 28 September 1996, when ZE759 was being flown by a MoD (PE) test crew. As the aircraft climbed away after an overshoot at Blackpool, it rolled uncontrollably and crashed into the sea. The crew ejected safely but the fact that it was one of the first aircraft to be rebuilt caused concerns that there might be a fault in the procedure. In the event, a loose article had jammed the taileron causing the loss of control. Although worrying, it meant that a simple technical error had caused the loss allowing the programme to continue. The remaining damaged aircraft were returned to service over the following years.

In the aftermath there were questions in Parliament and the MP for Bridgenorth, who was the local MP for RAF St Athan where the work was undertaken, spoke in defence of the RAF maintenance unit staff who had been implicated in the fiasco. He made it clear that the work had been sub-contracted and his words were released to the public through the official Parliamentary record, *Hansard*. In a response, Mr Arbuthnot, a defence minister at the time, said:

A negotiated settlement has been reached in respect of my Department's claim for structural damage to Tornado F3 aircraft while being modified by Airwork Ltd. During 1992–93. I am pleased to report that, of the 16 aircraft involved, 11 have been repaired and delivered back to the RAF and the remainder will be delivered progressively over the next few weeks, with the last due for delivery in May this year. One aircraft was lost in the crash off Blackpool in September 1996, the cause of which was not related to the modification programme on which Airwork had been engaged. The F3 aircraft were repaired by replacing the damaged centre fuselages with those from surplus F2 aircraft which had been earmarked for disposal. This was to ensure that the aircraft were returned to operational service as soon as possible. In choosing to replace the centre fuselage, the aircraft have been given valuable additional fatigue life. The overall cost of this work has been around £20 million. Taking this improvement into account, together with the costs which might have been incurred had arbitration been pursued, we have agreed that the Bricom Group, which owned Airwork at the time of the damage, will pay £5 million to the Ministry of Defence in settlement of our claim. [© Crown Copyright, Hansard]

Menzies Campbell MP, the Liberal Democrat Spokesman on Defence, was subsequently far more vociferous in a written answer, describing the deal as 'inadequate'. He went on:

This whole shabby episode arose out of the doctrinaire determination of the Minister of Defence to privatise essential repairs to front line aircraft. It turned into a financial disaster, and could easily have been a military one as well. Only the diligence of a sharp eyed RAF mechanic prevented a tragedy. Government Ministers past and present have a great deal to answer for. [© Crown Copyright, Hansard]

At about the same time as he was struggling to recover the Airwork airframes, my colleague in the Air Defence Department was hit by yet another tragedy with major implications to the F3 fleet. The RB199 Mk 104 turbofan fitted to the Tornado F3 is controlled by a digital electronic control unit, or DECU, which gave the pilot 'carefree handling' at all speeds and heights. A sensitive monitoring system checked vibration levels and the early indication of impending engine problems would be an amber 'VIB' caption on the telelight panel. If the fault progressed, a red 'Vib' caption warned of impending structural failure of the engine. Given a warning in the air, a suspect engine could be shut down and the aircraft recovered to base. After landing, a suspect engine could be changed, preventing catastrophic airborne failures. This early warning served the F3 community well.

After a rare Tornado F3 crash in 1995, an engine failure was suspected and the wreckage was recovered to allow them to be inspected. The S7 seal buried deep in the core of the engine was found to have failed, causing an uncontained disintegration of the engine. The flight safety implications were immediate and a further failure might occur at any time without urgent rectification. After a brief fleet grounding, a 'get well' programme was agreed and engines were returned to the manufacturer to undergo a refurbishment programme to fit new strengthened seals. Severe limitations were placed on how the engines could be operated in terms of heights and speeds and, inevitably, some engines were quarantined as being high hours and high risk. No manufacturer can surge the engineering effort to a level which satisfies the operators and engineers under such circumstances. Aircraft were grounded as engines were only slowly modified and crew currency suffered as a result. It was many months before engine supply returned to normal levels and allowed unrestricted operations to resume.

In one of the more bizarre episodes of my career as a staff officer, I became involved in an initiative to replace the Tornado F3. At high level within the MoD, a civilian adviser to the Minister of Defence was pushing to axe the Tornado F3 and replace it with F-16. The aircraft being offered as a replacement was an early F-16A with a first generation, limited-capability radar with stern-only weapons (as fitted to the European F-16s of the day) and no data link. Like the F3, the early generation F-16 was a totally different aircraft to the later versions, albeit more impressive at an airshow. Despite the legendary problems of Foxhunter and the F3's performance deficiencies, this really would have been a backward step. A later generation F-16 with AMRAAM and AIM-9L would have been a better alternative, despite inevitable protestations from the 'Navigator's Union', but it was not on offer. By then, the core capability envisaged for the F3 was for AMRAAM (albeit, austere AMRAAM), ASRAAM, and JTIDS, plus a towed radar decoy (TRD) and chaff and flares. Despite the attraction of a highly manoeuvrable addition to the order of battle, it would take years to introduce an F-16, even if bought off the shelf as with the UK F4J Phantom. Things as simple as flying clothing and safety equipment would have to be bought. Critically, leased aircraft can be acquired cheaply but it is often support costs which increase the price well above the original cost. A bargain to buy can become a financial drain with the cost of support. Additionally, an introduction of the F-16 into RAF service would have been a boon to US industry because it would have cast severe doubt over the viability of the Eurofighter project which was under intense scrutiny at the time and was subject to political delays among the partners. Had the RAF withdrawn from Eurofighter there was a definite risk the project would collapse. Despite my heritage flying the Phantom and being a huge advocate of American fighters, and despite being impressed with the efficiency of the F4J buy, this was not what the RAF needed. I was not alone in seeing this as an unwelcome diversion away from the task of fixing the problems that plagued the F3. Happily, sanity prevailed and F3 was upgraded, protecting the Typhoon programme.

The RAF was not the only air force experiencing problems with the delay in the Eurofighter deliveries. In the early 1990s, the Italian Air Force (IAF) realised that their aging F104 Starfighters would not survive long enough to be replaced by the Eurofighter Typhoon; they had been in service for many years and, without extensive maintenance, would slowly be grounded. The original in-service date for the Typhoon was an optimistic 1996, which was delayed to 2000 quite early in the project's life, not only for realism but to align with German operational plans. It was soon apparent that even that date would not be achieved, particularly as the Italians were receiving aircraft quite late in the delivery schedule. An interim solution was needed but, with the huge cost of procuring Typhoon, money was short. A number of options were considered including leasing F-16s from the USA, but a more realistic solution was to lease twenty-four Tornado F3s from the UK as Italy already operated the type. The UK had bought 165 air defence variants and, with the end of the Cold War, the numbers of F3s in service had been reduced to 100 to save money—part of the so called 'Cold War Windfall'. A planned attrition buy of an additional thirty-two airframes had already been cancelled because losses in front-line service had been low and they were not required. The upgrade of eighteen Tornado F2s to F2A standard was shelved, yet there was still a surplus of airframes that would otherwise have to be stored, sold, or destroyed. It was attractive to the British planners to offer this surplus to the Italians to tide them over.

After a swift staffing process, the F3 was selected by Italy and in November 1993 the lease agreement was signed. Selecting airframes was a complex juggling act. Few changes were needed in the front seat, although systems such as the auto wing sweep, which the UK had elected not to clear, were reviewed to decide whether they were to be included. In the back seat the picture was complex and many of the detailed discussions would fall to me as the operational sponsor. Like any smart customer, the Italian Air Staff wanted the best operational standard available. A radar standard had to be agreed, for which elements of the defensive aids suite would be offered, and whether the lease fleet would be fitted with data link was also negotiable. The Italian air staff wanted champagne but had a budget for lemonade, so there followed a hectic few months shuttling Italian experts between the manufacturer and RAF Coningsby. Each aspect of the aircraft's capability was explained, including what was fitted and what was planned in the immediate future. A specification was agreed and, in discussion with engineering staffs, we established whether sufficient additional airframes could be added to the modification programme. Additional modification kits had to be ordered and, inevitably, some would have to be diverted from RAF sources if the ambitious timescales were to be met. Crucially, I was keen that our own implementation plans should not be disrupted.

One of the more complex problems was whether the data link system could be included in the lease arrangement, as JTIDS required the new Stage 2 avionic system software standard to integrate the radical upgrade. If the Italians were to operate JTIDS it set the baseline weapon system standard. Unfortunately, JTIDS was American equipment so it was not in our gift to offer terminals as they would have to be procured under the Foreign Military Sales system direct from the USA. Decisions were taken, bids were made, and the Italians received a very capable version of the F3.

One of the thornier problems would be airworthiness approvals. Many of the capabilities were being operated by the RAF under service deviations pending approval of formal manufacturer's modifications. The Italians had no equivalent system and asked that each of these enhancements be endorsed by the manufacturer before delivery. Although the process was underway, it would take a number of years to work through the bureaucracy. After briefing the senior air staff on how the service deviation system worked, and proposing an Italian equivalent, there followed a good deal of discussion as the Italian generals digested the implications of assuming airworthiness authority and responsibility. It was a nervous time and for some months the lease was in jeopardy until realism finally prevailed. If the latest standard was to be delivered with the modifications, it would come with the responsibility.

Under the terms of the lease, the selected airframes had to be of a standard such that no major servicing was required during the ten-year lease period. Primary servicing would be undertaken in Italy but the aircraft would not return to the UK for deep servicing. This meant that providing low-hours airframes which had completed the '25 FI' programme would be vital. With the Airwork saga a recent nightmare, our own servicing schedule was in turmoil, so seeing yet more precious upgraded airframes stripped out from the front line to meet the lease requirement was traumatic. In addition, the return-to-works programme to rectify the problem identified with the S7 seals had reduced the flow of engines to the front line. In a routine savings measure, the engineering staff had been asked to reduce the rate of scheduled maintenance and spares provision for the F3's engines. The impact was that sixteen aircraft would be grounded on a rolling basis and when the measure was taken, as predicted, these aircraft were indeed lost to the front line. With the combined pressures, availability suffered and the Italian lease aircraft fitted with low hours RB199s compounded the problem. Although popular with the

MoD financiers, our own squadrons would suffer to provide an ally with a stop gap.

Italian Air Force pilots and navigators would train to fly the F3 at the Operational Conversion Unit at RAF Coningsby. There was a ready supply of Italian pilots but the provision of navigators was a problem. Although the Tornado GR1 was already in Italian service, navigators could not be spared, so some newly trained pilots were re-designated to train as navigators with the proviso that they would be kept current in their handling skills on the MB339 aircraft back in Italy. Their tour in the back cockpit would be followed by a front seat tour on the F3. Although it solved the numbers game, it caused friction. It had long been joked that RAF fast jet navigators were frustrated pilots. Although not true, on Italian Tornado F3 squadrons it would certainly be the case. At peak output, the capacity of the OCU was limited and the Italian Air Force had to man two squadrons during a rapid build-up. For that reason RAF crews were offered to give immediate experience and to ease the training burden. For the early years at least two experienced RAF crews per squadron helped to build up our ally's capability.

The first aircraft was delivered into service on 5 July 1995 and flown to the base at Gioia Del Colle where our own F3s had operated during Operation Deny Flight. The first squadron formed in 1996 and was followed in 1997 by the second squadron. The Italian safety record flying the F3 proved to be exceptional. The F3 saw operational service flying air-to-air missions over the Balkans during Operation Allied Force in 1999 and served well on both operational and QRA duties. However, in a bid to save money, some of the agreed modifications were cancelled in 1997.

The lease ended in an unusual way. With Typhoon further delayed and deliveries still some way off, the interim fighter would be needed for longer. With the agreed ten-year lease coming to an end, the Italian Air Force began to look at what would be needed to extend the service life beyond the planned period. The RAF F3s were being updated under the Capability Sustainment Programme and it was seen as vital to maintain viability, but this was expensive. In a bizarre twist, F-16As were leased from the USA and the F3s were returned for disposal. Few lease airframes re-entered RAF service and many were delivered directly to RAF St Athan where they were broken up for spares for the Tornado GR4 fleet. By December 2004, all the Italian F3s had been returned with one exception. A ceremony was held at the base at Gioia del Colle in 2004 to mark the end of the lease programme. A single Tornado F3 (MM7210 which had started life as ZE836) gave a flypast before being presented as a permanent museum exhibit.

The final chapter in the life of the Tornado F3 was the Combat Sustainability Programme, or CSP, and it had a chequered history. Reputations had suffered over the Tornado GR1 Mid Life Update which brought the bomber variant up to GR4 standard, and there was nervousness given the reputation of the F3. With limited funds, as an aircraft moves into its last five years of service, it becomes impossible to instigate a cost-effective modification programme. The time it takes for a modification to go through specification, design, and testing, is simply too long to equip the fleet in sufficient numbers within that time. For that reason, with ten years to go to the out of service date (OSD), a flurry of activity to identify which upgrades might be viable began.

It was clear that Typhoon would not be cleared for military tasks in time to allow the rundown of the F3 fleet by 2009. The F3 armed with Skyflash was already obsolescent as it was completely out-ranged by its potential opponents. The Russian AA-10A short-range Alamo, which was fitted to Iraqi Mig 29s, was a good match and carried by a formidable opponent. Drawn to the merge when guiding a Skyflash, the F3 would lose. The AA-10C 'long burn' Alamo was more than a match and appeared on many ex-Soviet fighters exported worldwide. The AA-12 Adder was an AMRAAM equivalent and was already appearing on Russian fourth-generation fighters such as the Su-27 Flanker, and the hugely improved SU-35 Flanker 'E'. Also widely proliferated was the updated and much more capable French-designed Matra 530D.

The weapons upgrade was vital to make the Tornado F3 viable for its final ten years of service, yet the term 'update' or 'upgrade' was taboo. If a programme was to be approved it would have to be run under the banner of sustainability. Any suggestion that Tornado F3 was being enhanced when billions had been invested in Typhoon was anathema to the financiers and spin doctors. The term 'taking a capability at risk' had become fashionable, which in layman's terms means that you allow a weapon system to 'wither on the vine'. To the accountants this is an attractive option as it is always the cheapest. To operators asked to step in harm's way it is much less popular. Although capability deteriorates, participation in keynote multinational exercises such as 'Red Flag' at Nellis AFB in Nevada continues. Critically, crews are still expected to succeed when their political masters commit them to an overseas intervention. To do so, equipment has to be prudently updated rather than being rushed into service when the latest overseas operation is announced.

A number of potential solutions were investigated to solve the F3 capability gap. Active Skyflash was a Matra BAe Dynamics programme to fit an active seeker head to the basic Skyflash missile. A further development of the motor meant that the missile would have a slightly longer range but it fell well short of the American Advanced Medium Range Air-to-air Missile or AMRAAM. Being active, the upgraded missile would be 'fire and forget', just like the Sidewinder. Inside the missile body, the electronics were digital so would be more compatible with the 'electric jet'. The missile body was the same as Skyflash so, mechanically, the interfaces were identical. Even so, software modifications would have been needed to the missile management system to allow the missile to be carried and fired. However, with the marginal improvement of Active Skyflash, the F3 would remain out-ranged by its principal opposition armed with the latest AA-10 Alamo missile. Additionally, a case to acquire yet another missile type was tenuous.

The only viable solution was to fit AMRAAM which is a beyond-visual-range air-to-air missile which can be used in all weather, both day and night. AMRAAM had already been procured to equip the Sea Harrier FRS2 and had been specified to equip Typhoon. It relies on the onboard radar of the firing aircraft for initial cueing and takes an initial flight path to a point in space, at which time it becomes 'active'. At that point its onboard radar illuminates the target and completes the intercept using its own data. Integrated into the Tornado F3 weapon system, the missile could operate in one of two modes. In austere mode, the missile took cuing information from the Foxhunter radar and launched using that tracking data. It would then receive no additional input from the F3 until its own radar updated the original cuing information. If a smart opponent was warned during this phase an evasion turn could put the AMRAAM outside its effective launch success zone, leaving it with insufficient aerodynamic performance to make the intercept. In the 'full up' mode, the Foxhunter provided a mid-course guidance to update to the missile. This meant that the missile could take a revised course and should still be able to achieve a kill, despite target evasion. It was this capability which was to cause rifts.

The programme had been mooted in the early 1990s and slowly gained momentum, albeit embroiled in politics. As a 'sustainment' programme, it was led by the RAF staff rather than the joint operational staff in the central staff, or the Tornado F3 Integrated Project Team. The IPT provided the usual detailed support in defining and contracting the various software modifications, but the Air Force Department would 'front up'. Of the fundamental constraints, lack of funding was inevitably at the fore. With Typhoon still under close scrutiny, any thought that the F3 was being 'improved' might lead to pressure to cancel the later but vital project. Some measures could be taken which made the F3 project more affordable. Missiles were already in service as AMRAAM had been bought some years earlier to provide a front-sector capability for the Sea Harrier FRS2. These missiles could be shared pending the further AMRAAM buy for Typhoon. With delays in Typhoon it was logical to earmark those missiles for the Tornado until the new type was declared operational, at which time they could revert to their intended use. Support systems were already in place to service those missiles so costs could be contained. With the demise of the Sea Harrier in March 2006 the original AMRAAMs were finally dedicated for F3 use. By offsetting costs in this way, scarce funds could be focussed on the software changes to the F3 weapon system.

The preferred option was to provide the 'full up' AMRAAM capability from the outset, and costings were produced to support the bid. As always, the first estimate caused a collective intake of breath and the accountants began to press for 'austere' AMRAAM. This was despite warnings from the front line, arguing that austere AMRAAM merely maintained a nervous status quo and gave no margin for developments among opposing threat systems. With a projected fifteen-year service life, during which many more threat developments were likely, the risk of obsolescence was still high. As the arguments followed, feasibility studies quantified the not insignificant integration challenge.

The first and easiest challenge was to mount the missiles onto the aircraft. AMRAAM is the same shape and size as the Skyflash so it slotted into the semi-conformal launchers under the Tornado quite easily. The Fraser Nash launchers were extremely powerful so no modification was needed to fire the missile. At that stage efforts turned to making the Foxhunter radar talk to the new weapon and this would tax the experts. The 'Holy Grail' for crews would be to use the track-while-scan, or TWS, to prosecute an attack against four JTIDS-designated hostile targets at long range and to fire four AMRAAMs against multiple targets before the attacking pilots even gained visual contact. That meant that the F3 could use its excellent speed capability to extend the range of the missile. A missile launched at Mach 2 at high level will travel much farther than a similar missile launched at 350 knots at low level. If this goal could be achieved, the F3 crew could return to base to re-arm without ever coming under threat from a hostile fighter. Avoiding air combat manoeuvring would negate the airframe limitations which had plagued the F3. Unfortunately, Foxhunter was 1970s technology rather than 1990s digital technology and deficiencies in the original design architecture were quickly evident. During its own update, the Tornado GR4 had been fitted with a military standard data bus to allow digital signals to be passed between electronic components. A similar electronic network would be needed to allow digital messages to be passed. The old processors which controlled the radar were obsolescent and had to be replaced. In parallel, the main computers which controlled the other avionics such as JTIDS were old and unfit to tackle the new jobs. This should have come as no surprise. Considering an analogy with one's own personal computer, anyone using a Sinclair Spectrum computer in the 1990s would have been the subject of derision, yet this was, in effect, the situation with F3. With an airframe expected to last twenty-five years plus, replacing obsolescent components was routine and CSP allowed a number of efforts to be coordinated. Although the cost was high, the value was higher, but identifying which project would 'front up' the money for the greater good proved challenging. As software engineers dug deeper, potential solutions were taken forward to full development and planners tried to identify funds.

The aim was achievable but expensive so, despite best efforts, the critics were not persuaded that the full AMRAAM capability was needed to match the fielded threat and, much to the dismay of the operational community, austere AMRAAM was endorsed. In a further blow, the software upgrades to display launch success zones in the cockpit were not approved. Crews would be forced to conduct mental gymnastics in the cockpit to decide when missiles could be fired in different tactical situations rather than relying on their displays. Although the missile was massively more capable, the potential had been compromised. Sometimes MoD logic was frustratingly opaque and common sense did not prevail. It would eventually cost more to achieve the same aim and it would take more time and effort and arrive in service much later.

The Combat Sustainability Programme was finally announced in March 1996, but it was to take until 2001 before realism finally set in. The planned out-of-service date for Tornado F3 was April 2010, although false optimism allowed the date to be brought forward to 2009 at one time. With Typhoon further delayed to 2006, many years late, the comprehensive handover plan made it clear that the Tornado F3 would be needed in significant numbers until at least 2010 to allow the Typhoon force to build up. The comprehensive testing to allow Typhoon to assume QRA duties would not be completed in time. New threat missiles had been fielded, as feared, and it was apparent that the full AMRAAM capability was vital if the F3, which was still deployed on operations, was to remain credible. The questionable decision to fit austere AMRAAM was revisited. In June 2001 a reluctant MoD was finally persuaded that a fully supported AMRAAM was essential, but the programme would be known as the AMRAAM Optimisation Programme and would become an integral element of what became known as the 'Stage 3' standard of weapon system. AOP was finally endorsed and the F3 received the update which would make it a truly capable fighter.

In the run up to the operational firings there were a number of 'AMRAAM scares' in the media, possibly stirred up by the pro Sea Harrier lobby which was smarting after the loss of the Navy capability. Under the dramatic headline 'RAF Abandons Missile System After Near Miss' it was suggested that the programme had been terminated after a stray missile had targeted a chase aircraft. The article picked up on the integration problems, suggesting that Foxhunter was not compatible with AMRAAM and that no plans were in place to replace the radar. Despite the claims that the Tornado F3 would never be able to effectively use AMRAAM, they were not well justified in the article. The article focussed on the fact that the AMRAAM had been fired 'blind' (without radar guidance) yet this was one of the modes which made AMRAAM attractive in air combat. It was an active missile after all. An RAF spokesman was rolled out to admit that integration problems were still being resolved.

The conclusion was that the government should be urged to reverse its decision to scrap Sea Harrier on the grounds that it was the only aircraft which could use AMRAAM—in reality, it had only recently been adapted. The Blue Vixen radar in the Sea Harrier was a more modern digital design which had been installed during a retrofit programme in 1993. The more modern design was the basis for the new radar in the Typhoon and was a generation ahead of Foxhunter, so integrating AMRAAM was a much simpler task. The electronic data buses needed to support the missile had already been installed and F3 was only then being modified with similar digital equipment.

Such misinformed reporting was comical to anyone who had ever been involved in a missile test. The early firings in 2002 would naturally begin by validating the simplest mode described as 'blind'. The chase aircraft takes pictures during an operational test firing and flies in loose formation behind the firing aircraft. Unless the missile failed dramatically and reversed its course there is no way it could threaten the chase aircraft and an AMRAAM seeker, which could search behind the aircraft, would indeed have been a radical breakthrough. Equally, if a chase pilot had flown his aircraft into a position where the missile could detect him before launch, he deserved the fright he would undoubtedly have received. Safety procedures were rigorous to minimise such risks and were well practiced. Even in its last years of service, Tornado F3 was the subject of hostile lobbying designed to favour other projects and deny it the capability which would tide the air defence force over until Typhoon was ready for service. A more likely conclusion would be that inter-service politics were in play at a time when the Sea Harrier was coming under financial pressure. The reality was that there simply were not enough Sea Harriers to meet the readiness requirements for air defence aircraft so F3 would run on until replaced by Typhoon, with or without Sea Harriers alongside.

In stark contrast, fitting a new infra-red missile had proved much simpler. By the time efforts were underway to fit AMRAAM, a programme had already been agreed to fit the Advanced Short Range Air-to-Air Missile, or ASRAAM. Bizarrely, the shorter range ASRAAM, a hugely capable infra-red guided missile, had been procured to provide self-defence protection for the Harrier GR7 fighter bomber. While a welcome addition to the inventory, there was no logic to providing a ground attack aircraft with such a complex missile, while the Tornado F3, as the principal air defence aircraft, soldiered on with the earlier generation AIM-9L Sidewinder. ASRAAM was earmarked for F3.

ASRAAM is an innovative design and much more capable than the Sidewinder it replaced. Although it uses infra-red guidance and tracks to its target passively, there the similarities end. It uses what is known as imaging technology. Rather than the old-style gimballed heads of the Sidewinder, the sensor uses a planar array seeker quite similar to the sensor in a digital camera. Instead of a spot heat source it produces a complex map of the heat signature of its target, so is much more accurate when tracking and more resistant to infra-red decoys. The missile differs from earlier generations in that it has only four control fins at the rear of the missile body and no forward control fins which reduces drag considerably. With its larger rocket motor, it is much faster than Sidewinder, accelerating to a higher Mach number over launch speed. With its bigger motor it also has a much greater range than earlier generation missiles, extending out to the limits of visual range. Its principal advantage is that it has a much-improved 'off boresight' capability, meaning it can see targets well off axis when sitting on the launcher rail. This means that in air combat, much more fleeting shots can be taken. The F3 need not be pointing directly at its target and the pilot could allow the radar to designate and cue the missile before launch, right out to the limits of radar coverage. Even if it cannot be designated before launch, a 'lock after launch' mode allows more flexibility, albeit with greater risk. Once it reaches its target the high-explosive blast fragmentation warhead is detonated by either laser proximity or impact fuse. The missile mounted onto the launcher rail used a standard coupling and was connected to the electronics via an umbilical lead. Modifications were needed for the missile monitoring system so that the new missile could be recognised and managed. Other than telling the seeker where to look for its target, the weapon aiming and employment principles were similar, so integration proved much less complex than AMRAAM. The increased range of the seeker head was to prove critical when employed tactically. Cued by the Foxhunter beyond visual range, even when targets employed defensive tactics to defeat a long-range AMRAAM shot, the ASRAAM seeker would already be locked and the pilot could use the target designator in the head-up display to aid visual acquisition. If the target turned back towards, an ASRAAM shot could be taken at the limits of visual range and far sooner than would ever have been possible using Sidewinder. While the F3 crew was still pulled towards the merge, the chances of entering an engagement with a missile in the air were increased.

An operational test programme ran in parallel and the Operational Evaluation Unit completed a series of test firings against QF4 drones at Eglin AFB in Florida in 2002 under service evaluation trials. This initial test was extremely successful, resulting in the destruction of two drones. A number of issues were identified, leading to software updates; a further standard was tested on the Aberporth ranges proving equally effective as three Jindivik drones joined the tally of 'kills'. A final standard with all the bugs fixed and improved capability against flares entered service shortly afterwards in 2003. Inevitably there were problems, but ASRAAM was without doubt a success.

One of the more innovative modifications to emerge for the Tornado was in its guise as the Tornado EF3. One of the fundamental roles in any air operation is SEAD, or suppression of enemy air defences, and more recently, DEAD, or destruction of air defences. During both Gulf wars and the Kosovo campaign, combined air operations packages were not tasked into hostile airspace without first attacking the enemy air defences and providing support jamming during the operation. This was a capability for which the UK had come to rely on the USA, having fielded only a limited capability with an anti-radiation missile known as ALARM during the Cold War. It was carried by a specialist Tornado GR1/GR4 squadron trained for the role and, although it was a complex and capable weapon, it was different to the US equivalent, the High Speed Anti-Radiation Missile, or HARM. Able to operate in three modes, corridor, loiter, and direct, ALARM was intended to punch holes in a Soviet Army attack formation, allowing allied bombers to penetrate into the rear areas without threat from anti-aircraft defences. In the loiter mode, the missile climbs to height and hangs suspended in a parachute. If the surface-to-air missile threat radar shuts down, the missile listens as it slowly descends. Should the radar begin to illuminate again, the missile is released and guides on the radar signal before detonating close to the radar dish. With the end of the Cold War it was thought the weapon had reached the end of its life, but Saddam's Soviet-like infrastructure reinvigorated its usefulness and a seeker head upgrade, tested in 2005, gave it an extended lease of life. Financial stringency had even affected the US, and the EF111 support jammer was scrapped in 1998 with the role being assumed by the US Navy with the EA6B Prowler. For that reason, support jamming was always a precious capability and assets were at a premium. The Prowler uses the AN/ALQ99 jamming suite and can jam surveillance radars, threat radars, and communications. It is supported in the role by the F-16 Wild Weasel, using the HARM and the AGM-88 HARM Targeting System. The Prowler has since been replaced by the EF18 Growler. More relevant was that the systems were extremely expensive and unaffordable within the constraints of the budget. Cheaper solutions were needed.

A Tornado EF3 carrying 1,500-litre fuel tanks, ALARM anti-radiation, and ASRAAM air-to-air infra-red missiles, a towed radar decoy pod, a Phimat chaff dispenser, and Vinten flare dispensers. (*Geoff Lee*)

Given the lack of SEAD forces, it was proposed that the F3 could be modified to provide an additional SEAD capability. In broad terms, a 'black box' similar to those used in self-defence jamming systems was built into the weapon system, allowing jamming techniques to be employed against threats the attacking forces were likely to encounter. By using the radar homing and warning system to alert the crew, the navigator could cue a jamming response against a threat. The innovative aspect was that best use was made of existing antennas on the airframe, precluding the need to cut metal or hang additional high drag pods on the pylons. To extend the capability further, ALARM missiles were fitted onto the pylons and integrated into the missile management system. The final enhancement was to fit the Enhanced Paveway II laser-guided bomb, giving the ability to destroy the radars and support cabins of a SAM complex. Once installed, the system was operationally tested to ensure that the techniques worked and to develop operational tactics against typical threats. It proved remarkably effective for a 'quick fix' concept. Crucially, none of these modifications affected the basic air-to-air functions so, not only could the EF3 attack the air defences, it could provide escort fighter cover for the attacking formation with its four AMRAAM and four ASRAAM missiles. Although the EF3 was offered to commanders, it never captured the imagination and, to the best of my knowledge, was not used in anger.

The logical extension would have been to integrate AN/ALQ99 pods onto the aircraft to extend the range of capability further. The basic capabilities could have been further integrated, but with the end of operations, the imperative disappeared, as did the funding. The base capability was declared to commanders, but with the demise of No. 11 Squadron in 2005, the EF3 was withdrawn from service and the capability was not replaced.

12

The Final Operational Standard

When the Tornado F2 entered service it was intended to fight over the North Sea facing a Cold War threat comprising mostly bombers employing heavy electronic jamming. Expeditionary operations were not envisaged and RAF Germany was the limit of projected deployments forward. The uneasy balance of power meant overseas adventures were tempered by risk. As Soviet fighters developed from the short-range Mig-21 Fishbed into the long-range air-to-air refuelled Su-27 Flanker, the F3 began to be challenged even in its intended role. With UN operations in Iraq, the Balkans, and Afghanistan, fighter threats emerged against which it was ill-equipped. Iraqi Mig-29 Fulcrums were fitted with air-to-air weapons which ranged from the AA-8 Aphid through the AA-10a Alamo, to the highly effective AA-11 Archer with its thrust vector control. Meanwhile the Soviets had introduced an anti-radiation version of the AA-10 Alamo known as the AA-10e which had the ability to recognise and home on the emissions of a threat radar. It could be designated and fired and would track passively without the crew who were targeted being aware of its presence. Without complex defensive aids, only the ability to recognise an attack and turn off the radar would prevent an engagement. With a planned service life of twenty-five years, it was clear that the F3 would have to be updated to keep pace with technological progress. Who could have envisaged a Spitfire which appeared in 1936, still being the RAF's front-line fighter in 1963—the era of the supersonic Lightning—without radical modifications being needed?

Take a look in the cockpit of a Tornado F3 preserved in a museum and it looks quite similar to the cockpit of one of the early Tornado F2s which were delivered to RAF Coningsby in 1984. To understand the real changes and why the final standard of F3 was different is to understand the software. For the first time software transformed a capability, despite relatively minor changes to the airframe and the cockpit. With the Stage 2 radar, Foxhunter came of age and by the time it arrived on the front line, it had changed radically from the immature Y List radar. The fundamental way the radar tracked a target was different, and 'cartesian tracking' replaced the original 'polar tracking' methodology. A new radar data processor with much enhanced capability drove the modified software. A new main computer with a massive increase in capacity replaced the tiny 32-kb computer of the Tornado F2. The problem of attacking specific targets within a hostile formation was transformed by incorporating a raid assessment mode allowing precise analysis. The missile monitoring system was further improved to allow the carriage of the latest generation of missiles. Automatic track-while-scan was finally introduced allowing the navigator to concentrate more on the tactical battle rather than struggle with manipulating the uncooperative radar. Improved identification systems such as Mode 4 IFF, a complex and more secure system, were complimented by fitting a Mode 4 interrogator similar to the original Mode 3 system from the early years. Additional systems, which analysed the nature of a target response and could identify the aircraft type by its electronic characteristics, finally gave an effective means to declare a target hostile from within the aircraft rather than relying on external inputs. The introduction of the Joint Tactical Information Distribution System, or JTIDS, revolutionised the way an engagement could be prosecuted and allowed new tactics to be adopted. Not only were details of hostile formations fed in from ground radars and the airborne early warning aircraft, but a formation leader was instantly aware of the position of his wingman and could adopt more fluid tactics.

The 'Stage 2' standard was further developed to adopt the Operation Granby modifications before the final modifications under the combat sustainability programmes incorporated the full AMRAAM and ASRAAM capability. Known by the catchy title of 'ASS6', or avionics software standard 6, the final modifications which became known as 'Stage 3', introduced a modern digital data bus to carry information between the sub-systems. The successor Identification friend or foe (SIFF) was added during the Combat Sustainability Programme in addition to the AMRAAM Optimisation Programme which followed.

Nothing could illustrate the progress of the F3 weapon system more graphically than to compare illustrations of the tactical plan display. The mode matured from the earliest display which simply showed the radar information in a geographical format, through the 'Stage 1' standard where refinements had made the display more user friendly to the quantum step forward at 'Stage 3' standard. In the final standard the addition of JTIDS and the massive increase in computing power over the Tornado F2 meant that a digital representation of geographical features was now shown. Gone was the need to use route lines. The host Tornado was represented by a Tornado symbol with a 'cheese wedge' to show the radar coverage. Radar tracks still appeared in the traditional way but data link tracks acquired a new format. The tactical picture and the situational awareness of the crew had been revolutionised.

Although not an F3 specific requirement, another huge step forward in the way in which aircrew debriefed their sorties was the introduction of the Rangeless Airborne Instrumentation and Debrief System, or RAIDS. It replaced the fixed Air Combat Manoeuvring Installation (ACMI) which had been built in the UK and

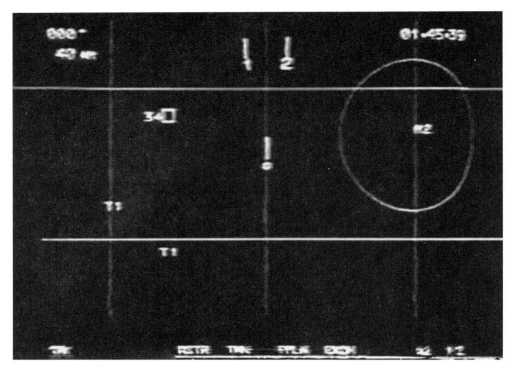

The original plan display in 1985. (*UK MoD Crown Copyright, 1984*)

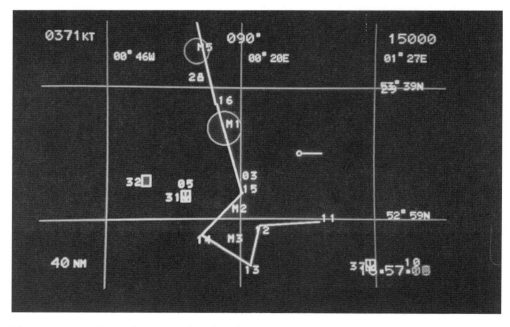

The east coast of UK drawn on the plan display using navigation lines. In use *c.* 1986. (*UK MoD Crown Copyright, 1986*)

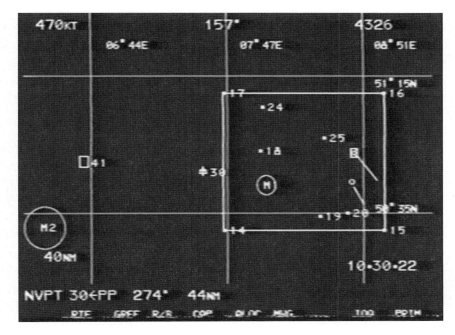

A fighter tactical area of responsibility drawn using navigation lines in 1993. (*UK MoD Crown Copyright, 1993*)

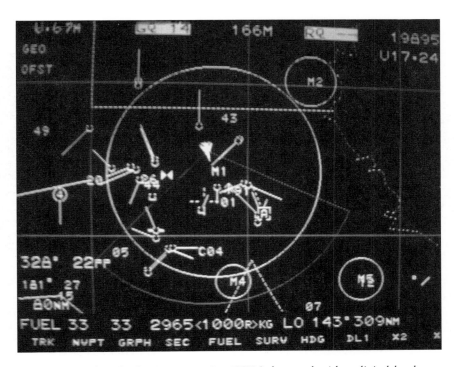

The ultimate plan display incorporating JTIDS data and with a digital landmass towards the end of the aircraft's service life. (*UK MoD Crown Copyright, 2010, courtesy of Kelvin Harris*)

Decimomannu in the 1980s, where fixed buoys on the ground received signals transmitted from a pod on each participating aircraft. RAIDS technology achieved the same level of fidelity as ACMI without resorting to fixed installations. Looking like a Sidewinder missile, a RAIDS pod fitted to each aircraft could establish a network between participating aircraft by sharing positional information, generating an air picture like a mini JTIDS network. Electronic 'bricks' mounted in each pod were downloaded into a debriefing station at the home base and could be used to reconstruct an engagement. Crews had progressed from simple scribbled notes on a kneeboard, hastily captured in the air, to precise three-dimensional reconstructions of where each aircraft was at any given moment. The debrief could be conducted at a home base, and could be stopped, rerun, and dissected in excruciating detail, thereby revolutionising aircrew debriefings and improving training value.

A system similar to ACMI is used during the iconic wargame called 'Exercise Red Flag' at the home of US military aviation, Nellis Air Force Base, Las Vegas, Nevada. Red Flag originally replicated the first ten sorties of World War 3, and the theory said that if aircrew experienced those missions in a controlled environment, mistakes would be less likely when called to fight. To move with the times, the scenarios were reconfigured to represent those which would be encountered on expeditionary detachments in Iraq or Afghanistan. I was privileged to spend three years as the Air Warfare Centre Liaison Officer at the USAF Warfare Centre and observed a number of Flag exercises. In November 1992, No. 29 (F) Squadron became the first Tornado F3 unit to participate, and the deployment became a regular feature on the schedule. The squadron's efforts set a high standard from the outset and on one mission, nineteen kills were claimed by the F3 crews for no loss. Despite the successes, it was telling that the F3 was often relegated in the pre-AMRAAM days to 'Red Air' duties with F3s simulating Russian Mig-23s, armed with older generation weapons. If acting as 'blue' fighters, the F3 would often be relegated to the night shift where night vision goggles and the two-man crew redressed the deficiencies in the Skyflash missile. The inclusion of JTIDS transformed the aircraft; a colleague, 'Giz' Taylor from No. 5 Squadron, described how JTIDS changed the way the F3 fought. His comments about Exercise Red Flag 99-2 are illuminating.

No. 5 (AC) Squadron received the Joint Tactical Information Distribution System, or JTIDS, in early 1996 as one of the first Tornado F3 squadrons to receive it. Known as the 'Force Multiplier', JTIDS was to give the F3 crew a huge increase in their situational awareness, or 'SA'—the cornerstone of any fighter crew to keep awareness of who they are shooting at or if they are being shot at. JTIDS was controlled by the navigator with a simple control panel and the data was loaded with a tape cassette into the main computer during start up. The network would then automatically synchronise. Initially, the Tornado F3 had its own data link network but was soon joined by the E3 Sentry which put out a surveillance picture of the whole 'war' (or exercise). Each F3 could contribute its own radar picture to the net receiving the picture from other Tornados in their formation and, once combined with the picture from the E3, situation awareness increased ten-fold. It quickly became apparent that new tactics could be employed to make up for the lack of range of the ageing Skyflash Missile. With some great weapons instructors on 5 Squadron, fresh ideas were introduced and trialled in the UK against both bombers and fighters. At low level, where the F3 had excess power, we could regularly 'sneak up' on a bomber package with our radar in standby—giving no advanced warning on the opponents radar warning receiver—while still receiving the air picture from F3s on combat air patrol or from the E3 which could be 100 miles away. Getting in among a bomber package would usually result in either a shot against the bomber or forcing them into a defensive reaction meaning they ran short of fuel or missed their pre allocated time on target.

The famous 'Exercise Red Flag' is held at Nellis AFB in Nevada USA and is known as 'The World's Biggest Air Defence Exercise'. The American aggressor squadrons, in their role as 'Red Air', fly F-16s painted in Russian colour schemes and employ Russian tactics or can adopt those of a potential enemy. Red Flag 99-2 was held from 26 Jan 99 to 5 Feb 99 and 5 (AC) Squadron were invited to participate as 'Blue Air' or friendly fighters. This would be the first time JTIDS would be used by the F3 and would work to our advantage. In the first few days we employed the new data link tactics and achieved good results. Fighter crews from other nations were very interested in our new piece of kit and visited our detachment after each mission to see how much our situation awareness had increased through use of JTIDS.

One fantastic mission, and one of the best days of my flying career, came on 4 February flying Tornado F3 ZE983. I was chosen to lead a 6-ship of F3s as Blue Force Leader. After discussion with the squadron weapons instructors, I came up with a plan that would hopefully out-fox the 'Red Air' F-16s and sanitise the airspace for the bomber package. It was vital that they get through and release their bombs on target, on time. The briefing is held on a huge stage in the Red Flag auditorium at Nellis in front of all the exercise participants and is quite a measure of one's confidence. I briefed my plan without questions and we launched with the JTIDS net working well. At 'vul time', or the time at which the combined air operation is deemed to begin, my 6-ship crossed the start line in 'wall' (line abreast with 2 mile spacing between fighters) at around 20,000 feet at 0.9 Mach. Together with another 20 fighters we swept the Red Flag range in an aggressive 30 mile wide wall looking for opponents. JTIDS rapidly gave us a perfect picture of where the threats lay and we soon had the 'Red Air' fighters on the defensive and running back to their haven in the west of the area. For the next 10 minutes we threatened the aggressors as soon as they felt able to re-enter the fight by committing fighters at appropriate times based on our outstanding air picture built by our own radars and the E3 Sentry. With the airspace clean, the bombers pushed through the hostile airspace on time. At the debrief they were thankful for their relatively simple run-in to the targets. We didn't lose any F3s on my watch and we claimed several valid kills on the 'Red Air' F-16s.

This story was repeated on more than one exercise, yet is rarely quoted by the detractors. As AMRAAM replaced the Skyflash, results improved yet further as 'fire and forget' coupled with the longer range missiles made tactics even more fluid. The F3 was coming of age.

Some aspects and capabilities never materialised. A passive tracking system was never fitted. An infra-red search track system such as that fitted to Typhoon or the Su-27 Flanker would have given a capability to operate in the presence of anti-radiation missiles such as the AA-10e Alamo. A helmet-mounted sighting system (HMS) was viable and a system was tested in a Tornado F2 under the Tornado Integrated Avionics Research Aircraft (TIARA) programme. With an aircraft which lacks agility yet is armed with a highly agile air-to-air missile such as ASRAAM which can be designated at high off- boresight angles, an HMS would have conferred a huge increase in capability. A pilot trapped in a combat 'circle of joy' could have used the HMS to lock his ASRAAM 'across the circle' without the need to point the fighter's nose at the target. The missile was more than able to make up for the aircraft's lack of agility by its own impressive performance and shots which were impossible would have become routine. Add to that the improvements in situation awareness which the HMS confers by projecting tactical information onto the visor, and the pilot's abilities would have been magnified. Crucially, colour displays were never introduced, although they would have been a huge step forward. Better defensive aids were always proposed but never funded. TRD remained an operational fit on a small portion of the fleet. A missile warning system suitable for a fast jet was always elusive and potential solutions were never sufficiently developed until late in the F3's service life. For that reason, unless crews detected a threat missile visually, they remained vulnerable to attack. Even if detected, the reaction times against a short-range threat were so short that it was doubtful whether a crew could save the aircraft. With the excruciatingly short flight times—as little as five seconds—a crew would have to be alert, as well as lucky, to see and react to a missile in flight. Many times during the darker days, proposals were made to replace the Foxhunter with the US AN/APG65 medium PRF radar or the Blue Vixen system, but despite its history, Foxhunter arguably matched these capabilities by the end of its service life.

So might things have been done better? With an unlimited budget, a resurgent Cold War and Air Defence of the Homeland as a number one priority, Tornado F3 might have attracted more resources earlier. More comprehensive development and operational testing in the early 1980s might have identified the deficiencies before introduction to service and the hasty 'Granby' modifications would have been unnecessary. With more funding, the 'Granby' modifications and the JTIDS capability would have been incorporated fleet wide, preventing the fleet-within-a-fleet problems. An active jammer specified from the outset would have avoided the near eviction from Operation Deny Flight. The full AMRAAM capability implemented from the inception would have prevented the frustrations of 'austere' AMRAAM.

The final capability was good but it was achieved through patient staff work using the limited funding to make best headway past a reluctant procurement system. A perfect procurement programme is impossible and, with limited funding, something is always better than nothing, whereas nothing is always the easier option. Indisputably, the final weapon system standard would have been unrecognisable to the early Tornado F2 crews. Although externally the airframe appeared the same, under the skin there was a quantum change. The foibles of the F2 had been replaced by a mature weapon system driven by a capable radar which launched some of the most effective air-to-air missiles in the world. Those who compare the two aircraft in the same breath are misguided.

A combat aircraft has a finite service life and a target of twenty-five years for the Tornado Air Defence Variant was not unreasonable. As is always the case when an aircraft retires, even with an aircraft as unloved as the F3, there is a sense of sad regret. The Tornado F3 was no exception.

Epilogue
The Demise

I would have loved a final sortie in the Tornado F3 equipped to the final standard before retiring, but my flying career ended in the Falkland Islands in 1994 when the 'Stage 1' standard was the baseline. Of the fourteen air defence squadrons in service in 1991, only eight survived the post 'Cold War Windfall' as the Phantom and Lightning were retired. Even the Tornado F3 fleet was trimmed back early. Opportunities to take command of a squadron declined and competition for the highly prized appointments became fierce. My time in command of No. 1435 Flight was to be my last flying tour.

The Tornado F3 had a remarkable safety record with only thirteen aircraft lost in RAF service over its operational life, which compares favourably to the much higher loss rates of its immediate predecessors, the Lightning and the Phantom. As a comparison, ten English Electric Lightnings were lost in accidents in 1971 alone. Even so, this does not make it easier to accept the loss of the aircrew who died in accidents and they will always be remembered.

The retirement eventually ran quite closely to the original plans. In October 2009 the National Audit Office announced the drawdown of the Tornado F3 force one year earlier than planned to ease manning shortfalls. It suggested that the F3's operational tasks would be progressively handed over to the Typhoon beginning in 2009. The reality was different.

Drawdown had begun much earlier with No. 23 (F) Squadron at RAF Leeming being retired in February 1994 as a savings measure. Under the Strategic Defence Review, No. 29 (F) Squadron disbanded at RAF Coningsby in October 1998, followed by No. 5 Squadron in September 2002, further reducing the numbers of air defence aircraft on the front line. The Tornado Operational Conversion Unit, No. 56 (R) Squadron, like its Phantom predecessor, relocated to RAF Leuchars in March 2003 leaving RAF Coningsby to prepare for the arrival of the Typhoon. Next came the retirement of the Leeming units. No. 11 Squadron was first to go in October 2005, being replaced by Typhoon and becoming one of the earliest squadrons to operate the new fighter at RAF Coningsby. In April 2008 No. 25

Squadron followed, leaving RAF Leeming to operate just its Hawk target facilities squadron. RAF Leuchars became the F3's final home and the OCU was subsumed within No. 43 (F) Squadron in April 2008, as only a small number of crews were needed to man the squadrons until retirement. The fleet was reduced from thirty-six to twelve aircraft from September 2009 with the remaining crews meeting only the Northern Quick Reaction Alert (Northern Q) commitment. By then operational training had been reduced to a minimum with QRA as the priority; crews focussed exclusively on QRA to the detriment of other operational training. The penultimate squadron, No. 43 (F) Squadron disbanded in July 2009 with the last unit, No. 111 (F) Squadron, finally giving up its aircraft on 22 March 2001, bringing the career of the Tornado F3 to an end. This was a year later than the planning date, although many felt that the date had been pulled forward.

A hangar party was held at RAF Leuchars to mark the F3's retirement and was attended by aircrew and groundcrew from every squadron that had operated the aircraft during its twenty-five-year life. A formal ceremony was held to mark the retirement attended by former squadron commanders and those who had been associated with the aircraft. The Parade Reviewing Officer was Air Chief Marshal Sir Michael Graydon, a former Station Commander at RAF Leuchars and a fine fighter pilot. The final flights from RAF Leuchars took place on 28 March 2011 as the last aircraft were flown to RAF Leeming for disposal. ZH554 landed at RAF Leeming to be delivered to the 'Reduce to Produce' (RTP) facility, in company with ZE734 and ZE791, both of which sported commemorative colour schemes. 'Scimitar' formation broke into the Leeming circuit and ended the story.

As always, the test establishment holds the accolade for being the last to operate a particular type. Crews at Boscombe Down were still flying ZH552 as late as June 2012, although the aircraft was scrapped later that year. The TIARA aircraft was still flying in early 2011, but has since been grounded. It holds the record for length of service. ZD902, one of the earliest Tornado F2s, first flew on 4 September 1984. I flew the aircraft on No. 229 OCU where it served from 10 May 1985, continuing for over twenty-six years, although for most of that time, not on the front line.

The RTP programme was conceived to recover essential spares from F3s to support the Tornado GR4 force. Many of the components were common and could be reused to reduce future running costs for the bomber fleet. Once stripped, components which were of no use to the front line were reduced to scrap metal and recycled. Ironically, this meant that many F3s which might otherwise have found their way into a museum were broken up and sent to scrap dealers. For Phantom operators, the sight of the Phantom Graveyard at Wattisham was very sad. For F3 operators there were similar scenes in the North of England and in Wales.

Happily, many airframes still survive. The cockpit of a Tornado F2, ZD938, survives at Doncaster Aero Museum on the site of the former RAF Doncaster. It is slowly being renovated to its original condition by its owner Simon Pulford. ZE887 survives in the RAF Museum at Hendon and sits alongside Phantom

XV424 in the Main Hall. ZE760 is the Gate Guardian at RAF Coningsby and was the eighty-third Tornado off the production line, serving with No. 5 Squadron and No. 229 OCU at RAF Coningsby, where it survived a wheels-up landing. It was then transferred to No. 43 (F) Squadron at RAF Leuchars before being leased to the Italian Air Force serving with 36 Stormo at Gioia Del Colle as MM7206. It returned to RAF Coningsby in 2003 and was presented to the station to mark the retirement of the Tornado F3 at RAF Coningsby on 22 July 2003. It now sits opposite the Phantom Gate Guardian, XT891.

Many aircraft did not survive. The Italian lease aircraft were mostly broken up at RAF St Athan after being delivered back to the UK. My own aircraft, ZE253, AT019, which featured on the No. 56 (R) Squadron print, first flew on 9 March 1987 and was delivered to No. 56 Squadron later that month. It was flown to RAF St Athan on 27 November 2001 where it was stored before finally being scrapped. The final single sticker ZG799, AS147, which I delivered into service on 24 Mar 1993, was sent to the RTP programme at RAF Leeming before being scrapped on 6 June 2008.

Another fine example survived and was refurbished by Jet Art Aviation based at Selby in Yorkshire and will remain in private hands. It was auctioned at Silverstone and was bought by a former Tornado F3 flyer, hopefully to find a home in a collection. The aircraft, ZE256, served on No. 229 OCU at RAF Coningsby. Chris Wilson, the director of the company, is an ex-RAF technician and refurbishes airframes for display in museums and collections. Luckily he rescued this fine example of the twin-stick Tornado F3 from the clutches of the RTP programme and has returned it to its former glory. Designated AT020 and delivered into service on 2 April 1987, it was one of the first Tornado F3s to arrive at Coningsby. It flew with both No. 29 Squadron and No. 56 Squadron at Coningsby before heading north to end its service life at RAF Leuchars, where it was retired. Shipped by road to its temporary home near Selby, the airframe was repainted and carries ZE343 and No. 11 Squadron colours on the right-hand side. The cockpit was carefully restored, and with the exception of the JTIDS panel in the rear cockpit, is virtually complete.

One aircraft, ZE728, met a more interesting fate when, after decommissioning, it became a piece of artwork on Gateshead's Quayside. It began its journey at a scrap yard in Seaham, County Durham, before being melted down at a local foundry and recast into a bell which can be rung by any member of the public who feels the need.

A mission simulator survives and has been restored almost to its original condition by its owner Simon Pulford. Three units were produced by Rediffusion and were delivered to each main operating base at RAF Coningsby, RAF Leeming, and RAF Leuchars. The simulators were transportable and were mounted in large wheeled containers to allow them to be relocated to a new operating base if the need arose. The concept proved difficult in practice and the Coningsby simulator never left its plinth before being retired once the F3 moved north. Unlike their predecessors, there were no hydraulic jacks to simulate flying, although the seat

The cockpit of Tornado F2 ZD938 at Doncaster Air Museum.

Tornado F3 ZE887 at the RAF Museum, Hendon.

Chris Wilson of Jet Art Aviation with Tornado F3 ZE256.

Tornado F3 ZE760 on the gate at RAF Coningsby.

base moved a little, giving a limited feel. Originally without graphics, a simplistic system was installed later in life. It is now mounted on a trailer, albeit minus its graphics screen and can be moved to air shows to allow the public a chance to sit in an F3 cockpit.

In analysis of its chequered history, what can be said of the Tornado F3? In comparison with the bomber variant, the F3 was a much more capable airframe. It had bigger engines, more fuel, flew faster, and was a more aerodynamic design. The question is, can you turn a bomber into a fighter? Most experts would argue that the answer is no. The F-15, F-16, F-18, and to a certain extent, the F-14, were all designed as fighters and made a successful transition to become bombers. The F-15E is arguably the most capable airframe of its generation. I would struggle to identify many designs which were adapted in the opposite sense. The F3 certainly did not adapt well and even in its final days, only weapon system upgrades made up for aerodynamic deficiencies. The Tornado F3 never made that final step to become a truly capable fighter, although it was a long way down the road. In my opinion, and some would disagree, the biggest error was not to fit a helmet mounted sight. With AMRAAM for the beyond-visual-range fight coupled with an HMS/ASRAAM capability close- in, the F3 would have been a feared opponent at any altitude. Even so, the progress it made over the years was never understood, even by informed critics, and it retired unloved and well underestimated. NATO training opponents still felt cheated and maybe a little embarrassed when removed from the fight by an F3. They should not have. It was a capable opponent in an arena where the gravest mistake is to underestimate the enemy.

Looking for quotes to reflect the Tornado's life was a challenge and this maybe reflects its reputation—it simply never evoked the same emotions as its peers. I cannot honestly say I felt the same adrenaline buzz that I often experienced after flying a sortie in the Phantom. Even so, the F3 probably did most things slightly better and many things much better than my old mount. I can leave others to reflect on the reason why.

A number of celebrities helped by offering an insight. Gordon Ramsey, after a flight in a No. 43 Squadron F3, said, 'Do you know what, I can't eat a f*****g thing. I've lost my appetite!' Apt for a chef and typical of his television persona. Damon Hill, comparing the F3 to his Williams Formula 1 racing car after his flight and just before his first Grand Prix win in Hungary, said, 'It's a bit slow as you let off the brakes but you can beat me from 400 to 600 knots.' A typically humorous response from a national hero.

A number of interesting facts emerged during my research; some have already been mentioned but are worthy of repeating:

- The Tornado F3 served with the Royal Air Force, the Royal Saudi Air Force and the Italian Air Force. Oman ordered eight aircraft but the order was subsequently cancelled.
- The first Tornado F2 was delivered to RAF Coningsby on 5 November 1984. ZD901 (AA) was flown by the BAE test pilot Jerry Lee with Air Vice Marshal Ken Hayr, the Air Officer Commanding No. 11 Group, in the back cockpit. The second Tornado F2, ZD903 (AB), was flown by David Eagles with OC No. 229 Operational Conversion Unit, Wg Cdr Rick Peacock-Edwards, in the rear cockpit.
- Four Tornado F3s from No. 29 (F) Squadron circumnavigated the world from west to east, departing in August 1988. They completed 26,000 miles in eleven weeks, visiting Oman, Malaysia, Thailand, Australia, Singapore, Samoa, Hawaii, USA, and Canada.
- The longest flight by a Tornado F3 was flown by Wg Cdr Rick Peacock-Edwards and Flt Lt Dave Gledhill on 24/25 November 1986, lasting ten hours fifteen minutes during a deployment to Masirah, Oman, for Exercise Swift Sword 86.
- The shortest flight was claimed by a number of crews, mainly because it was rare to log less than five minutes in the authorisation sheets: Flt Lt Roy Macintyre and Flt Lt Ian Evans flew ZE785 from Dishforth to Leeming on 4 April 1989, claiming just five minutes. The F3 had a crack in the taileron and was cleared for the short sortie to recover to base. Flt Lt Jamieson and Wg Cdr Clive Duance flew another five-minute sortie in ZE258 on 17 February 2005. After engine fluctuations on take off, the sortie was aborted turning downwind to land immediately.
- The shortest night flight was flown on 5 January 1989 by Flt Lt Dave Hunt and Flt Lt David Lewis in ZE731. The aircraft was recovering from RAF Waddington to RAF Coningsby after a diversion.
- The longest unrefuelled flight across the Atlantic by an RAF fighter was completed by the crew of ZE155 on 24 September 1987.
- The last single-stick Tornado F3, ZG799, was delivered to RAF Coningsby by Flt Lt Ian 'Shiney' Simmons and Sqn Ldr Dave Gledhill on 20 November 1993.

- The final delivery flight was flown from BAES Warton to RAF Coningsby on 24 March 1994 by the Air Officer Commanding No. 11 Group who flew ZH599, the last trainer variant of the Tornado F3, with OC No. 56 (R) Squadron, Wg Cdr Pete Coker, in the back seat.
- ZE338 was the first RAF F3 to emerge from the Capability Sustainment Programme on 15 May 1998.
- The pilot who flew the most hours in the Tornado F2/F3 was Roy McIntyre, who amassed 4,565 hours. The highest number of hours were flown by navigator Colin 'Wiki' Wills who flew a staggering 4,942 hours, only just missing the elusive 5,000-hours accolade.
- And the most bizarre F3 fact of all? The *Guinness Book of Records* grants a record to the Tornado F3 for carrying the fastest airborne piper. A chief technician from No. 43 Squadron played his bagpipes at Mach 2 in the rear cockpit of a Tornado F3, flown from RAF Leuchars—a feat which can no longer be beaten.

Tornado F3s of No. 56 (Reserve) Squadron at dawn at Florennes airbase.

Appendix

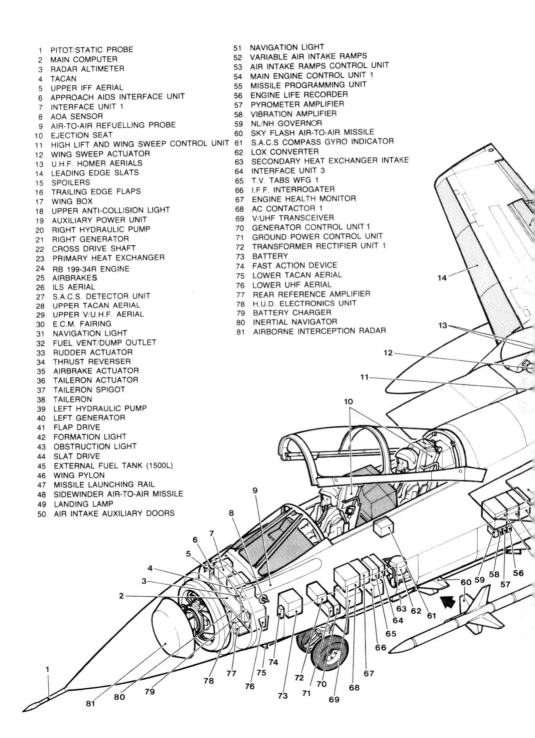

1 PITOT/STATIC PROBE
2 MAIN COMPUTER
3 RADAR ALTIMETER
4 TACAN
5 UPPER IFF AERIAL
6 APPROACH AIDS INTERFACE UNIT
7 INTERFACE UNIT 1
8 AOA SENSOR
9 AIR-TO-AIR REFUELLING PROBE
10 EJECTION SEAT
11 HIGH LIFT AND WING SWEEP CONTROL UNIT
12 WING SWEEP ACTUATOR
13 U.H.F. HOMER AERIALS
14 LEADING EDGE SLATS
15 SPOILERS
16 TRAILING EDGE FLAPS
17 WING BOX
18 UPPER ANTI-COLLISION LIGHT
19 AUXILIARY POWER UNIT
20 RIGHT HYDRAULIC PUMP
21 RIGHT GENERATOR
22 CROSS DRIVE SHAFT
23 PRIMARY HEAT EXCHANGER
24 RB 199-34R ENGINE
25 AIRBRAKES
26 ILS AERIAL
27 S.A.C.S. DETECTOR UNIT
28 UPPER TACAN AERIAL
29 UPPER V/U.H.F. AERIAL
30 E.C.M. FAIRING
31 NAVIGATION LIGHT
32 FUEL VENT/DUMP OUTLET
33 RUDDER ACTUATOR
34 THRUST REVERSER
35 AIRBRAKE ACTUATOR
36 TAILERON ACTUATOR
37 TAILERON SPIGOT
38 TAILERON
39 LEFT HYDRAULIC PUMP
40 LEFT GENERATOR
41 FLAP DRIVE
42 FORMATION LIGHT
43 OBSTRUCTION LIGHT
44 SLAT DRIVE
45 EXTERNAL FUEL TANK (1500L)
46 WING PYLON
47 MISSILE LAUNCHING RAIL
48 SIDEWINDER AIR-TO-AIR MISSILE
49 LANDING LAMP
50 AIR INTAKE AUXILIARY DOORS
51 NAVIGATION LIGHT
52 VARIABLE AIR INTAKE RAMPS
53 AIR INTAKE RAMPS CONTROL UNIT
54 MAIN ENGINE CONTROL UNIT 1
55 MISSILE PROGRAMMING UNIT
56 ENGINE LIFE RECORDER
57 PYROMETER AMPLIFIER
58 VIBRATION AMPLIFIER
59 NL/NH GOVERNOR
60 SKY FLASH AIR-TO-AIR MISSILE
61 S.A.C.S. COMPASS GYRO INDICATOR
62 LOX CONVERTER
63 SECONDARY HEAT EXCHANGER INTAKE
64 INTERFACE UNIT 3
65 T.V. TABS WFG 1
66 I.F.F. INTERROGATER
67 ENGINE HEALTH MONITOR
68 AC CONTACTOR 1
69 V/UHF TRANSCEIVER
70 GENERATOR CONTROL UNIT 1
71 GROUND POWER CONTROL UNIT
72 TRANSFORMER RECTIFIER UNIT 1
73 BATTERY
74 FAST ACTION DEVICE
75 LOWER TACAN AERIAL
76 LOWER UHF AERIAL
77 REAR REFERENCE AMPLIFIER
78 H.U.D. ELECTRONICS UNIT
79 BATTERY CHARGER
80 INERTIAL NAVIGATOR
81 AIRBORNE INTERCEPTION RADAR

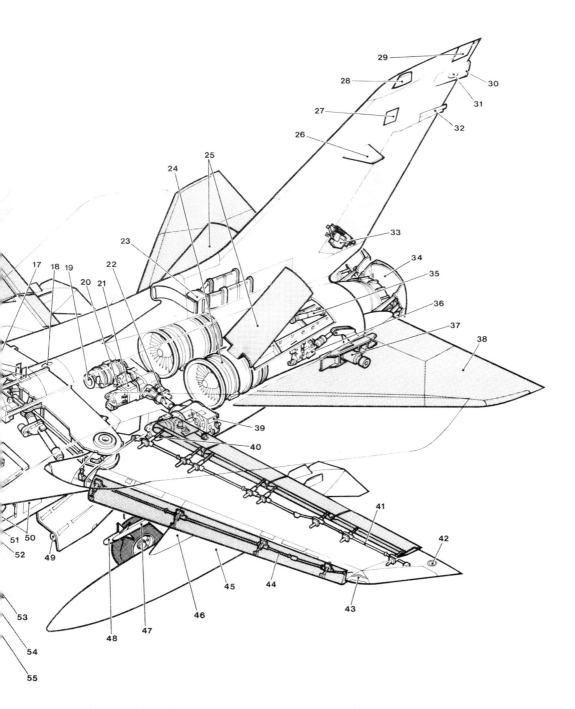

Tornado F Mark 3 Schematic. (*UK MoD Crown Copyright, 1985*)

FRONT COCKPIT

Left Console

1	Engine start panel
2	Throttle box
3	Wing sweep lever
4	Pilot's hand controller
5	AOA and accelerometer lighting dimmer
6	CCS station box
7	Food and drink containers
8	Wander lamp
9	OXYGEN ON/OFF switch
10	CRASH bar
11	CVR control panel
12	SPILS control panel
13	CSAS control panel
14	Canopy JACK RELEASE handle
15	AFDS control panel
16	CANOPY JETTISON handle
17	FLAP emergency override switch
18	AIRBRAKE emergency-in switch
19	FLAPS selector lever
20	ANTI-DAZZLE lamps switch
21	TAXI NOZZLE selector

Main Panel

1	TAE, NEXT TGT and clutter indicators
2	AP/THROT engaged indicator
3	Attention-getter
4	Attitude Direction Indicator (ADI)
5	Angle of attack indicator
6	LATE ARM switch
7	Weapon control panel No 2 (pilot's)
8	HUD unit and control panel
9	HUD camera
10	RPM indicators
11	Fire extinguisher buttons
12	Accelerometer
13	FUEL FLOWmeter
14	Attention-getter
15	Remote frequency/channel indicator
16	ILS marker light
17	Approach progress indicator
18	Take-off monitor lights
19	AAR READY and FULL lights
20	Standby compass
21	OXY flow indicators
22	NH/NL changeover switch
23	Hydraulic pressure gauges
24	Engine temperature indicators
25	FUEL contents indicator and selector buttons
26	Emergency power switch and indicator light
27	Hydraulics UTILITIES TEST switch
28	HYDRAULICS selector switches
29	Central warning panel
30	Brake selector lever
31	BRAKES triple pressure gauge
32	Nozzle area indicators
33	Three-axes TRIMS indicator
34	HSI and servo altimeter test button
35	RAPID TAKE-OFF panel
36	HSI MODE selector
37	OTF and AGG selector/indicators
38	Electronic Head-Down Display (EHDD)
39	Rudder PEDAL ADJUST handle
40	LAND/TAXI lamps switch
41	Flaps, slat, wing sweep and airbrake position indicator
42	BRAKES TEST button
43	SELECTIVE/EMERGENCY JETTISON buttons
44	Landing gear emergency lowering handle
45	Landing gear selector handle
46	Servo altimeter
47	Horinzontal Situation Indicator (HSI)
48	Combined Speed Indicator (CSI)
49	Vertical Speed Indicator (VSI)
50	LP COCKS switches
51	LIFT DUMP indicator
52	REVERSE THRUST override switch and indicators
53	Landing gear position indicator
54	Arrester HOOK button/indicator
55	Nosewheel steering mode selector
56	Radar altimeter
57	Master armament safety switch
58	Left anti-glare shield and HUD CP dimmers

Right Console

1	Safety pin stowage
2	Fuel control panel
3	CANOPY internal control handle
4	VHF/UHF control panel
5	SEAT RAISE/LOWER switch
6	Environmental control panel
7	Fuel temperature indicators
8	EXTERNAL LIGHTS switch panel
9	LAMPS test panel
10	Document stowage
11	APU AUTO TEST switch
12	Governor test switch
13	THROTTLE ROCK TEST indicators
14	INTERNAL LIGHTS control panel
15	Intake ramps control panel
16	Engine and GENERATORS control panel
17	HUD CAMERA control panel
18	TACan control panel
19	ILS control panel

Tornado F Mark 2 front cockpit decodes. (*UK MoD Crown Copyright, 1985*)

REAR COCKPIT F Mk 2

Left Console

1   Weapon control panel No 1
    (navigator's)
2   RADAR control panel
3   Document container
4   Wander lamp
5   OXYGEN ON/OFF switch
6   Canopy JACK RELEASE handle
7   EMERGENCY UHF control panel
8   CANOPY JETTISON handle
9   SACS control panel

Main Panel

1   Landing gear position
    indicator
2   OXYGEN test button, contents
    and flow indications
3   Angle of attack indicator
4   J1 (D-band jamming) indicator
5   TUNE FAIL indicator
6   Radar roll ring locked
    indicator
7   TOTAL FUEL contents indicator
8   Left TV tabular display unit
9   Right TV tabular display unit
10 IFF INTERROGATOR control
    panel
11 Visual identification offset
    control panel
12 Central warning panel

13 Attention-getter
14 Altimeter
15 Artificial horizon
16 Combined Speed Indicator
    (CSI)
17 Secondary heading display
    panel
18 Next target indicator
19 Target accept indicator
20 Navigator's hand
    controller
21 TV tabular DISPLAY SHIFT
    switch
22 Radar display control
    panel
23 Attention-getter
24 Radar clutter indicator
25 Radar altimeter low height
    indicator

Right Console

1   Safety pin stowage
2   IFF control panel
3   CCS station box
4   Miscellaneous switch panel
5   Command ejection selection
    lever
6   VHF/UHF control panel
7   External lights master switch
8   HF control panel
9   SEAT RAISE/LOWER switch
10 LAMPS test panel

11 ECS airspray dump valve
12 Document/food and drink
    container
13 INTERNAL LIGHTS control
    panel
14 Main computer control
    panel
15 Inertial navigator panel
    control and display unit
16 Navigation/attack mode
    control panel
17 Cockpit voice recorder

Tornado F Mark 2 rear cockpit strike version decodes. (*UK MoD Crown Copyright, 1985*)

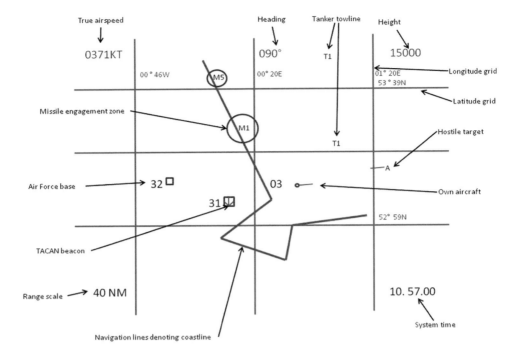

Tornado Plan display decode.

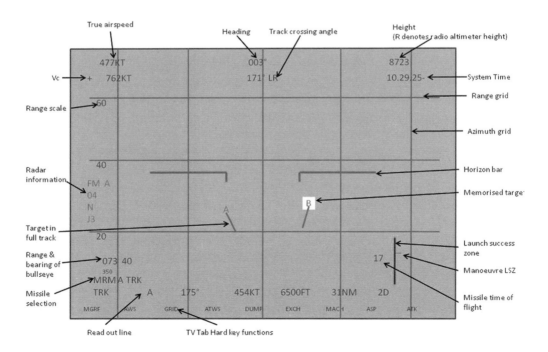

Tornado radar display decode.

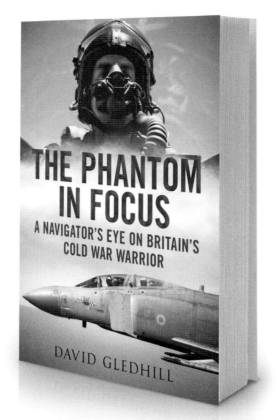

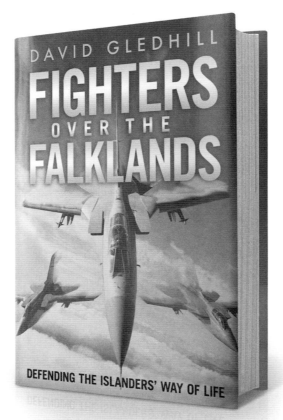